BIG VOICES
OF THE AIR

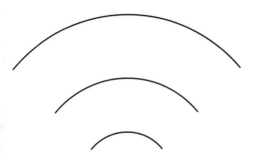

BIG VOICES
OF THE AIR

The Battle over Clear Channel Radio

James C. Foust

Iowa State University Press
Ames, Iowa

James C. Foust is an associate professor of journalism at Bowling Green State University, where he teaches courses in broadcast journalism, journalism law and ethics and desktop publishing. He has worked as a television news videojournalist and in commercial and industrial video production.

Cover and book design by Justin Eccles

Orders: 1-800-862-6657
Office: 1-515-292-0140
Fax: 1-515-292-3348
Web site: www.isupress.edu

∞Printed on acid-free paper in the United States of America

First edition, 2000

Library of Congress Cataloging-in-Publication Data

Foust, James C.
    Big voices of the air: the battle over clear channel radio / James C. Foust
        p. cm.
    ISBN 0-8138-2804-X
    1. Radio frequency allocation—United States—History—20th century. 2. Radio broadcasting policy—United States—History—20th century. I. Title.

HE8698 .F68 2000
384.54'524'0973—dc21   99-055027

The last digit is the print number: 9 8 7 6 5 4 3 2 1

Contents

	Acknowledgments	vii
	Acronyms	ix
1.	Introduction	3
2.	Anarchy in the Ether	13
3.	The Greatest Static Eliminator We Know Of	39
4.	Meet Mr. Big	79
5.	The Clear Channels Are on Trial	107
6.	Heads It's Clear Channels, Tails It's Regionals	145
7.	A Romance Needs Cultivation	185
8.	Conclusion	221
	Bibliography	229
	Index	239

Acknowledgments

This book began as a paper written for Dr. David Mould's media historiography class at Ohio University in 1993. Since that time, the study has grown and evolved through conference papers, a dissertation and journal articles. I am indebted to many people who have helped me over the years in bringing it to its present form; however, any factual errors that appear in the book are my responsibility.

Although the work has gone through substantial changes since my dissertation, my committee provided the initial spark and enthusiasm that carried me through the ensuing six years. Dr. Patrick Washburn, my dissertation advisor, has been a tremendous critic, mentor and friend and has offered me invaluable support since signing off on the title page. Dr. Mould, Dr. Robert Stewart and Dr. Michael Flemister also served on my committee and offered both excellent ideas and encouragement to continue working.

Dr. Louise Benjamin and Erwin G. Krasnow read earlier versions of this manuscript, and I am thankful for their ideas, which

I have tried to incorporate to the best of my ability. I am also thankful to others who have either read portions of the manuscript or offered more general encouragement and support, including Art Neal, Robert Turner, Herman Haas, Bob Letsinger and Catherine Cassara.

The study, of course, would not have been possible without many visits to various archival collections. I must thank the Bowling Green State University Department of Journalism and the Bowling Green State University Faculty Development Committee for providing financial support. I am grateful to all of the people who helped me access the material I needed to complete the project, including Joe Fields and C. David Mayfield at the American Farm Bureau Federation, Clay Peterson at the National Farmers Union, Dave Hayes and Marty Covey at the University of Colorado, Katherine Reagan at Cornell University, Tab Lewis at the National Archives and Wayne Vriesman of the Clear Channel Broadcasting Service. I also thank Ward Quaal, Hollis Seavey, Jack DeWitt, Roy Battles and William Potts for providing their perspectives. David Hilliard of Wiley, Rein and Fielding has gone far beyond the call of duty to facilitate my work over the past six years. This study would not have been possible without his generosity and help.

Judi Brown at the Iowa State University Press has shown great enthusiasm for this project, and her encouragement and concern have been invaluable over the past 18 months. I also thank my parents, who have always been there when I needed them.

I save the greatest debt of gratitude for my wife Cathy, who came into my life at about the same time as this project. In the inevitable competition between the two, she has always innately known when to offer encouragement, when to offer ideas, when to offer diversions and when to stay out of the way. Without her help, encouragement, friendship and love, this book would not have been possible. I'm not sure where I would be without her, but I am sure it would be a darker and much less pleasant place.

Acronyms

ABS	Association for Broadcast Standards
AFBF	American Farm Bureau Federation
AIRS	Associated Independent Radio Stations
APA	Administrative Procedure Act
ASCAP	American Society of Composers, Authors and Publishers
AT&T	American Telephone and Telegraph
BMI	Broadcast Music, Inc.
BRECOM	Broadcast Emergency Communications
CBS	Columbia Broadcasting System
CCBS	Clear Channel Group Broadcasting Service
CCG	Clear Channel Group
DBA	Daytime Broadcasters Association
DCB	Defense Communications Board
FCC	Federal Communications Commission
FRC	Federal Radio Commission
GE	General Electric
NAB	National Association of Broadcasters
NAEB	National Association of Educational Broadcasters
NARBA	North American Regional Broadcasting Agreement
NARBS	National Association of Regional Broadcast Stations
NBC	National Broadcasting Company
NFU	National Farmers Union
NIB	National Independent Broadcasters
OWI	Office of War Information
RBC	Regional Broadcasters Committee
RCA	Radio Corporation of America

BIG VOICES OF THE AIR

CHAPTER ONE

Introduction

As AM radio embarked upon its so-called Golden Age in the early 1930s, the industry's structure had been in many ways dictated—or at least endorsed—by government regulation. Among the most significant of these structural requisites was a tripartite arrangement of individual stations in which power, frequency and hours of operation were assigned according to each station's class. Atop this allocation structure were the clear channel stations, which were assigned maximum power and given permission to broadcast on frequencies of which they had exclusive—or nearly exclusive—use. The Federal Radio Commission (FRC) reserved 40 of these frequencies in 1928 for the purpose of providing radio service to remote rural listeners, especially during nighttime hours. While hundreds of stations crowded onto the remaining 56 frequencies of the broadcast band, at night only one station was permitted to operate on each clear channel, ensuring, the FRC said, "clear reception of the station's program up to the extreme limit of its service range."[1]

In an effort to provide long-range rural service, then, the FRC established a class of stations with more power, more range and larger potential audience than other classes of stations. These advantages, of course, led to increased revenue and prestige as well. "From 1930 to 1950—give or take a few years on either side—the clear channel stations reigned supreme," *Broadcasting* magazine noted in the early 1960s. "They were the big voices of the air. ... [T]heir programs and commercials rang loud and clear during the day and rose to a roar at night." The clear channel stations, all of which were either owned by or affiliated with national networks, carried the most popular national programming and attracted most of the national spot advertising revenues; thus, they could afford to supplement network-supplied national programming with elaborate locally produced fare. Stars such as Doris Day, Red Skelton and Andy Williams got their start performing on clear channel stations, and many of the best known early radio shows such as *The WLS National Barn Dance* and *Grand Ol' Opry* originated on clear channel stations.[2]

However, behind the scenes and out of earshot of the clear channel stations' vast audiences, a battle was being waged over the future of clear channel broadcasting. On one side were proponents of the clear channels—led by the clear channel stations themselves—who sought increased power and the maintenance of the stations' exclusive status. On the other side, opponents—led in large part by less powerful stations fearing the dominance of clear channel stations—opposed power increases for clear channel stations and called for the duplication or breakdown of clear channels by assigning additional stations to clear frequencies. The debate had begun even before the FRC's 1928 allocation plan, but it increased in intensity during the 1930s when one clear channel station, WLW in Cincinnati, Ohio, received experimental authorization to broadcast with 500,000 watts—10 times the existing limit. Clear channel stations saw the WLW experiment as the precursor to significant power increases for *all* clear channel stations, but at the same time the Cincinnati station's massive coverage area and aggressive marketing tactics fueled the outcry against the "clear channel monopoly."

Even after WLW's experimental license was revoked in 1939, the debate over clear channels continued. Following World War

II, the Federal Communications Commission (FCC), which had succeeded the FRC in 1934, initiated a comprehensive examination of the clear channel structure. Over the next 16 years, the commission established a voluminous record of evidence on clear channel broadcasting, considering proposals to grant clear channel stations up to 750,000 watts, to relocate clear channel stations to areas where they could provide better rural service, to break down the clear channels and to assign clear channel licenses to noncommercial, governmental and educational interests. All the while, the commission also kept an eye on Congress, which sporadically conducted clear channel investigations of its own.

The debate over clear channels was the first significant intra-industry dispute in AM radio, and until at least the mid-1940s it was arguably the most important regulatory matter before the FRC and FCC, its inherent importance amplified by the intricate relationship it had to many of the radio industry's other regulatory debates. The clear channel issue was, in fact, the keystone to the entire system of broadcasting. Questions about network dominance of radio, the negotiation of international broadcasting agreements, allocations to noncommercial interests and accommodating post-war demand for new broadcast stations all hinged to a significant degree on the outcome of the clear channel debate. Beyond that, resolution of the dispute also could have a significant impact on the development of new broadcast services such as FM radio and—to a lesser degree—television, both by determining whether such services would complement or replace AM radio and by establishing the entities that would be poised for commercial success in these new technological venues.

Despite the importance of the clear channel issue, remarkably little has been written about it. There has been no published comprehensive examination of the clear channel battle, and a single law review article on the topic concentrates on an analysis of the FCC's decision rather than the debate's historical significance. This dearth of literature has led to the clear channels getting short shrift in general broadcasting histories as well, with most mentioning the issue little if at all. And while the histories of individual clear channel stations have attracted the attention of some broadcast scholars, so far these, too, have addressed the clear channel debate only tangentially.[3]

In broader terms, broadcasting historians also have neglected the factionalism of the radio industry during radio's Golden Age and the role of specialized interest groups in intra-industry regulatory debates. Instead, scholars of this era have concentrated in large part on the growth and dominance of the national networks, ignoring the internecine battles within the industry. While the networks were without doubt important, and in some ways dominant players in broadcast regulatory debates, their viewpoint was by no means the only one presented by the commercial industry. This fact is perhaps best understood when considered within the context of the work of Robert McChesney, who has evaluated the united front offered by the nascent commercial industry against calls for a noncommercial broadcast structure in the late 1920s and early 1930s. In *Telecommunications, Mass Media and Democracy*, he argued that the so-called American system of advertiser-supported, commercial broadcasting developed not because it was preordained as the most democratic option but because commercial interests were able systematically to exclude reformers from serious participation in the policy-making debate. "[T]he commercial broadcasters and their allies in Washington, D.C.," he noted, "continually postponed, eliminated, or defused any public examination of the American broadcasting system or any discussion of alternative models."[4]

But while McChesney observed that the commercial industry "marched in lockstep" against the reformers during the late 1920s and early 1930s, the situation was significantly different during the clear channel debate, which began in earnest just as McChesney's study ends. Having effectively vanquished the threat from noncommercial critics and having crystallized the commercial structure as the status quo, the commercial interests broke into individual factions, fighting amongst themselves for regulatory policies that would be most favorable to their particular interests. The terms of the fight, however, were dictated by business; despite rhetoric to the contrary, groups opposed one another not for any larger duty of serving public interest but for financial reward. The arguments of the noncommercial interests that remained were largely ignored, as the clear channel issue was decided within a commercial framework and from among a series of commercial alternatives.[5]

An important aspect of this fracturing of the commercial industry is how various groups pursued their agendas through lobbying government officials and building public support for their positions. Success in these ventures, of course, required framing policy positions in terms likely to elicit government and public support. Such activity is a staple of interest groups in all areas of policy making, yet empirical studies of how interest groups pursue their goals are far rarer than theoretical studies in the political science literature, leading one scholar to characterize the area as "theory rich and data poor." Communications historians, in particular, have largely neglected such empirical study, despite the fact that interest groups are acknowledged as an important component of the policy-making process. Notable exceptions, of course, are the work of McChesney and others on the debate over noncommercial broadcasting in the 1930s, the literature on the breakup of the American Telephone and Telegraph (AT&T) monopoly and Joel Brinkley's examination of the origins and development of high-definition television (HDTV). Still, however, the role of commercial interest groups in regulatory debates during the formative years of broadcast regulation has received scant attention.[6]

Erwin G. Krasnow, Lawrence D. Longley and Herbert A. Terry provided what is probably the most complete theoretical framework of the broadcast policy-making process. In this systems approach, policy is determined by interaction among six entities: the FCC, the industry, Congress, the courts, citizens' groups and the White House. Three of these, the courts, citizens' groups and the White House, began active and continuing participation in broadcast policy making only after the mid-1960s; thus, during the time of this study clear channel policy emerged largely from interaction among the FCC, the industry and Congress. The general pattern of policy making, according to Krasnow, Longley and Terry, is that participants place demands upon the policy making system, offering support for these demands in the form of legal and ideological symbols that imply service to the public. As participants' demands are often in conflict with one another and normally no participant possesses the strength to dominate the process, the resulting policy outcome is more often than not "mutual accommodation among participants." Thus, policy making normally embraces incremental change over radical solutions.[7]

Krasnow, Longley and Terry also pointed out that the FCC relies on the industry for much of its technical data, lacking the budget and resources to gather such information on its own. Thus, the commission is forced to defer to the industry when evaluating existing services and assessing the likely impact of future innovations. "[T]he line between gaining a familiarity with an industry's problems and becoming biased thereby in favor of that industry is perilously thin," they wrote. "It is difficult for commissioners and their staff to operate closely with an industry without seeing its problems in industry terms." Moreover, many commission personnel either came from the regulated industry or plan to enter it when they leave the commission, leading to something of a revolving door between the agency and the industry. In fact, the relationships between interest groups and government regulators often resemble a complex web that is nearly impossible to untangle.[8]

This book considers the clear channel debate from a policy-making perspective, concentrating on the role of commercial interest groups in the process. Specifically, the study examines the formation and operation of the Clear Channel Broadcasting Service (CCBS) and its precursor, the Clear Channel Group (CCG). A trade organization funded by independent (non-network owned) clear channel stations, the CCBS in 1941 hired a full-time director and established a permanent Washington, D.C., office. Soon, the group built a significant presence at the FCC and in Congress, leading Llewellyn White, in his 1947 critique of the broadcast industry, *The American Radio,* to call it "the most powerful radio lobby in the capital." The CCBS, White maintained, did "more than all other groups combined to maintain the *status quo* among clear channel plum-holders."[9]

Chapter 2 examines the pre-history of the clear channel debate, concentrating on the rapid growth of radio from an engineering curiosity to a system of broadcasting that attracted significant public and commercial interest. The industry's commercial structure and the regulatory decisions made during this time frame (roughly from 1919 to 1929), played a large part in determining the conduct of the clear channel debate over the remaining time of the study.

Chapter 3 chronicles the debate over clear channels in the 1930s, marking the emergence of specialized trade organizations, such as the Clear Channel Group, to represent various factions of the commercial industry. The debate over clear channels, which had carried on since the 1920s, took on added urgency at this time as WLW's superpower experiment hardened the arguments of both pro- and anti-clear channel interests.

In Chapter 4, the formation of the Clear Channel Broadcasting Service is examined, concentrating on how the new group sought to broaden the work of the pro-clear channel interests beyond engineering arguments and into public "education" about clear channels. From 1941 to 1944, the new group attempted to build support for the notion that clear channels were performing a public service by providing radio programming to rural listeners. At the same time, it attempted to fight individual duplications of clear channel frequencies, notably the FCC's decision to allow a Boston station to operate full-time on KOA's clear channel frequency.

Chapters 5 and 6 chronicle the extended clear channel proceedings, Docket 6741, initiated by the FCC in 1944. Chapter 5 examines the time period from 1944 to 1948, in which various industry factions argued their positions before the FCC and the Senate Interstate and Foreign Commerce Committee, which held hearings on the clear channel issue in 1948. Chapter 6 chronicles the years between the end of FCC hearings and the ultimate resolution of Docket 6741 in 1963. During this time, changes in the broadcast industry—brought on by the emergence of FM radio and television—significantly altered the terms of the clear channel debate.

Chapter 7 examines the efforts of the Clear Channel Broadcasting Service to elicit the support of farm groups, notably the American Farm Bureau Federation and National Farmers Union, in the clear channel debate. By attempting to improve and promote farm programming on clear channel stations, attending farm conventions and providing coverage of farm group activities, the CCBS attempted to convince powerful farm groups to support the clear channels' efforts to increase their power.

The Conclusion in Chapter 8 assesses the clear channel debate from a broader perspective, arguing that commercial interest groups serve to limit the terms of policy debate while simultaneously validating the commercial broadcast structure.

This study seeks not only to examine an important but neglected broadcast policy debate but to provide a broader sense of how regulatory issues are framed, argued and resolved. Such understanding is valuable not only for what it reveals about the clear channel debate but for what it can tell us about other communications policy debates as well. Today, commercial communications interests—be they a single corporation or a group with similar concerns—arm themselves with lobbying power and resources that dwarf the CCBS and the groups that opposed it. Yet the goals and strategies are much the same, and the Clear Channel Broadcasting Service, in its interaction with government entities, the general public and other groups, helped establish the outlines and strategies of policy pursuit that are still used today.

NOTES

1. FRC, *Second Annual Report* (Washington, D.C., 1928), 48–49.

2. "Clears Tops for 20 Years," *Broadcasting*, October 15, 1962, 29.

3. See Jeffrey Smulyan, "Power to Some People: The FCC's Clear Channel Allocation Policy," *Southern California Law Review* 44 (1971): 811; Erik Barnouw, *A Tower in Babel: A History of Broadcasting in the United States to 1933* (New York: Oxford University Press, 1968); Erik Barnouw, *The Golden Web: A History of Broadcasting in the United States, 1933–1953* (New York: Oxford University Press, 1968); Christopher H. Sterling and John M. Kittross, *Stay Tuned: A Concise History of American Broadcasting* (Belmont, Calif.: Wadsworth Publishing Company, 1990); Lawrence W. Lichty, "The Nation's Station: A History of Station WLW" (Ph.D. Diss., Ohio State University, 1964); and Jerry Wayne Rinks, "We Shield Millions: A History of WSM, 1925–1950" (Ph.D. Diss., University of Tennessee, Knoxville, 1993).

4. Robert W. McChesney, *Telecommunications, Mass Media and Democracy* (New York: Oxford University Press, 1994), 257.

5. McChesney, *Telecommunications, Mass Media and Democracy*, 6.

6. See R. Douglas Arnold, "Overtilled and Undertilled Fields in American Politics," *Political Science Quarterly* 97 (1982): 97; McChesney, *Tele-*

communications, Mass Media and Democracy; David Paul Nord, "The FCC, Educational Broadcasting, and Political Interest Group Activity," *Journal of Broadcasting* 22 (Summer 1978): 321–38; Alan Stone, *Wrong Number: The Breakup of AT&T* (New York: Basic Books, 1989); Jeffrey E. Cohen, *The Politics of Telecommunications Regulation: The States and the Divestiture of AT&T* (Armonk, N.Y.: M.E. Sharp, 1992); Steve Coll, *The Deal of the Century: The Breakup of AT&T* (New York: Atheneum, 1986); and Joel Brinkley, *Defining Vision: The Battle for the Future of Television* (New York: Harcourt Brace, 1997).

7. Erwin G. Krasnow, Lawrence D. Longley, and Herbert A. Terry, *The Politics of Broadcast Regulation* (Third Edition) (New York: St. Martin's Press, 1982), 33, 139–41.

8. See Krasnow, Longley and Terry, *The Politics of Broadcast Regulation*, 48–49; and Jeremy Tunstall, *Communications Deregulation: The Unleashing of America's Communications Industry* (New York: Basil Blackwell, 1986), 195.

9. Llewellyn White, *The American Radio: A Report on the Broadcasting Industry in the United States from the Commission on Freedom of the Press* (Chicago: University of Chicago Press, 1947; repr., New York: Arno Press, 1977), 148.

CHAPTER TWO

Anarchy in the Ether

Testifying before the Senate Interstate Commerce Committee in 1926, Stephen B. Davis of the Department of Commerce said that the existing radio structure had developed almost by accident. "The present broadcasting situation does not represent any conscious plan," he told the committee. "It is not any set-up; nobody started out with any idea of any kind to work out a result. In other words it is the result absolutely of growth."[1]

Davis' comments provided an apt assessment of the manner in which broadcasting regulation originated in the early and middle 1920s. Existing laws—designed to facilitate the use of radio in point-to-point communication—did not adequately provide for the explosive growth of radio broadcasting in the 1920s. Thus, the Department of Commerce, which had been granted limited authority to regulate radio, faced the challenge of reining in a technology that was spiraling out of control. For the most part, it attempted to do this through a process of cooperation with the nascent commercial industry, a strategy that was continued by the Federal Radio Commission (FRC) when it was created in 1927.

Such collaboration naturally led to regulations that favored the commercial broadcasters over experimental operators and noncommercial stations.

The most important legacy of early regulation was by far the process of allocation, in which individual stations were assigned frequencies, power and hours of operation. Indeed, allocation set the parameters for all regulatory issues that would follow, as the process established who would be powerful and who would not be—both in engineering and in political, social and economic terms. Indeed, many pioneering broadcasters—especially noncommercial stations and experimenters—eventually either were allocated out of the system or given unfavorable assignments, while wealthy commercial interests received the most desirable allocation grants.

An integral assumption of the allocation plans pursued first by the Department of Commerce and then by the FRC was that stations would be assigned frequency, power and operating hours according to their class. At the top of this class structure were what came to be called the clear channel stations, intended to provide wide-area rural service by using high power on a frequency that was cleared of other stations at night. Like the allocation plan at large, the assignment of clear channel stations during this time established the parameters for the debates that would come in ensuing decades.

RADIO IN THE WORLD WAR I ERA

At first, radio was used chiefly for point-to-point communication, adding voice transmission to the model established by the telegraph. In its early years, radio provided the greatest benefit to the maritime industry, giving shipping companies a way to track cargo and allowing commercial, passenger and military vessels to contact land stations in emergencies. Regulation, too, envisioned radio chiefly as a tool for maritime point-to-point communication; the United States' first radio law, the Wireless Ship Act of 1910, merely required all ocean-going steamers carrying more than 50 people to have radio communications apparatus and a skilled operator on board. More significantly, the Radio Act of 1912 authorized the Secretary of Commerce and Labor to grant licenses, "revocable for cause," to radio operators and required each radio station to designate a specific broadcast frequency and "to use the minimum amount of energy necessary to carry out any communications desired."[2]

With the exception of a number of "amateur" hobbyists, most users of radio in the 1910s were involved in maritime industries. Transoceanic communication appeared to offer radio's most financially lucrative opportunity, and in the years leading up to World War I, a number of disputes arose over the ownership of various patents crucial to establishing such point-to-point radio communications systems. These disputes centered on the high-power Alexanderson transmitter patented by General Electric, the diode vacuum tube controlled by British Marconi, and the Audion vacuum tube, a modification of the diode tube owned by American Telephone and Telegraph (AT&T). When the war began, the U.S. government, wanting to be sure to have crucial radio equipment available to it, created a patent pool, vowing to protect companies from claims arising out of the use of patented technologies. In the interest of national security, the government also took over all high-powered radio transmitters—many of them operated by Marconi's American arm—and in 1917 ordered stations operated by amateur experimenters off the air.[3]

At the conclusion of the war, it became clear that the U.S. government did not want to turn the high-power transmitters back over to Marconi, nor did it approve of General Electric's plans to build several Alexanderson transmitters for Marconi and to give the British company exclusive use of the technology. Eventually, General Electric's Owen D. Young formed a separate entity, Radio Corporation of America (RCA), to keep the Marconi operations under the control of Americans. GE and RCA then signed cross-licensing agreements, and American Marconi's assets were passed to the new corporation. Having acquired the Marconi assets, GE and RCA now controlled American rights to the diode vacuum tube, and in July 1920, GE, RCA and AT&T signed an agreement to pool their radio patents. The next year, United Fruit Company and Westinghouse joined the pool, bringing their respective patents to the venture. Under the terms of the agreements, RCA, whose stock was controlled by GE, Westinghouse, AT&T and United Fruit, would administer the patent pool and sell radio receivers manufactured by Westinghouse and GE. AT&T was given exclusive rights to sell radio transmitters to interests outside the patent pool and to engage in "radiotelephony for hire." RCA, GE, AT&T and Westinghouse also were authorized to manufacture radio transmitting and receiving equipment for their own use. Although no one had yet envisioned a commercial broadcasting structure, the alliance formed in an attempt to reap radio's potential for long-distance communication would prove extremely influential when broadcasting did develop.[4]

THE BIRTH OF BROADCASTING

Ironically, radio hobbyists stumbled upon the concept of broadcasting long before the commercial concerns envisioned anything more than point-to-point communication. A number of amateurs began transmitting music, news and other "programming" for the benefit of their fellow experimenters soon after World War I. One of these, Dr. Frank Conrad, who operated amateur station 8XK in Pittsburgh, began playing phonograph records over his station in 1919 and soon was receiving requests from listeners. Eventually, the growing popularity of Conrad's broadcasts attracted the attention of his employer, Westinghouse, which decided to finance a station that would broadcast on a regular schedule to create a market for the company's receiving sets. On October 27, 1920, Secretary of Commerce Herbert Hoover, using his authority under the Radio Act of 1912 to authorize such "land" stations, granted Westinghouse a permit for station KDKA, the first commercial broadcasting license ever issued by the U.S. government. KDKA's first broadcast—the returns of the Harding-Cox presidential race on November 2—attracted an audience estimated in the thousands and proved to be a watershed event in the development of broadcasting.[5]

Radio broadcasting grew somewhat slowly after the initial KDKA broadcast; by the end of 1921 the Department of Commerce had issued only 30 broadcast licenses. But six months later the radio boom was on. By the beginning of 1923, more than 500 broadcast stations had been licensed, and an estimated 2 million radio receivers were in use. For the most part, the early stations were not run by operators who wished to make money directly from broadcasting; the vast majority of stations were operated by radio and electrical manufacturers or dealers who hoped to stimulate radio set sales by giving buyers something to listen to. Educational institutions operated about 12 percent of broadcast stations; newspapers and other publishers were close behind. Still, the concept of advertising to provide support for broadcasting had not yet developed, and while the total number of stations grew steadily throughout the early and middle 1920s, many stations were forced to go off the air for financial reasons.[6]

Radio's growing use for broadcasting also led to serious problems with interference. In December 1921 Hoover authorized two frequencies specifically for land-based broadcasting, thus providing additional space for stations that had formerly operated on maritime frequencies. One of these frequencies, 833 kHz, was to be used for "news, concerts, lectures, and such matters," while the other, 618 kHz, was designated for crop reports and weather forecasts. Although there were no expressed power limits, most early broadcasters used between 100 and 500 watts, a very small amount of power by later standards. Nonetheless, nearly 600 stations shoehorned onto two frequencies created a situation that was far from optimal, and the numerous stations that jumped on and off of these designated frequencies merely made matters worse. The Radio Act of 1912, however, gave the Secretary of Commerce no regulatory guidance on broadcasting, and Hoover himself lacked the engineering expertise to solve the worsening interference problems. Thus, the Secretary of Commerce organized a conference to bring together government and industry representatives to discuss the radio situation and to make recommendations to Congress for more comprehensive radio regulation. As it turned out, however, four "National Radio Conferences" would be held before Congress acted.[7]

The conferences, held between 1922 and 1925, developed not only the basic structure of the American broadcast system but the way that structure would be maintained and modified through government and industry cooperation. Louise Benjamin, in her 1998 assessment of the radio conferences, noted that they were driven by what historian Ellis Hawley called an "associative state," where private and public entities combine "to meet societal needs for national reform and steady economic expansion." Indeed, the radio conferences came to be dominated by the powerful commercial interests in the nascent industry, especially AT&T, Westinghouse, RCA and GE, and the recommendations of the conferences were for the most part favorable to these entities. Much of what ultimately was codified in the Radio Act of 1927, in fact, came from the discussions that took place at these four industry/government meetings.[8]

Although Hoover believed that the industry should be able to work out the details of how broadcasting would develop, he told delegates at the first conference that there had to be some government regulation to avoid "national regret that we have parted with a great national asset into uncontrolled hands." Commercial interests called for establishing order by emphasizing large stations while doing away with what they called "indiscriminate" broadcasters. One GE representative, in fact, said that smaller stations should "learn to keep out of it," while a Westinghouse delegate called for a "complete" national radio service provided by 12 to 15 stations using high power.[9]

The conference ultimately recommended that radio licensees be assigned frequencies, power and ranges according to the type of service they offered, with the Secretary of Commerce to have authority to regulate the medium. These recommendations became part a proposed radio bill in Congress in 1923; and while the proposal passed the House, it stalled in the Senate Interstate Commerce Committee, largely as a result of industry opposition. RCA and AT&T particularly objected to placing so much power to regulate the industry in the hands of the Secretary of Commerce, especially with regard to his ability to refuse licenses to groups believed to be monopolizing radio. In the meantime, Hoover moved on his own to attempt to relieve interference, authorizing the creation of Class B stations, the forerunner of high-power clear channel outlets. Given their own reserved frequency—750 kHz—Class B stations were authorized to use between 500 and 1,000 watts of power. Additionally, Class Bs were prohibited from playing phonograph records and were required to maintain a sufficient quality and quantity of spare parts "to insure continuity and reliability of the announced schedule of service." If conflicting Class B stations in a particular area could not work out time-sharing arrangements for the frequency, they would be moved into the band with the lesser stations, which were now designated as Class A.[10]

Existing stations that qualified for Class B operation were moved to 750 kHz, as were new applicants who could meet the power and programming requirements, with Hoover issuing the first Class B licenses in September 1922. The programming and equipment prerequisites, naturally, limited Class B operation to relatively wealthy broadcasters: two stations each owned by Westinghouse and AT&T were among the first Class B licensees, along with GE's WGY; most of the rest of the Class Bs were owned by large-market newspapers or department stores. By the end of 1923, 30 Class B stations were using 750 kHz, while more than 500 stations crowded onto the remaining two frequencies. This immediately lessened interference among the more powerful stations, creating what Sterling and Kittross called a "privileged class," but did little to help other broadcasters. Those stations, Erik Barnouw noted, "were still crammed into what had become an inferno of the unfavored, an underworld of 360 [meters], a place of howls and squeals and eternal misery, from which escape seemed difficult." With the situation on the Class A bands remaining chaotic, and with no legislation forthcoming from Congress, Hoover convened another radio conference in March 1923.[11]

This time, Hoover instructed Commerce Department staffers to meet more closely with industry representatives before the conference began. Westinghouse began its own publicity campaign, urging the elimination of "inefficient" broadcast stations and calling for a two-tier system of high-power national and low-power local stations. "Would not 25 high class stations located in large metropolitan areas where talent and resources were available, supplemented by local stations operating on small power, be the best way to serve the American public?" Westinghouse asked. There was agreement, however, that three frequencies were not enough to meet the demands of the growing broadcast industry, and thus the conference recommended opening up the entire range of frequencies between 550 and 1350 kHz, with stations to be assigned on channels spaced 10 kHz apart. This would create 81 broadcast frequencies, each designated for one of two types of

FIGURE 2.1   Daytime groundwave and skywave signal paths.

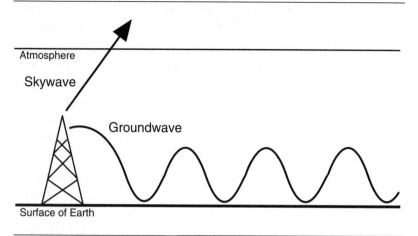

stations. Fifty of the channels—those at the "low" end of the band from 550 to 1040 kHz—would be reserved as "territorial wave frequencies" with one high-power station operating on each, while on the remaining 31 frequencies, lower-power stations would be assigned.[12]

Hoover implemented a modified form of the conference's recommendation on May 15, 1923. He allocated the band from 550 to 1350 kHz for broadcasting but allowed the low-power stations using 833 kHz, now designated as Class C, to remain there. Eventually, Hoover moved the more powerful Class C stations into the Class A area and forced weaker stations—including a large number of educational and religious stations—into time-sharing arrangements on other frequencies. In the meantime, the band was split above and below the 833 kHz anomaly. Forty channels were designated for Class B stations, which would operate with between 500 and 1,000 watts and fulfill the intended role of the "territorial wave frequencies" recommended by the conference. The remaining 36 frequencies would be assigned to Class A stations with a 500-watt power limit.[13]

CLEAR CHANNELS AND THE DEBATE OVER HIGHER POWER

The reservation of 40 frequencies for Class B stations created

FIGURE 2.2   Nighttime skywave signal path.

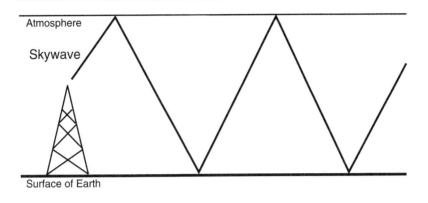

the basis of the clear channel structure that remains to this day. It was also the culmination of engineering opinion, based on several unique characteristics of the AM broadcast band, that reserving "clear" frequencies was crucial to providing rural service. Although much about the propagation of radio signals was not yet understood in the 1920s, engineers knew that transmitters in the AM band emit two kinds of signals: a groundwave signal that travels along the ground from the transmitting tower and a skywave signal that travels skyward from the tower (Fig. 2.1). During the day, the skywave signal is of no use to earthbound receivers as it simply travels through the atmosphere and into space. At night, however, changes in a portion of the ionosphere known as the Kennelly-Heavyside Layer cause the skywave to be refracted back to earth, where it then "bounces" back and forth between the earth's surface and the ionosphere (Fig. 2.2). Skywave signals enable listeners to hear stations in the AM band over great distances—far greater, in fact, than would be possible with only groundwave radiation.

The nature and use of skywave signals would be at the heart of the debate over clear channels for the next half century as a number of characteristics of the skywave signal affected the implementation of the clear channel structure. First, skywaves are usable chiefly during nighttime hours, although studies in the 1950s

power were General Electric's WGY, RCA's WJZ and AT&T's WEAF.[17]

At the fourth and final radio conference, held in 1925, Hoover noted his pleasure with the higher-power experiments, calling them "not only harmless ... but advantageous":

> Power increase has meant a general rise in broadcasting efficiency; it has meant clear reception; it has helped greatly to overcome static and other difficulties inherent in summer broadcasting, so as to give us improved all-year service. Whatever the limit may be, I believe that substantial power increase has come to stay, and the public is the gainer from it.

The fourth conference also urged continuation of efforts to decrease the number of broadcast stations, resolving that no new stations be licensed until the number of existing stations was reduced.[18]

THE CHAOS OF 1926 AND THE CREATION OF THE FRC

Hoover had orchestrated the radio conferences as a means to facilitate industry self-regulation. Allowing the industry to set the parameters under which it would operate was in keeping with the secretary's pro-business stance and provided guidance for him to control the quickly developing medium. In the absence of more comprehensive radio regulation, Hoover operated under the broad terms of the Radio Act of 1912 and used the recommendations of the radio conferences as a means to "fill in the blanks" of the radio structure. The system was showing signs of working, at least from the standpoint of owners of powerful radio stations. The industry was calling the shots, operating through Hoover and his radio conferences as Congress failed to pass comprehensive radio legislation.

Still, there was doubt as to what power was vested in the Commerce Department by the Radio Act of 1912 almost from the moment the law was passed. In that same year, the U.S. attorney general advised that the radio act required the Secretary of Commerce to issue a license to anyone who applied for one as long as

he or she was a U.S. citizen. A test of what, if any, discretion the
Commerce Department had in issuing licenses, however, did not
come until 1923, when the Court of Custom Appeals held that the
Secretary of Commerce had no authority to deny a license. The
case arose after Hoover refused to grant a license to New York's
Intercity Radio Company for wireless telegraphy because there
was no available frequency that would not cause interference to
existing stations. The court ordered Hoover to grant Intercity a
license on a frequency that would cause the least interference,
which Hoover subsequently did. For the time being, though, the
secretary maintained his discretion in the broadcast band as no
broadcast stations challenged his power under the Intercity ruling.[19]

In the course of following the mandates from the third and fourth
radio conferences to reduce the clutter in the broadcast band,
however, Hoover began to run afoul of a number of broadcasters.
Many of the stations displaced by the secretary's efforts to pare
down the number of broadcasters during 1924 and 1925 went qui-
etly, especially educational and noncommercial broadcasters who
were in large part relegated to undesirable frequencies or restric-
tive time-sharing agreements. The grumblings that did arise
prompted Hoover to say that he would welcome a test case to more
definitively proscribe his powers. Zenith Radio Corporation's
WJAZ obliged Hoover in 1926 by ignoring the secretary's order
that the Chicago station share a wavelength with Denver's KOA.
When WJAZ moved to another frequency, Hoover brought suit.
In April, an Illinois District Court ruled against Hoover and what
it called "the play and action of purely personal and arbitrary
power." Hoover asked the Justice Department what power he still
possessed under the 1912 Radio Act, and acting attorney general
William J. Donovan opined that the Secretary of Commerce had
no power to determine or restrict power, frequency, hours of operation or terms of licenses other than those specifically spelled
out in the act. "[T]he present legislation is inadequate to cover
the art of broadcasting, which has been almost entirely developed
since the passage of the 1912 Act," Donovan wrote. "If the present
situation requires control, I can only suggest that it be sought in
new legislation, carefully adapted to meet the needs of both the

present and the future."[20]

With little other choice, Hoover abandoned his attempts to control the broadcast band, essentially issuing licenses to all who requested them. The number of broadcast stations, which had fallen to about 500 under his control, swelled to nearly 700 by 1927. Chaos ruled the broadcast band as stations increased power, moved to new frequencies and changed hours of operation as they wished. Commissioner Orestes H. Caldwell later described what he called the "anarchy in the ether":

> [M]any stations jumped without restraint to new wave lengths which suited them better, regardless of the interference which they might thus be causing to other stations. Proper separation between established stations was destroyed by other stations coming in and camping in the middle of any open spaces they could find. ... Some of the older stations also jumped their power, increasing 5 to 10 times their output. ... Indeed, every human ingenuity and selfish impulse seemed to have been exerted to complicate the tangle in the ether.[21]

Finally, on February 21, 1927, Congress enacted the first radio legislation designed to deal specifically with broadcasting, the Radio Act of 1927. The new legislation created the Federal Radio Commission, intended as a temporary body that would take responsibility for licensing broadcast stations for one year, at which time such authority would shift to the Secretary of Commerce. Under the 1927 Radio Act, the FRC was given broad authority to classify radio stations, assign frequencies to individual stations, set broadcast power and time limitations and make whatever other regulations it deemed necessary to facilitate radio communication and limit interference between stations. Congress gave the commission no specific criteria for evaluating applicants competing for limited spectrum space but merely required it to make decisions based on "public interest, convenience, or necessity," a vague concept borrowed from public utilities law.[22]

One of the reasons Congress finally moved to remedy the chaotic broadcasting situation of 1926 was that radio was rapidly becoming a profitable enterprise. By 1927, advertiser-supported broadcasting, largely facilitated by interconnecting stations into "networks" or "chains," gave stations a way to make a direct profit from their broadcast operations. By connecting stations, programming could be shared and advertisers could reach a greater number of listeners. Individual stations—especially those located in smaller cities—could receive quality network programming, thus allowing them to attract more local sponsors. National sponsors, of course, made radio profitable for the networks, and each network also owned a number of stations, including powerful outlets in large markets such as New York and Chicago. Having such a significant stake in the success of broadcast allocation, the networks, already developing a potent lobbying presence in Washington, D.C., and the National Association of Broadcasters (NAB), which formed in 1923 to promote commercial use of the airwaves, pressured Congress to do something about the chaotic broadcasting situation.

The networks had grown to dominance with a speed rivaled only by the explosive growth of radio itself in the 1920s. AT&T was the early pioneer in the interconnection of stations, largely because under the terms of the 1920 patent pool agreements it had the exclusive right among pool signatories to engage in toll broadcasting. By the end of 1925, AT&T had put in place a 26-station network, charging advertisers $2,600 per hour for time on 13 of those stations. RCA also experimented with networking, although because AT&T refused to allow it to use telephone lines to connect the stations, it had to use inferior telegraph lines. RCA was, of course, also hindered by the fact that under terms of the patent agreement it could not support its radio operations through toll broadcasting.[23]

In 1926, however, RCA purchased AT&T's radio assets, including WEAF and its network operations, and folded them into a new entity, the National Broadcasting Company (NBC). NBC would now operate both the "Blue" network, formed from RCA's chain with WJZ New York as the key station, and the "Red" network, based on AT&T's more impressive WEAF network. Under terms of RCA's purchase of AT&T's radio concerns, NBC could now engage in toll broadcasting and also use AT&T's telephone lines to interconnect its stations. By the end of 1927, there were 48 stations affiliated with NBC. That same year, another network, which would become Columbia Broadcasting System (CBS), formed with 16 stations.[24]

FRC ALLOCATION EFFORTS

The Federal Radio Commission endorsed the development of network broadcasting by obliging network-affiliated stations and quickly abandoning plans to completely reallocate the broadcast frequency spectrum in favor of evolutionary solutions that would accommodate the majority of existing broadcasters with a minimum of disruption. To this end, the commission instructed its allocation committee to consider "power, priority, past conduct and program quality" when evaluating new allocation plans. "The committee will be directed to find a place in its allocation scheme for each station in the order of its apparent value to listeners, and will relegate those stations which seem to be of little or no value to frequencies on which they can make little trouble," the commission noted.[25]

The FRC interpreted its public interest mandate to mean that allocation decisions should be made with an eye toward providing listeners with the radio service they desired. And listeners' desires were judged, for the most part, to be the existing programming offered by the dominant commercial broadcasting industry. "The future of radio broadcasting is in your hands," Commissioner Henry A. Bellows told the League of Women Voters in April 1927. "The broadcasters exist solely to serve you as listeners; they charge you nothing and they ask only your good will." The FRC was thus decidedly reluctant to address programming in allocating frequencies and instead relied largely on engineering issues. "[H]ow shall we measure the conflicting claims of grand opera and religious services, of market reports and direct advertising, of jazz orchestras and lectures on the diseases of hogs?" Bellows asked. Naturally, such reliance on technical considerations favored wealthy broadcasters—especially network affiliates—that had the facilities necessary to render the most technically superior service. At the same time, the commission's reluctance to consider diverse program types and its reliance on technical criteria meant noncommercial broadcasters would receive less favorable frequency, power and operating time assignments.[26]

In its first six months, the FRC reassigned a number of inter-fering stations and removed stations from frequencies reserved for Canada. While these measures helped radio reception in met-ropolitan areas, they did little to lessen the "heterodyning" inter-ference caused by two stations on the same frequency in rural ar-eas. In November 1927, the commission mandated the band of frequencies from 600 kHz to 1000 kHz "to be maintained free from heterodynes or other interference" and ordered stations operat-ing on those frequencies to facilitate this goal by time-sharing, power adjustments or other means. The FRC itself transferred many stations out of the band, leaving the most powerful stations intact. "Stations adversely affected in some instances must be martyrs to the cause of better radio," the commission explained. "Over these cleared channels it will thus be possible for rural and remote listeners to pick up stations in all sections of the coun-try."[27]

The assignments created under the November 1927 plan formed the basis of the clear channel allocation plan that remains largely intact to this day. Although several of the frequencies were not "clear" in the sense of having only one station operating on them, the commission had explicitly stated that the purpose of this band of frequencies was to render high-power service to rural areas, free from the interference of other stations. On several frequen-cies, two or more dominant stations shared time, while on others stations signed off after dark. Still other frequencies had stations assigned full-time along the East and West coasts. The commission's inclination to accommodate rather than plan also led to clear chan-nels being assigned to stations in large metropolitan areas, rather than in areas where they could more effectively provide rural ser-vice. Four clear channel stations were located in New York City, for example, and four were in Chicago.[28]

The FRC's piecemeal approach, especially its clearing of fre-quencies for powerful network stations in the East and Midwest, angered many in Congress, including Washington senator Clarence C. Dill, who was a co-author of the Radio Act of 1927. Members of Congress from the South and West believed that the FRC was giv-ing undue preference to stations located on the East Coast and in the Midwest to the detriment of listeners in other parts of the country. As a result, when Congress voted to extend the FRC for another year, it attached the so-called Davis Amendment to the FRC's authorization. Named after its author, Representative Ewin Davis of Tennessee, the amendment required the FRC to allocate broadcasting facilities equally among the five zones of the country and to provide "fair and equitable" radio facilities among states. Once again, however, the legislation provided little direction on how the FRC was to carry out or assess the success of such a plan, so the commission eventually settled upon a complex "points" system based on wattage and hours of operation. Ironically, given the Western zone's massive land area, the Davis Amendment impeded efforts to equalize radio service to that area. The Federal Radio Commission, and later the Federal Communications Commission, continued to tinker with the quota system until the Davis Amendment was repealed in 1936.[29]

In the meantime, however, the FRC, after discontinuing the licenses of mobile broadcasters and deleting more than 60 stations judged not to be serving the public interest, began work on a general reallocation plan to comply with the Davis Amendment. Still, the commission set out to disturb the existing structure as little as possible "in order that a minimum of inconvenience shall result to the public." Throughout discussions of various plans, the commission also cited "almost perfect unanimity of opinion" that powerful clear channel stations to provide rural service should be the keystone of any allocation structure. The only terms of debate with regard to clear channels were how much power they should be allowed and how many of them to allocate. Engineers offered various plans including from 25 to 50 cleared channels and maintained as "purely physical fact" that they were the only way to "provide high-class programs" to rural areas.[30]

It also was essentially a given that the allocation spots for clear channel stations would be given to the most powerful broadcasting interests, especially the chains. Because of the commission's intention to upset the existing allocation as little as possible and its reliance on stations' existing technical ability to broadcast with high power, it was largely a foregone conclusion that the "new" allocation plan would look a lot like the one that already was in place. Commission secretary Carl Butman defended this circular logic by likening radio broadcasting to the railroad industry, where, he said, the biggest railroads were the best. "These trains are, of course, high powered, given right of way, and best serve the public because they maintain their schedules, and so with the broadcasting stations I have in mind." He stated that in the early 1920s the large electric and radio interests were the only ones "that saw the possibilities of high-powered broadcasting [and] had the engineering backing and financial ability to undertake such station construction." Since that time, he noted, "they have maintained their stations efficiently and rendered good programs and obeyed the radio laws in every instance." This attempt to fit radio regulation into a transportation model of understanding was common during the 1920s and still exists to a great extent in modern regulation. In other instances, commission engineers noted that the chains' experience in broadcasting was greatest and that "they will probably continue to lead the field." The lone opposition on the commission to the outlines of the new allocation plan came from acting chairman Ira E. Robinson, who decried the reliance on testimony from "big business minded" engineers. "I want to go on record that I shall ever oppose the use of the air, undoubtedly belonging to all of the public, being 'grabbed' by private interests," he wrote.[31]

In August 1928, the FRC announced General Order 40, which set out its new allocation plan. Forty of the AM band's 96 frequencies, while not designated clear channel, were reserved for only one station operating at night. These 40 frequencies were divided among the five zones, with each zone assigned eight clear frequencies. Of the remaining 56 frequencies in the broadcast band, 35 were designated as regional channels with two to three stations in each zone, 15 were designated as local channels and the remaining six were reserved for the exclusive use of Canada. The clear channel assignments essentially mirrored those proposed in the FRC's 1927 allocation, although frequency shifts meant that the exclusive channels were no longer in a single block. The allocation plan met the FRC's objectives of establishing order in the broadcast band, doing so with a minimum of disruption to existing stations and meeting the vague requirements of the Davis Amendment, but these objectives mandated an allocation system that was less than ideal. "The disadvantage [is] that the allocation's structure is fortuitous rather than logical or planned," J.D. Dellinger, the FRC's chief engineer, pointed out, noting that if the commission would have started from scratch it could have created a much more logical framework for efficiently assigning stations. Still, the rationalization of the commercial structure of broadcasting under General Order 40 led one radio engineer to call it "Radio's Emancipation Proclamation."[32]

One of the allocation plan's most glaring weaknesses was its endorsement of shared-time and limited-time stations. In many cases, rather than delete stations, the commission assigned conflicting broadcasters to time-sharing arrangements, where, for example, two stations would broadcast on alternate days of the week. On 11 of the designated exclusive frequencies, in fact, stations were forced to share time, despite the fact that the commission had previously called such arrangements "uneconomic." General Order 40 also assigned daytime-only stations on 10 frequencies and limited-time stations on 13 more; these assignments, of course, were intended to fit more stations into the broadcast band during hours when they would not interfere with other stations' secondary service. General Order 41, released just days after General Order 40, mandated that daytime stations not operate past the average time of sunset each month at the location of their transmitters. Later, the FRC established criteria for limited-time stations as daytime hours plus any time not being used by other stations on the same frequency. For example, a limited-time station located in the West could broadcast in the evening hours if the dominant station to the east had already signed off. The commission noted, however, that it was within the discretion of the dominant station to reclaim such extended hours of operation if it desired. Naturally, a large number of daytime and limited-time stations would eventually want to increase their hours of operation, despite the fact that the commission noted that if it allowed them to do so "the operation of the entire [allocation] plan will be ruined."[33]

The only major commercial station to lose its clear channel assignment in the 1928 allocation was General Electric's WGY in

Schenectady, New York, which was reduced to a limited-time assignment with KGO of Oakland, California, on 790 kHz. GE owned KGO as well, but objected to restrictions on WGY's operating hours. It appealed the FRC's decision to the Court of Appeals for the District of Columbia, arguing in essence that the FRC had refused to renew its license and thus was depriving the station of its property rights. While the court refused to accept that station licensees possessed property rights, it agreed that the FRC should not have limited WGY's operating hours. Noting the station's record of performing "great experimental work" and the large population in its listening area, the court ruled that full-time operation by WGY was in the public interest. The FRC thus restored it to full-time in March 1929, allowing both it and KGO to use the same frequency.[34]

By the beginning of 1930, the FRC was receiving complaints of interference between exclusive stations broadcasting on frequencies near each other, especially in the Eastern zone. In April, the commission issued General Order 87, shifting the zone assignments of 15 exclusive frequencies with the goal of providing greater frequency separation between interfering stations. The owners of three of the affected stations—Westinghouse (KYW Philadelphia), Stromberg-Carlson (WHAM Rochester) and the Courier-Journal Company (WHAS Louisville)—appealed the FRC's decision and secured a restraining order against the shifts. The stations argued that the FRC was proposing a modification of their licenses without holding hearings and noted that none of the stations had requested a changed assignment, and the commission eventually abandoned the efforts to shift the frequencies. In November 1931, the commission adopted rules and regulations affirming the basic allocation of 1928 but referring to the 40 exclusive frequencies as clear channels for the first time.[35]

Throughout the late 1920s and early 1930s, as the FRC watched over the rapid development of a network-dominated commercial radio system, Congress continually decried the "chain monopoly" in radio broadcasting. Central to this criticism was the dominance of networks—especially NBC—over clear channel assignments and that those clear channel stations that were not owned by networks quickly affiliated with them. Edward Nockels, manager of the

Chicago Federation of Labor's nonprofit WCFL, noted that "the radio air has been monopolized so that the Big Power interests, Big Business, and the Big Newspaper interests have gotten all the cleared radio channels and nobody else has a 'peep-in.'" WCFL and other noncommercial groups, such as the Missionary Society of St. Paul the Apostle's WLWL, campaigned unsuccessfully for single clear channel assignments while each network possessed several.[36]

The chain dominance led to the duplication of programming as the lure of network programming's profitability and wide audience prompted stations to sharply curtail local programming. Many listeners complained that the broadcast system seemed to consist of a lot of stations running the same shows at the same time. In 1928, the FRC proposed to squelch duplication on clear channels by prohibiting stations located less than 300 miles apart from airing the same programming during evening hours, but it quickly rescinded the plan. The FRC said that it found that listeners objected to curtailing network programs. "People protested and said they wanted the New York programs," Commissioner Harold LaFount told Congress. A year later, the commission rejected a motion that would have prohibited stations using more than 5,000 watts from broadcasting chain programs.[37]

CONCLUSION

In the course of a decade, radio broadcasting had grown from an experimental curiosity to a medium of communications that had attracted both the interest of listeners and the money of capitalism. Along the way, a system of allocating frequencies had arisen largely from experimentation and chance, and it was open to criticism on many fronts. Clear channel stations, which had developed from early experiments with long-distance broadcasting, were now a key component in the allocation plan; however, they were also at the center of criticism of the emerging commercial broadcasting system and of brewing disputes over frequency assignments, hours of operation and broadcasting power.

The commission's attempt to accommodate an existing structure rather than implement a new allocation plan also created problems that would plague allocation policy for decades. Time-sharing arrangements among two or more stations on one frequency were cumbersome and led to disputes among the stations. Daytime-only stations, wedged into the broadcast band and hampered by continually changing hours of operation, began to push for fulltime operation, or at least greater stability. Clear channel stations, broadcasting during the evening and nighttime on exclusive frequencies, would inevitably pursue even higher power; at the same time opponents would look to duplication of the clear channels as a way to provide more room for other stations. Although the systematized allocation that had developed by 1928 succeeded in establishing order out of the chaos of broadcasting's nascent years, it was in many ways an unsustainable house of cards that played stations against one another. For the next three decades, the clear channel dispute would be the most significant of these intra-industry squabbles.

NOTES

1. Senate Committee on Interstate Commerce, *Radio Control: Hearings on S. 1 and S. 1754*, 69th Cong., 1st Sess. (Washington, D.C., 1926), 17.

2. Radio Act of 1912, Public Law No. 264, 62nd Cong., August 13, 1912.

3. Christopher H. Sterling and John M. Kittross, *Stay Tuned: A Concise History of American Broadcasting* (Belmont, Calif.: Wadsworth Publishing Company, 1990), 30, 45–46; Susan J. Douglas, *Inventing American Broadcasting, 1899–1922* (Baltimore: Johns Hopkins University Press, 1987), 285; and Erik Barnouw, *A Tower in Babel: A History of Broadcasting in the United States to 1933* (New York: Oxford University Press, 1968), 47–48.

4. See Barnouw, *A Tower in Babel*, 59–60; Sterling and Kittross, *Stay Tuned*, 55–58; and Douglas, *Inventing American Broadcasting*, 290.

5. Radio Act of 1912.

6. See Christopher H. Sterling, *Electronic Media: A Guide to Trends in Broadcasting and Newer Technologies, 1920–1983* (New York: Praeger, 1984), 5; and Edward F. Sarno, Jr., "The National Radio Conferences," *Journal of Broadcasting* 13 (Spring 1969): 193; and Sterling and Kittross, *Stay Tuned*, 63.

7. See CCBS, *Summary History of Allocation in the Standard Broadcast Band* (Washington, D.C.: Press of Byron S. Adams, 1948), 6; Radio Act of 1912; and Sarno, "The National Radio Conferences," 190.

8. See Louise Benjamin, "Working It out Together: Radio Policy from Hoover to the Radio Act of 1927," *Journal of Broadcasting and Electronic Media* 42 (Spring 1998): 221–22; Sarno, "The National Radio Conferences," 189; and C.M. Jansky, Jr., "The Contribution of Herbert Hoover to Broadcasting," *Journal of Broadcasting* 1 (Summer 1957): 241, 244.

9. See Sarno "The National Radio Conferences," 192; and Department of Commerce, *Minutes of Open Meeting of Department of Commerce Conference on Radio Telephony*, February 27 and 28, 1922, FCC Library, Washington, D.C., 21, 33.

10. See Benjamin, "Working It out Together," 224; and Department of Commerce, *Radio Service Bulletin No. 64*, September 1, 1922, 10.

11. See Department of Commerce, *Radio Service Bulletin No. 66*, October 2, 1922, 10; Sterling and Kittross, *Stay Tuned*, 83; and Barnouw, *A Tower in Babel*, 122. The term "meters" refers to an alternate method of designating broadcast frequencies used in the early days of radio.

12. See Benjamin, "Working It out Together," 227; and CCBS, *Summary History*, 9.

13. Barnouw, *A Tower in Babel*, 179

14. FCC, *Daytime Skywave Transmissions*, 24 FR 7755 (1959).

15. CCBS, *Summary History*, 10.

16. Department of Commerce, *Recommendations for Regulation of Radio* (Washington, D.C., 1924), 5, 6, 14.

17. Department of Commerce, *Radio Service Bulletin No. 92*, December 1, 1924, 11–12.

18. Department of Commerce, *Proceedings and Recommendations for Regulation of Radio* (Washington, D.C., 1925), 3, 21–23.

19. See Radio Communication: Issuance of Licenses, 29 Op. Atty. Gen. 579 (1912); Hoover v. Intercity Radio Company, 286 Fed. 1003 (1923); and George Harry Rogers, "The History of the Clear Channel and Super Power Controversy in the Management of the Standard Broadcast Allocation Plan" (Ph.D. Diss., University of Utah, 1972), 78.

20. See Barnouw, *A Tower in Babel*, 180; United States v. Zenith Radio Corporation, 12 F. 2d 614 (1926); and Federal Regulation of Radio Broadcasting, 35 Op. Atty. Gen. 126 (1926).

21. See Robert W. McChesney, *Telecommunications, Mass Media and Democracy* (New York: Oxford University Press, 1994), 16; and FRC, *Annual Report* (Washington, D.C., 1927), 10–11.

22. McChesney, *Telecommunications, Mass Media and Democracy*, 18.

23. FCC, *Report on Chain Broadcasting* (Washington, D.C., 1941), 5–7.

24 . FCC, *Report on Chain Broadcasting*, 7, 8, 15, 21.

25 . FRC Minutes, April 29, 1927, 27, Meeting Minutes, Microfilm 1.1, RG 173, National Archives, College Park, Md. (hereafter referred to as NACP).

26 . See McChesney, *Telecommunications, Mass Media and Democracy*, 20; and FRC, *Annual Report*, 7.

27. FRC, *Second Annual Report* (Washington, D.C., 1928), 8–11, 42, 70–77.

28. FRC, *Second Annual Report*, 77.

29. See House Committee on Interstate and Foreign Commerce, *Regulation of Broadcasting: Half a Century of Government Regulation of Broadcasting and the Need for Further Legislative Action*, 85th Cong., 1st Sess. (Washington, D.C., 1958), 17–18; FRC, *Second Annual Report*, 11, 13, 117; and "Danger Signals Ahead of Radio," *Broadcasting*, October 15, 1931, 28.

30. See FCC, *Second Annual Report*, 14–16; Orestes H. Caldwell to Commission, July 26, 1928, 20-2 Memorandums, General Correspondence, 1927–1946, RG 173, NACP; *Agreements and Differences*, April 24, 1928, 66-4 Allocation, RG 173, NACP; Confidential Memo, August 13, 1928, 66-4 Allocation, General Correspondence, 1927–1946, RG 173, NACP; and McChesney, *Telecommunications, Mass Media and Democracy*, 35–36.

31. See Carl H. Butman to Orestes H. Caldwell, February 2, 1928, 20-2 Memorandums, General Correspondence, 1927–1946, RG 173, NACP; Mary S. Mander, "The Public Debate About Broadcasting in the Twenties: An Interpretive History," *Journal of Broadcasting*, 28 (Spring 1984): 167; S.C. Hooper to Commission, July 18, 1928, 66-4 Allocation, General Correspondence, 1927–1946, RG 173, NACP; and

McChesney, *Telecommunications, Mass Media and Democracy*, 35.

32. FRC, *Second Annual Report*, 48–50; J.D. Dellinger to Broadcast Committee, August 22, 1928, 66-4 Allocation, General Correspondence, 1927–1946, RG 173, NACP; and McChesney, *Telecommunications, Mass Media and Democracy*, 34.

33. See FRC, Press Release, April 11, 1928, 66-4 Allocation, General Correspondence, 1927–1946, RG 173, NACP; FRC, *Second Annual Report*, 50, 54; and Report of Special Allocation Advisory Group, April 20, 1928, 66-4 Allocation, General Correspondence, 1927–1946, RG 173, NACP.

34. General Electric Co. v. FRC, 31 F. 2d. 630 (1929), 633, 634.

35. See Westinghouse Electric and Manufacturing Company v. FRC, 47 F. 2d. 415 (1931); Saltzman v. Stromberg-Carlson Telephone Manufacturing Company, 46 F. 2d. 612 (1931); Courier-Journal Company v. FRC, 46 F. 2d. 614 (1931); FRC, *Fourth Annual Report* (Washington, D.C., 1930), 66–69; and CCBS, *Summary History*, 31.

36. See McChesney, *Telecommunications, Mass Media and Democracy*, 20–21, 33; Rogers, "The History of the Clear Channel and Super Power Controversy," 106–7; and Nathan Godfried, *WCFL: Chicago's Voice of Labor, 1926–78* (Urbana: University of Illinois Press, 1997), 80.

37. See "WLWL Campaigns for Clear Channel," *Broadcasting*, July 1, 1932, 8; FRC Minutes, September 8, 1928, 47, Meeting Minutes, Microfilm 1.1, RG 173, NACP; and FRC Minutes, November 5, 1929, 277, Meeting Minutes, Microfilm 1.1, RG 173, NACP.

CHAPTER THREE

The Greatest Static Eliminator We Know Of

In the late 1930s, WLW's signal was so powerful that some said that you did not even need a radio to hear it. Farmers near the station's transmitter in Mason, Ohio, northwest of Cincinnati, said they could hear WLW coming from their barbed-wire fences. Various instances of the station's programs coming from other metal objects were reported as well, and it was said that if you attached a light bulb to a strand of wire and stuck it in the ground near WLW's 831-foot tower, it would light. The station, in fact, rewired several homes near the transmitter site after owners complained that their lights stayed on even when they were switched off.[1]

Although some of these reports are likely apocryphal, it is true that from 1934 to 1939 WLW broadcast with more power than any other station in the United States because it had secured "experimental" authorization from the Federal Radio Commission in 1932 to increase its output to 500,000 watts. The Cincinnati clear channel outlet that had already dubbed itself "The Nation's Station" could now legitimately claim that as more than a mere slogan: in a

1935 postcard survey conducted by the Federal Communications Commission, rural listeners in 13 states listed WLW as their first radio choice. It was thus not surprising that WLW wanted to make its 500,000-watt license permanent and that other clear channel stations sought similar consideration for themselves as well.[2]

WLW's high power formed the backdrop for the debate over clear channels in the 1930s. Although there would be no major changes in policy regarding clear channels during the decade, the arguments over the WLW experiment presaged the debate that would come after World War II. As a result of WLW's superpower operation, clear channel proponents showed that higher power on clear channels was an efficient way to improve rural radio service, but at the same time the terms of policy debate shifted from engineering aspects to social, political and economic concerns. Although in practice the increased emphasis of the Federal Communications Commission (FCC) on such matters merely cemented the status quo commercial radio structure, clear channel stations could not overcome the perceived negative effects of the superpower operation. The clear channel structure was preserved, but what was beginning to seem as the natural tendency for power limits to be revised upward every few years stopped. Fifty thousand watts remains the regular limit for AM broadcast stations to this day, and the 500,000-watt WLW transmitter of the late 1930s is still the most powerful ever used regularly in the United States' standard broadcast band.

The debate of the 1930s also was important because it marked the emergence of station interest groups. Although networks and radio giants such as RCA and Westinghouse had maintained a lobbying presence since the beginning days of regulation and the National Association of Broadcasters (NAB) represented the overall broadcast industry, during the 1930s groups of stations began to organize their own representative groups. The most notable of these was the Clear Channel Group (CCG), formed by a number of independent clear channel stations in 1934. In response, a group of regional and local stations came together as the National Association of Regional Broadcast Stations (NARBS), which would oppose the CCG's overtures for higher power. Although the groups would become more formal and the techniques more sophisticated in later decades, the terms of the clear channel debate were largely set by the end of the 1930s.

HIGHER POWER AND THE WHITE AREAS

WLW always had been a pioneer in high-power broadcasting. Powel Crosley, Jr., who owned the station as part of the Crosley Corporation manufacturing conglomerate, began his broadcasting career in 1921 with experimental station 8CR's 20-watt transmitter; the station boosted its power to 50 watts and became WLW in 1922. He pioneered use of 500 watts and 5,000 watts, and WLW was among the first stations to use 50,000 watts on a regular basis. In 1932, the Federal Radio Commission granted Crosley's request for a license to operate experimental station W8XO at night with up to 500,000 watts on WLW's 700 kHz frequency. The license was approved, according to the FRC, to "permit development of more powerful transmitters for study of service area, fading, interference, and increased service to the public at increased powers." Central to such a study was improving service to rural areas, which, despite the reservation of high-power clear channels since 1928, still lagged well behind urban areas in quality and choice of signals.[3]

Indeed, this problem was especially pronounced during nighttime hours, when skywave interference played havoc with reception in the AM band. The FCC estimated during the 1930s that more than half of the land area of the United States did not receive primary (groundwave) service from any radio station. In this area of nearly 1.7 million square miles, there were more than 21 million people; during the evening hours when most people listened to radio, residents in these areas received service only via less reliable skywave signals, usually provided by clear channel stations. By the end of the 1930s, these sections of the country without primary nighttime service had come to be called White Areas because on maps showing shaded signal coverage these areas remained white, as shown in Figure 3.1. The majority of the White Area land was west of the Mississippi; however, most of the White Area population resided in the East. Providing more reliable service to the White Areas would be at the center of the debate over clear channels for the next half century.[4]

FIGURE 3.1   Shading indicates areas receiving primary (groundwave)
service at night from one or more broadcast stations (as
computed by the FCC's engineering department).

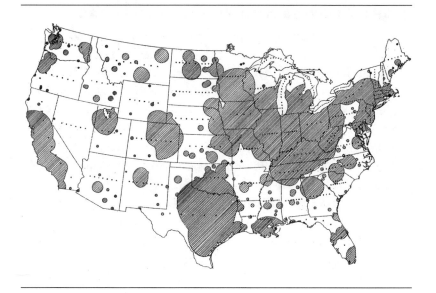

The attempt to improve rural service in large part drove the
steady power increases for clear channel stations throughout the
late 1920s and early 1930s. Soon after announcing General Order
40 in 1928, the commission set the power limit for exclusive channels at 25,000 watts. However, it authorized the use of up to 50,000
watts on an experimental basis to ascertain what, if any, interference higher power would cause. Chairman Ira Robinson opposed
power in excess of 10,000 watts, as did Commissioner Harold
LaFount, who called the higher limit "excessive, extremely dangerous and not in the public interest at this time or in the immediate future."[5]

By 1929, however, seven exclusive stations had the capability
to broadcast with 50,000 watts, although only four—WEAF, WGY,
KDKA and WLW—were doing so; the majority of exclusive stations used 5,000 watts, and a few used between 10,000 and 30,000
watts. In June 1930, the commission announced that it would grant
authorization for 50,000 watts on up to 20 of the exclusive frequencies after holding hearings to determine which stations were

most likely to provide improved rural service by increasing power. The examiner who oversaw these hearings in the fall of 1930 recommended that all 40 channels be granted 50,000 watts. "With all clear channel stations operating with power output of 50 KW, the rural listener, without increased cost to him, would receive greatly improved and additional radio broadcasting reception," he noted. "The pioneers and promoters of the radio art deserve the gratitude and appreciation of the general public for the marvelous contribution they have made to the progress of the present age." The commission, however, adhering to its original intention, granted 50,000-watt authorization to only 20 stations, although in September 1933 it opened all clear channel stations to 50,000-watt power.[6]

But in the early 1930s, Crosley was one of only a handful of broadcasters in the country who possessed the financial ability and willingness to construct and operate a 500,000-watt transmitter. In all, the superpower facility cost nearly $350,000 to build, and about $120,000 a year more to operate than a comparable 50,000-watt transmitter. Moreover, the use of power levels higher than 50,000 watts on a regular basis was uncharted territory. The commission had given General Electric permission to experiment with up to 200,000 watts over WGY in the late 1920s and would later grant similar authorization for Westinghouse's KDKA, but both of these studies were sporadic and variable, aimed more at developing equipment than studying service area. The intent of WLW's experiment, on the other hand, was to provide regularly scheduled broadcast service. The commission could study the effects of higher power on rural service, and Crosley—through increased coverage area and advertising rates on WLW—would benefit as well. "Crosley envisioned WLW's call letters beaming across the seas and from one end of the U.S. to the other," one writer noted. He also hoped to increase sales of his low-cost, low-sensitivity receiving sets, which, if unable to tune in lesser stations would at least be able to pick up WLW's booming signal.[7]

The WLW 500,000-watt transmitter was the result of a cooperative effort among the Crosley Corporation, Westinghouse, General Electric and RCA. It was both a physical behemoth and an electrical wonder: 26-foot-high tubes required 1,200 gallons of cir-

culated water each minute to keep them cool, and the audio trans-
former weighed 88,000 pounds. "The most powerful broadcasting
station in the world!" WLW's promotional department breathlessly
noted. "It is inanimate ... it is neuter ... yet it lives ... it speaks ...
it sings. This giant is your servant." An editorial in *Broadcasting*
magazine proclaimed Crosley "no less a pioneer in his own sphere
than the great American trail blazers and railroad builders of the
nineteenth century," noting that his willingness to finance a
500,000-watt operation "took courage as well as foresight." Crosley
himself estimated that his coverage would increase 25 times, and
he boasted that the station "might be picked up anywhere in the
world."[8]

WLW engineers tested the new transmitter at night throughout
the first quarter of 1934 and sporadically broadcast during the
day as well. Although given the experimental designation W8XO,
the station normally broadcast WLW's regular programming
schedule. On April 3, 1934, Crosley applied to the FRC for authorization to operate WLW full-time using the 500,000-watt transmitter. The FRC granted the request on April 17, and on May 2
Crosley formally dedicated the "new" WLW, calling the powerful
transmitter "the greatest static eliminator we know of." As part of
the dedication ceremonies, President Franklin D. Roosevelt
pressed a gold telegraph key on his desk, ostensibly to power up
the new transmitter; however, in reality the new power did not
start until the tubes had taken a few minutes to warm up. Roosevelt
joined others such as David Sarnoff, Guglielmo Marconi and Albert
Einstein in congratulating Crosley. "I feel certain that WLW will
give the people of our country and those in our neighbor nations a
service managed and conducted for the greater good of all,"
Roosevelt said. From a public relations standpoint, Crosley could
scarcely have done better: not only were respected radio pioneers
and inventors speaking in favor of his new powerful station, the
president seemed to be giving his blessing as well. Higher power
for clear channel stations was being made to seem a natural evolution of science, a public service gesture and a demonstration of
American know-how.[9]

FORMATION OF STATION INTEREST GROUPS

Although the WLW experiment was intended to assess the effectiveness of increased power on the clear channels, the number of frequencies with only one station broadcasting at night had been decreasing since the 1928 allocation. Of the original 40 frequencies designated as clear by General Order 40, only 32 remained clear by the end of 1934. The first clear channel was duplicated less than six months after the implementation of General Order 40, when the FCC was forced to reinstate WGY's full-time operation, subsequently allowing the Schenectady station to broadcast full-time on the clear channel occupied by KGO in San Francisco. With the exception of two frequencies made available for use by Canada, all of the remaining affected frequencies had been duplicated by consent of the dominant clear channel station. In other words, dominant stations had allowed certain daytime or limited time stations to operate full-time on their frequencies; in many cases, this consent came as a result of payment made to the dominant station. The remaining clear channel stations, however, claimed they were subjected to "every conceivable sort of pressure" to allow such duplications of their frequencies, and at the same time feared that the increasing number of duplications by consent would make the commission more likely to authorize mandatory duplications.[10]

One of these clear channel stations was Nashville's WSM. KPCB, a limited-time station in Seattle operating on WSM's 650 kHz frequency, sought permission to broadcast full-time and enlisted the help of Washington senators Clarence C. Dill and Homer Bone, who buttonholed Tennessee senator Kenneth McKeller in an effort to pressure WSM to consent to the duplication. Dill, of course, was a leading authority on radio in Congress. McKeller approached Edwin W. Craig, who operated WSM as part of the National Life and Accident Insurance Company, but Craig opposed the duplication and asked his chief engineer, John H. (Jack) DeWitt, to draw up a technical study showing that KPCB's full-time operation would disrupt WSM's nighttime coverage. "I was pretty careful to say that it would interfere with WSM's signal," DeWitt later said, "although I must admit that it [KPCB] was awfully far away."

TABLE 3.1   First stations to join the Clear Channel Group

KFI	Los Angeles, California	Earle C. Anthony, Inc.	640 kHz
KNX[a]	Hollywood, California	Western Broadcast Co.	1050 kHz
WBAP	Ft. Worth, Texas	Carter Publications, Inc.	800 kHz[b]
WFAA	Dallas, Texas	A.H. Belo Corporation	800 kHz[b]
WGN	Chicago, Illinois	WGN, Inc.	720 kHz
WHAM	Rochester, New York	Stromberg-Carlson Manufacturing Co.	1150 kHz
WHAS	Louisville, Kentucky	Louisville Times Co.	820 kHz
WJR	Detroit, Michigan	WJR, The Goodwill Station	750 kHz
WLS	Chicago, Illinois	Agricultural Broadcasting Co.	870 kHz
WLW	Cincinnati, Ohio	Crosley Radio Corp.	700 kHz
WOAI	San Antonio, Texas	Southland Industries, Inc.	1190 kHz
WSB	Atlanta, Georgia	Atlanta Journal Co.	740 kHz
WSM	Nashville, Tennessee	National Life & Accident Insurance Co.	650 kHz
WWL	New Orleans, Louisiana	Loyola University	850 kHz

[a] Became ineligible for CCG membership when purchased by CBS in December 1936.

[b] Shared time on frequency.

In reality, clear channel stations such as WSM sought to protect their frequencies from duplication not necessarily because of interference that would result under present conditions but because of interference with higher-power operation. And many clear channel stations—WSM included—believed that higher-power authorization was imminent, especially in light of the ongoing WLW experiment. Those stations that desired increased coverage and power in the future, therefore, took great pains to preserve their clear channels.[11]

The experience heightened Craig's anxiety over the duplication of clear channels, whether through individual consent, FRC policy change or the operation of foreign stations on U.S. clear channels. In May 1934, he called together a group of clear channel station representatives who were in Chicago for an advertising meeting and found that the owners of several other clear channel stations shared his concerns. The group agreed that it should petition the FCC to investigate the overall clear channel structure, with the assumption being that such an inquiry would "establish beyond argument the necessity of clear channels for serving rural and small-town America."[12]

In an effort to more uniformly represent their interests, the stations formed the Clear Channel Group (CCG), electing Craig chairman. The organization allowed any station holding an unduplicated clear channel and "interested in preserving the channel as clear" to join but prohibited membership by network-owned clear channel stations. At the time, networks—NBC and CBS— owned 12 clear channel stations. Initially, 14 stations joined the CCG, as shown in Table 3.1. Only one eligible station, KSL in Salt Lake City, chose not to. Nonetheless, KSL contributed to the CCG's technical studies and—according to CCG members—was "in full sympathy and agreement" with the group.[13]

Forming the Clear Channel Group not only allowed the clear channel stations to pool their resources, it also—by prohibiting the membership of network-owned stations—let the "independent" clear channel stations insulate themselves from monopoly charges leveled at networks. The membership of the Clear Channel Group, in fact, included five stations owned by newspapers, three owned by companies involved only in broadcasting, two by electrical or radio equipment manufacturers, and one each by a life insurance company, an automobile distributor, a farm journal, and a university. Although all of the CCG members were affiliated with one or more networks, since they were independently owned, they believed they could reasonably argue that they were not part of any network monopoly. During the CCG's tenure, the prohibition on the membership of network-owned stations was for the most part merely a public relations move, although several members of the group resented the networks' willingness to allow frequencies to be duplicated in order to further their own interests, such as had happened when WGY duplicated KGO's clear channel in 1929. Craig maintained that individual licensees of clear channel stations had no right "to bargain away the rights of the listening public by so-called consent."[14]

Although Craig spearheaded the formation of the Clear Channel Group and the Clear Channel Broadcasting Service, Louis Caldwell was a much more significant influence in developing the group's strategy. As the Federal Radio Commission's first general counsel, Caldwell was largely responsible for General Order 40 and since that time had become legal counsel for at least nine different clear channel stations. He was also the first chairman of both the American Bar Association's Standing Committee on Radio Law and the Federal Communications Bar Association, and he was acknowledged by the latter group as "the foremost authority on communications law." Along with championing the commercial, network-linked system of broadcasting, Caldwell believed in powerful clear channel stations as the most important links in the overall allocation scheme. In a 1932 article in *The Journal of Radio Law,* he decried the piecemeal breakdown of the clear channel structure through individual duplications, characterizing it as "the relentless process of corrosion which is working toward the eventual destruction of clear channels." He called the United States' 50,000-watt power limitation "a curious compound with a large ingredient of psychology caused by hostility against 'high power' on the part of a few members of Congress who have confused high power, clear channels, and chain programs with the supposed menace of a radio trust." This artificial power limit, Caldwell wrote, served only to deprive rural listeners of adequate radio service:

> This means the reduction or elimination of broadcast service to rural areas in favor of additional service at urban centres in which the advertiser is more interested. Rural listeners have no organization through which to give effective voice to their rights and interests. ... [H]igh power stations on clear channels are indispensable if our rural population is to receive broadcasting service.

This argument, which tied together the interests of clear channels and rural listeners, would be echoed by Caldwell and clear channel proponents for the next several decades. Clear channel stations sought the maintenance of their exclusive status and increased power, they said, because they were looking out for the interests of rural listeners.[15]

As a result of the initial CCG meeting in Chicago, Caldwell drew up a petition, calling for the Federal Communications Commission—which in July 1934 had supplanted the FRC—to investigate the clear channel structure, which he contended was "in imminent danger of a total or partial breakdown with corresponding

destruction of rural broadcast service." The FCC obliged, order-
ing a study of the utilization of the broadcast band, especially as it
related to clear channels. In addition to technical studies, the commission also proposed a postcard survey to find out what classes
of stations rural residents listened to. However, efforts to turn the
survey into anything even approaching a referendum on commercial, network-dominated programming were rebuffed by the commission. Tracy Tyler of the National Committee on Education by
Radio suggested to Commissioner Hampson Gary that the FCC
expand its survey to ask rural listeners about their views on radio
advertising, but Gary responded that the allocation survey was
intended to gauge what classes of stations rural residents listened
to, not the type of programs they liked. "The entire allocation
survey does not touch on the question of programs," he replied.
So the questionnaires, sent to nearly 106,000 rural residents,
merely asked respondents whether they owned a radio, how old it
was and the call letters of their four favorite radio stations.[16]

More than 32,000 questionnaires were returned, and the results showed that 76.3 percent of listeners relied primarily on clear
channel stations for their radio entertainment. "The general conclusion," the commission said, "was that the average rural listener
is dependent upon secondary service from clear channel stations,
frequently hundreds of miles away." The survey also indicated
that WLW had particularly impressive coverage of the rural population. It was the first choice of listeners in 13 states from Michigan to Florida, and in six other states, among them Texas, it was
the second overall choice. The survey demonstrated, according to
the commission, "the effectiveness of the use of higher power in
extending the coverage and rendering increased service to rural
listeners."[17]

Early in 1936 the FCC announced its intention to fold the clear
channel inquiry into hearings in October on the entire AM allocation structure, vowing to collect information "not only in its engineering but also in its corollary social and economic phases." The
repeal of the Davis Amendment in June 1936 made the upcoming
hearings even more significant; no longer constrained by the un-
workable quota systems among the five zones, the commission
would now have a freer hand in deciding allocation matters. Still,

before the hearings began it became obvious that no radical changes would be made in the allocation structure, with the FCC citing a desire to pursue "evolution, experimentation and voluntary action" rather than more substantive solutions. The commission's additional intention to seek "cooperation with the industry in solving the basic radio problems confronting the nation" ensured that whatever changes would be made in the allocation would be favorable to the continuing development of the commercial system.[18]

In anticipation of the FCC hearings, the CCG, which had functioned only informally since its formation in 1934, picked up its pace considerably. By the middle of 1936, Caldwell was on retainer as legal counsel, and the group had authorized a budget of $25,000, with the money to be raised by assessing each member monthly "dues" of approximately $125. From the beginning, the CCG pursued a technical defense of clear channels, as well as a technical justification for power increases on them. A three-man committee composed of CCG station engineers started working on technical studies, and a Washington, D.C., engineering consulting firm was hired to help. Member stations also pooled their resources to gather technical data, and during the summer of 1936 CCG engineers enlisted station cooperation to perform signal strength studies on duplicated channels. Even the results of the 1935 postcard survey were treated as an engineering justification for clear channels, with Caldwell assuring group members that it would be an important weapon in the upcoming hearings: "While the facts set forth in the survey are, or ought to be, a matter of common knowledge and common sense, this is the first time they have been proved; this is of immeasurable advantage in freeing the issues of loose claims and political considerations."[19]

Despite the fact that most CCG members had applied for power in excess of 50,000 watts, there was considerable discussion at planning meetings over whether the group should promote superpower. Some members—such as WLW—were obviously eager to pursue increased power, but others were not. Still other members had what Craig called a passive attitude: they were willing to increase power if it was the only way to preserve their nighttime exclusivity, but because of the uncertain economic climate brought on by the Depression, they were not eager to do so. Unable to reach a strong consensus, the group's executive committee passed a nebulous resolution, noting support for 50,000 watts as a *minimum* power for clear channel stations. The resolution would guide the group's testimony throughout the hearings, as Caldwell and others concentrated on defending the value of clear channels for providing rural coverage while leaving the door open to possible superpower. If stations wished to pursue higher power, the group noted, they could do so on an individual basis.[20]

As the Clear Channel Group was preparing for the fall hearings during the summer of 1936, regional stations also were organizing. At the July meeting of the NAB, several regional station representatives tried unsuccessfully to push through a resolution against superpower. The NAB tabled the resolution, noting that the issue—a divisive one among its membership—was not one in which it should become involved. Soon after, John Shepard III, owner of four regional stations and New England's Yankee Network, spearheaded the formation of the National Association of Regional Broadcast Stations (NARBS), retaining its own engineering consultant and legal counsel. NARBS sought power increases for regional stations from 1,000 to 5,000 watts and opposed superpower for clear channel stations; it called the reservation of clear channels "an uneconomic waste of potential radio facilities." In recruiting members, NARBS noted that presenting the regional case as a group would be more cost-effective and more impressive from the FCC's standpoint, and it also pointed out that regional stations had to oppose the presentation of the Clear Channel Group or else they would have no recourse if the FCC decided to grant superpower. Eventually, NARBS recruited more than 80 dues-paying regional stations. It, too, created a framing of its position that emphasized concern for listeners: it said that its membership of "progressive regional stations" had come together "with the hope and purpose of doing everything possible to improve radio service to the American people."[21]

The formation of NARBS and the Clear Channel Group was indicative of the larger trend toward factionalization in the commercial industry. 1936 was a pivotal year in this trend, with *Broadcasting* magazine noting that "more feeling and bitterness has been engendered in broadcasting ranks than at any time since organized broadcasting began." The upcoming allocation study, of course, was one reason for this discord, as groups of stations maneuvered to preserve and enhance their positions in the broadcast band. Music copyright was also a divisive issue, as affiliated stations opposed the networks' extensions of agreements with the American Society of Composers, Authors and Publishers (ASCAP) in 1935. Crosley formed the short-lived Associated Independent Radio Stations (AIRS) in the spring of 1936 to fight the networks on the copyright issue, signing on Shepard and several other clear channel, regional and local stations. AIRS, Crosley noted, would "combat all forms of inequitable exploitation" directed at independent stations by the networks. He also was supported by the National Independent Broadcasters (NIB), formed in the early 1930s to promote independent stations with national advertisers. Thus, the 1936 NAB convention became the venue for a showdown on the copyright issue, exposing the existing and developing fractures in the commercial industry. As a result of the convention, the NAB established its own library of music for broadcast use, eventually forming Broadcast Music, Incorporated, (BMI) as a rival to ASCAP. Significantly, the various disputes in the broadcasting industry of the 1930s showed that bitter rivals on one issue, such as Shepard and Crosley, were not above forming alliances on others.[22]

ALLOCATION HEARINGS OF 1936

Despite the FCC's announced intention to pursue issues beyond engineering concerns, Caldwell believed that the clear channels' engineering testimony would trump the less demonstrable and "objective" testimony on programming and economic effects. Thus, the group continued to concentrate on assembling engineering exhibits to show the technical value of clear channels and the benefits of superpower. However, in the fall of 1936, Caldwell, through conversations with commission personnel, began to realize that the Clear Channel Group could not ignore the social and economic consequences of superpower. "[I]t is becoming increasingly obvious," he told members just 11 days before the hearings began, "that economic and social issues are going to prove just as important as technical issues and perhaps more important." He encour-

vice, Maland's testimony was designed to assuage fears that clear
nnel stations—whether with 50,000 watts or 500,000—were
naging economically to other classes of stations. To this end,
WHO president noted that overall radio advertising volume
l grown more than 50 percent between 1933 and 1935 and that
classes of stations were sharing in this bounty. Maland, in fact,
sented a model in which local advertising business would be
ven to local and regional stations by clear channel power in-
ases, as such advertisers could not afford and would not need
coverage provided by superpower stations. Above all, he ar-
l that economic and social issues would take care of themselves
e commission followed the CCG's technical advice:

[T]here is no conflict, as is sometimes claimed, between sound eco-
omic and social principles and sound technical principles. Ad-
erence to the latter will further the public or social interest, and
the same time will further the industry's true economic interest.
is non-adherence to sound technical principles that leads to un-
onomic and anti-social consequences.

an argument, of course, played to the larger issue of the com-
ial industry's dominance of the American broadcasting sys-
What was good for the commercial industry, Maland con-
d, would be good for radio listeners.[30]
ul D.P. Spearman, testifying for NARBS, also endorsed the
soundness of an allocation structure based on industry eco-
cs but said that regional stations, as the "backbone of Ameri-
roadcasting," were in the best position to serve the public.
ugh Spearman maintained that NARBS believed social and
omic considerations outweighed "questions of mechanics," his
ment was merely that the allocation plan should favor com-
al regional stations rather than commercial clear channel
ns. The main substance of the NARBS argument was based
alism, as Spearman noted that local and regional stations
in a better position to provide service to rural areas and small
than distant clear channel stations. He opposed 500,000-
ower increases for clear channel stations, noting that they
not provide unique programming worthy of such coverage.

aged stations to begin compiling data on the "unique rural character" of clear channel programming, and he enlisted WHO president Joseph Maland to make a presentation downplaying any adverse effects of superpower on other classes of stations.[23]

As the hearings were set to begin, most observers agreed that
the focal point was the superpower issue; *Broadcasting* magazine
called it "the knottiest problem" before the commission. Any significant alteration to the allocation structure would have to address the clear channel issue, either by granting clear channel stations more power, maintaining the status quo, duplicating the clear
channel frequencies or relocating clear channel stations for more
efficient rural coverage. Many believed that WLW's experimental
license was a precursor to further power increases for clear channel stations, and even if the commission did not approve superpower, it might alter the allocation structure in a way that would
affect other classes of stations as well. It was not surprising, then,
that in anticipation of the October 1936 hearings the commercial
broadcasting industry fractured into such interest groups as the
CCG and NARBS. And while noncommercial interests testified as
well, their fate was already largely determined; now and in the
future, the battles in broadcasting would be fought among commercial interests. FCC chairman Eugene O. Sykes, a longtime
friend of the commercial industry who also had served on the Federal Radio Commission, set the tone for the hearings when he
opened the first session by noting that "requests for allocation of
broadcast facilities to particular groups or organizations will not
be considered."[24]

Proponents of reserving frequency space for noncommercial
stations were permitted to testify, although their calls for substantial realignment of the broadcast structure fell on deaf ears.
Howard Evans of the National Committee for Education by Radio
testified hopefully that the commission's intention to examine the
social effects of allocation "suggests a totally different standard
than the commission has used hitherto in making decisions about
allocation." He noted that the division of stations into classes was
unfair, especially to the noncommercial stations that were clus-
tered into the lower classes. "[T]he Commission has allowed in-
equality and unfairness to develop to an extent which undermines

the whole system of American broadcasting," he said. Similarly, representatives of other educational interests, including the National Association of Educational Broadcasters, called on the FCC to "look beyond its technical decisions to the social consequences of its acts." The FCC's chief engineer, T.A.M. Craven, however, was dismissive of the noncommercial interests. Again and again, Craven insisted that allocation was purely an engineering concern and that consideration of programming was not appropriate, given the "very little space" available for broadcasting. Craven's conduct in response to the noncommercial interests who opened the hearings clearly established that while the commission may be considering the social, political and economic effects of various allocation schemes within the existing commercial structure, it was not willing to consider the social, political and economic shortcomings of that structure.[25]

Edward Nockels of Chicago's WCFL presented a scathing critique of the existing broadcast structure, especially the dominance of the commercial interests. "Is it in the public interest, convenience and necessity that all of the 90 channels for radio broadcasting be given to capital and its friends and not even one channel for the millions who toil?" he asked. The clear channel structure, he contended, was particularly unsuited to providing public service, as the networks, "gluttons of monopoly and dedicated to the furtherance of selfish interest" controlled most of the time on clear channel stations. Granting 500,000-watt licenses to clear channel stations, Nockels said, would only make the situation worse. The only broadcasters that would be able to afford such facilities, he noted, would be the networks or other large commercial enterprises.[26]

The testimony of the Clear Channel Group presented the basic outline of the argument that would be used by clear channel proponents for the next five decades. Of paramount importance, the CCG argued, was providing radio service to rural areas of the country that presently lacked it, and the only way to do that was through the use of clear channels and high power. Once again invoking a transportation model, Craig likened broadcast service to train tracks, noting that the foremost issue was implementing a technical plan that provided usable "tracks" of radio service. The

questions of the kinds of programming to be
tracks and the licensees of stations on them, Cra
separate—and far less important—issues. As
edged that duplication of network programmin
thy of FCC study, but he noted that the com
impinge on individual stations' programming
erated the CCG members' "independent" stat
presence of ownership by people who are in a
or region in which the station is located" w
tance.[27]

Craig also decried the piecemeal duplicatio
on several of the original 40 clear channels
the duplications, he acknowledged, were una
plained that pressure for duplicating other cl
cies had now become contagious, causing des
vice. "A bait is dangled before the eyes of
wants a new station, or better facilities for
Caldwell later testified, "while every clear
defend its rural coverage ... against all com
the regulations." The CCG called on the FC
by consent and preserve those clear cha
unduplicated.[28]

In keeping with the CCG's resolution, Cra
for minimum power of clear channel statio
said that every CCG member would be willi
it was the only way to preserve clear chann
Craven whether the Clear Channel Group s
tion for its member stations, sidestepped
you make a mistake by talking about the
Caldwell insisted. "It isn't whether the st
entitled. It's the rural public." While clea
doing a good job of providing rural servic
tions, Caldwell contended, rural listeners
service than city dwellers. Although Cald
engineer, his exchanges with Craven prov
couch engineering issues in public service

While Craig and Caldwell emphasized
ing as the only technically feasible way to

Whatever original programming clear channel stations now provided, he predicted, would be cut as the financial demands of operating 500,000-watt transmitters siphoned money away from programs. Hedging his bets somewhat, Spearman said that if the FCC did authorize 500,000-watt operation, it should consider all classes of stations for such power, granting it only to those "located where they will actually render unique service which cannot be duplicated by any other means—if such areas exist." He also attacked the 1935 postcard survey, calling the results "superficial and open to question"; nonetheless, he contended that most rural listeners did receive adequate radio service, disputing the existence of the White Areas.[31]

Local stations without network affiliation were represented by the National Independent Broadcasters, whose president, Edward A. Allen, noted that "the local station has been in the position of Lazarus dependent upon the crumbs from the table of Dives." Allen did not directly address the issues of clear channels and superpower but asked that the FCC consider the importance of small, independent broadcasters in future allocation plans. However, the group's legal counsel, George O. Sutton, said that reservation of clear channels was discriminatory and caused overcrowding in the rest of the broadcast band. He also said that low-power stations had difficulty selling commercial time because of many advertisers' worship of power. "'The Nation's Station' is a term which they have taken with a certain amount of literalness," he said. Granting superpower to clear channel stations would exacerbate these difficulties and "threaten the economic stability of every class of station below [them]," Sutton noted.[32]

The two major networks urged caution on superpower, realizing that granting tenfold power increases to a series of clear channel stations might upset the existing network structure. Lenox Lohr, president of NBC, urged the commission to be cautious in increasing power levels but noted that his network was prepared to take its stations to 500,000 watts if the opportunity arose. Lohr also reacted favorably to a theoretical structure including 30 superpower clear channel stations. He contended that it would be "entirely beneficial to the public." CBS's William Paley expressed similar sentiments but cautioned that the network might be forced to drop smaller affiliates if superpower licenses were granted. He doubted, however, that superpower would have any substantial effect on rural service and in fact speculated that it might harm urban service. He also expressed concern that if clear channel stations were forced—either by regulation or economic pressure—to raise their power, it might siphon money away from ongoing development of high-band (FM), television and facsimile experiments.[33]

The most contentious portion of the hearings came when Crosley testified, as WLW's 500,000-watt operation became a lightning rod for concerns about the social and economic implications of clear channels. Commissioner George Henry Payne, a progressive Republican and former Bull Mooser who had alerted newspaper reporters to the possibility of "hot news" with Crosley on the stand, grilled WLW's owner about the station's operating practices. The commissioner alleged that Crosley refused to accept advertising from rival products to those manufactured by Crosley concerns, that he instructed the station's news department not to publicize labor disputes, and that he refused to allow minority groups on the station. Although Crosley denied the charges, Payne was able to produce a smoking gun in the form of station memoranda taken by newscaster Norman Corwin after he was fired by the station in 1935. Corwin had given the material to the American Civil Liberties Union, which in turn gave it to Payne. Among the memos was one instructing that "No reference to strikes is to be made on any news bulletin broadcast over our stations." Corwin, who later went on to have a successful career with CBS, was fired by WLW after suggesting that the no strikes policy might hurt the station's credibility in the event other media were reporting on a particular walkout.[34]

In later testimony, Frank Weizenecker of Cincinnati's Central Labor Council affirmed charges that WLW refused to cooperate with labor interests. "We contend that this station WLW is operated solely in the interest of Crosley and not in the public interest," he said. Craven was obviously angered by Payne's orchestration against Crosley, and likely by the commissioner's deviance from engineering issues. When asked by Chairman Sykes if he had any questions for Weizenecker, Craven curtly replied, "No,

sir. I am an engineer, sir. I have no questions." *Broadcasting* magazine also was indignant, calling Payne's display "the most brazen
piece of political demagoguery we have ever seen perpetrated at a
public hearing on radio." But despite the disagreement of some
with Payne's methods, he expressed a concern that would ultimately lead to the discontinuance of WLW's superpower license
and would play a large part in thwarting future clear channel power
increases: the concentration of power in the hands of a few owners, who—like Crosley—might be reluctant to let other views be
heard.[35]

WLW's aggressive marketing campaigns also hurt the broader
efforts of the clear channel stations to secure higher power. The
station's advertisements in trade magazines carried the notice of
500,000 watts prominently, and some promotions during 1935
graphically showed the Cincinnati station as equal to 10 50,000-
watt stations. Advertising rates on the station increased as well.
In January 1934, before the superpower experiment, the station
charged $990 for an hour of evening time on the station; an hour
during the day cost $495. By the end of 1934, the same nighttime
hour had increased to $1,200, and a daytime hour was $600. Still,
WLW maintained that it was not earning an unusual profit as a
result of the 500,000-watt experiment. Station manager James
Shouse submitted that although the station's profits had increased
steadily during the superpower period, expenses had risen at a
higher rate as WLW spent more on programming and transmitter
maintenance.[36]

At the same time, some stations located near Cincinnati complained that they were unable to secure national spot advertising
because of WLW's coverage. Stations in Indianapolis and Charleston, West Virginia, said that they were regularly refused national
advertising because WLW's signal already covered their audience.
An analysis of advertisements in Indianapolis newspapers during
1938, in fact, showed that national spot advertisers devoted more
space to promoting programs on WLW than they did on two Indianapolis stations combined. In one instance, an advertising
agency asked WCHS in Charleston, which carried advertisements
for Cincinnati's Red Top Brewing Company, to rebroadcast a WLW
program sponsored by Red Top and to distribute 10,000 circulars

promoting the program in Charleston. The station manager said that his station could not carry a program promoting WLW broadcasts since it would undermine his efforts to build an audience for the station's local programming. In reply, the advertising agency handling the Red Top account warned that the station's refusal "will probably be closing the door to any further business we may have with WCHS." The agency noted that it would likely affect advertising on two other West Virginia stations owned by the same company. Although WLW initially was unaware of these tactics and immediately insisted that the agency cease using such threats when it found out, the episode illustrated the economic power that was inherent in WLW's high-power operation.[37]

Nonetheless, as the hearings concluded on October 21, 1936, many observers felt that a case had been made for at least a limited expansion of high-power stations. "All signs point to an eventual lifting on the limit of power," said *Broadcasting; Business Week* predicted that the clear channel stations were "virtually assured" of getting superpower. The hearings had produced what the FCC called "perhaps the largest amount of potential information on radio broadcast transmission ever assembled in any single investigation," more than half a million words, not including exhibits. "Practically every group of broadcast stations having a particular problem that is separate and distinct from the problems facing the industry was represented and presented testimony," the FCC noted.[38]

FCC ANALYSIS OF ALLOCATION DATA

The FCC's first step in bringing a social and economic perspective to bear on the hearing data was, ironically, asking its engineering department to analyze the data. The engineers, headed by Craven, found this something of a daunting task, given the fact that "we do not consider that engineering training alone is sufficient to make [us] 'economists.'" Thus, they promised merely to "utilize our best judgment to apply a dispassionate engineering form of analysis to this subject." By placing the responsibility for analyzing the social and economic data in the hands of engineers— especially engineers as adamant as Craven—the commission was essentially guaranteeing that no significant changes to the broadcast structure would be recommended, as the engineers would naturally be resistant to suggesting radical changes to a system that was founded largely on engineering principles. Still, that resistance to radical changes in the broadcast structure did not necessarily preclude higher power, as many engineers had traditionally embraced raising power limitations as a natural evolution of expertise in the art of radio engineering.[39]

The FCC also hired an economics professor, Herman S. Hettinger of the Wharton School of Finance and Commerce at the University of Pennsylvania, on a 30-day retainer to analyze the data presented at the hearings. At first, Caldwell opposed Hettinger's selection because he had worked as a consultant for NARBS. "I have no doubt as to Hettinger's integrity," he wrote. "but [I am] apprehensive of unconscious bias on his part in making findings on issues affecting groups by which he has been employed." But after a meeting in early January 1937 with Craven, Caldwell dropped his protest. The chief engineer assured Caldwell that he would be able to go over the report and "make corrections" if necessary. Caldwell also was shown a preliminary draft of the FCC engineering department's report on the October 1936 hearings and advised CCG members that it was "favorable to its contentions on all important issues."[40]

In a preliminary report issued in January 1937, the engineering department noted that the overall system of allocation was sound and dismissed the requests of "special groups" to reserve broadcast frequencies. The report recommended leaving the existing allocation largely intact, keeping at least 25 channels clear with only one station operating at night at a power of at least 50,000 watts. On the remaining frequencies reserved for clear channel broadcasting by the 1928 allocation, the report called for maintaining the status quo of duplicated operation pending international negotiations. While acknowledging that higher-power operation for clear channel stations was "technically sound and ... in accord with scientific progress," the report cautioned that "social and economic factors ... may outweigh in importance engineering considerations." The report did, however, recommend raising the nighttime power of most of the regional stations to 5,000 watts and the power of local stations to 250 watts.[41]

The engineering department's final report, released six months later, again argued essentially for the maintenance of the status quo. "[T]he Engineering Department has adopted the premise that the existing policy of the Nation, as expressed in the organic law enacted by the Congress of the United States, is fundamentally sound," the report contended. "The Engineering Department knows of no facts or legal reasons for suggesting a radical change in this fundamental law, and we feel that basically the American system of broadcasting has been proved beyond question to be the best for our country." Pointing to the fact that listening time and receiver sales were up, the report concluded that the radio structure was based on "sound public policy."[42]

Given the engineering department's assumptions, it is not surprising that the report advised against any radical changes in the broadcast structure. In effect, the report paid lip service to social, economic and political concerns of broadcasting without allowing them to upset the structure that was already in place, claiming that the data collected at the hearings was "insufficient to justify at this time a revolutionary course." The report endorsed the overall allocation structure, dismissing as impractical plans that would equalize the power and coverage of stations. Networks, according to the report, were doing an excellent job of providing "desirable live talent" to the public and would prove indispensable in times of national crisis. "[T]he evidence shows that the network system of distribution has made the world's finest programs available to thousands of communities, large and small, programs which they prefer and which they would be unable otherwise to enjoy," the engineers noted. The report also refracted the danger of network monopolies by pointing out the distinction between chain companies and the affiliated stations. Affiliates should not be considered party to any perceived network monopoly, the report noted, because they were merely "exercising their power of decision" to contract with chain companies. Such an argument, of course, pleased Clear Channel Group members, who had hoped to crystallize just that distinction.[43]

The report also was complimentary to the clear channel stations, especially their role in providing rural signals, "one of the most important social services rendered by broadcasting." It defended the location of clear channel stations in large metropolitan areas, contending that it would be economically impractical to construct stations in isolated areas and that only population centers could provide an appropriate pool of talent for clear channel programming. But although the report termed power of less than 50,000 watts on clear channels "wasteful use of a frequency," it urged caution on superpower. "There may be a point at which competition [between superpower and regional and local stations] becomes destructive and results in impaired service to the public," it warned. The report stressed that superpower should not be excluded from consideration but said that the hearings had not demonstrated a need for 500,000-watt service. Its final recommendation was that no changes be implemented until international aspects of allocation could be ironed out. "With the growing use of radio by our neighboring nations," it warned, "a chaotic situation is fast developing."[44]

NEGOTIATING INTERNATIONAL AGREEMENTS

Prior to 1937, there were no formal broadcasting agreements among the countries in the Western Hemisphere, although Canada and the United States negotiated informal arrangements in 1928 that were formalized in 1932. This division of the available frequencies between the two countries, however, left no open frequencies for other broadcasters in the Western Hemisphere, so when countries such as Mexico and Cuba developed broadcasting systems, frequency disputes were inevitable. During the early 1930s, several stations in the United States experienced interference from Mexican stations, especially high-power outlets near the American border that operated between U.S. frequencies. Among the Mexican station operators were John R. Brinkley and Norman Baker, both of whom had their American licenses revoked for broadcasting bogus medical remedies. Brinkley's station XER, located just across the Rio Grande from Del Rio, Texas, used at least 75,000 watts under authorization from the Mexican government, and Baker similarly operated XENT; both stations directed their signals at the United States. "In general, the programs [carried by the Mexican stations] are more objectionable than those carried by the two former American licensees when operating in the United States," the FCC noted. Several Cuban broadcasters also interfered with U.S. stations.[45]

Finally, in the spring of 1937, the United States, Mexico, Canada and Cuba held a preliminary conference and agreed to enter into negotiations, scheduled to begin in November in Havana. Caldwell accompanied the U.S. delegation to Havana as an observer for the Clear Channel Group. At the conclusion of the FCC hearings in 1936, there had been some question within the CCG as to whether it should disband, but the group ultimately decided to continue, noting the need for "educating the rural public (and Congress) as to the necessity for clear channels and the undesirability of blocking increases in power on such channels." Member stations agreed, however, that the group should continue to fight merely for the preservation of clear channels and permission to use power in excess of 50,000 watts, not involving itself in stations' individual applications for superpower licenses. Caldwell, however, stuck to his belief that superpower should be the cornerstone of the group's efforts to preserve clear channels. "The best defense against duplication consists in the showing of future possibilities of use of clear channels with increased power," he said. As for the Havana negotiations, the CCG sought to prevent anything that would either deteriorate the definition of clear channels or force the United States to give up rights to its existing clear channel frequencies. Finally, the CCG hoped that the Havana agreement would contain no power limitation on clear channel frequencies, thus allowing the United States and foreign countries to raise power. The CCG, of course, had no particular interest in allowing broadcasters in other countries to use more than 50,000 watts, but it hoped that other countries' use of increased power would encourage the United States to do the same.[46]

An agreement, which came to be known as the North American Regional Broadcasting Agreement (NARBA), was reached on December 13, 1937. Joining the original four participants in the agreement were the Dominican Republic and Haiti. The channel and station classifications followed closely those that were emerging from the FCC engineering department, namely maintaining the tripartite channel setup (clear, regional and local) and then providing subclassifications of stations operating on those channels.

Of the 106 channels in the standard broadcast band, 59 were designated as clear channels, 41 as regional channels and six as local channels. The United States was given priority on 32 clear channels, while Cuba was given one and Mexico and Canada six each. Stations with nighttime exclusivity on clear channels were designated Class I-A, while duplicated clear channel stations were designated Class I-B. Secondary stations operating on clear channels and providing protection from interference to the dominant station were designated Class II. Regional stations were designated as Class III-A or Class III-B depending on power, and local stations were designated as Class IV.[47]

The agreement also provided different levels of protection for Class I-A and Class I-B stations. The signals of Class I-A stations were to be free of interference from other countries within the entire land area of the dominant station's country, and under no circumstances could another country assign a nighttime station on a clear channel within 650 miles of the border of the dominant clear channel station's country. Class I-B stations received lesser protection, based chiefly on the stations' existing service areas. While limiting the power of Class I-B stations to 50,000 watts, the NARBA treaty authorized Class I-A stations for a minimum of 50,000 watts.[48]

Meanwhile, there was a rising tide of indignation against the FCC, usually focusing on the commission's role in—if not fostering, then at least turning a blind eye toward—monopoly control of radio broadcasting. The network structure was frequently the focal point of criticisms, although WLW's experimental license called attention to the power—and arrogance—of the clear channel stations as well. The same week that the FCC engineering department released its preliminary report on the allocation hearings, President Roosevelt recommended to Congress that the FCC be absorbed by the Department of Commerce. Agencies such as the FCC, a presidential committee said, were "a headless 'fourth branch' of government," which could not be controlled by Congress, the president or the courts. An almost continuous series of bills had been introduced in Congress calling for investigations of the FCC, the "radio monopoly," or both. At one time in 1937, no less than four resolutions were pending to investigate the control of radio. "We have dictatorships in America," said Representative W.D. McFarlane of Texas, "when 300 or less people have an absolute monopoly in the molding of public opinion through undisputed control of radio stations, newspapers and motion pictures." McFarlane particularly criticized FCC experimental licenses—such as the one granted to WLW—as "not worthy of the name."[49]

The press had picked up on the criticisms of the FCC as well. An article in the *Saturday Evening Post* called the commission "one of the strangest, and potentially, most dangerous of Washington's thriving bureaucracies." *The Nation* speculated that if even half the charges of FCC malpractice were true, it was "one of the most corrupt federal agencies in history," while *Business Week* predicted that an inquiry of the FCC would find "many a delicious tidbit of scandal to chew upon." President Roosevelt was able to stave off a formal investigation of the FCC—at least temporarily—by appointing Frank McNinch as chairman after the death of Anning S. Prall in October 1937. McNinch, the former mayor of Charlotte and chairman of the Federal Power Commission, was instructed by Roosevelt to clean house at the FCC, and upon taking office, he promptly did away with the commission's tripartite structure (telephone, telegraph and radio sections) and guided the commission to a 5–1 decision against allowing the publicity-hungry Payne to participate in disbarment proceedings against two FCC lawyers who claimed Payne was biased against them. Craven, meanwhile, was promoted to commissioner.[50]

THE SUPERPOWER HEARINGS

As the power limitation on clear channel stations was both the most significant and the most controversial portion of the FCC's allocation deliberations, the FCC scheduled hearings before its newly formed Superpower Committee consisting of Chairman McNinch and Commissioners Payne, Craven and Norman S. Case. Following those hearings, the committee would consider whether to continue WLW's experimental superpower license, which had been designated for hearing by Commissioner Payne in early 1938.

The first set of hearings, held during June 1938, were a veritable replay of the portions of the 1936 hearings that dealt with superpower. The Clear Channel Group continued to urge approval of superpower on a case-by-case basis, supporting power increases for other classes of stations "where appropriate." Once again, the CCG took pains to separate itself from the perceived chain monopoly and emphasized the independence of its members. "[T]he chief bulwarks against the acquisition of too much power by anyone else are to be found precisely in this Group," Craig testified, "if it had not been for them, there would be much more danger of monopoly in this country than there actually is." Later, Caldwell said that clear channel stations were unfairly lumped into criticisms of monopoly power in radio. He noted that CCG members sought only "to join hands and to share expense in protecting rural broadcast service against being degraded or destroyed by interference."[51]

The commission also heard from several groups calling for the duplication of clear channels and continuation of the 50,000-watt power limit. NARBS presented a plan that showed the additional service provided by adding stations to selected clear channel frequencies. C.M. Jansky, appearing for New York's WOR, said he knew of no reason clear channels occupied by stations on the East Coast could not be duplicated by stations on the West Coast. The NIB reiterated its opposition to superpower, and CBS and the American Civil Liberties Union registered opposition as well. While publicly holding to the notion that duplication at 50,000 watts would cause interference, in private the Clear Channel Group acknowledged that nighttime exclusivity at the present power level made little sense. Caldwell admitted to members that NARBS made "a rather effective" presentation. "If the power maximum is to remain at 50 kw.," he told the group, "no effective answer can be made to duplication."[52]

The most significant argument against higher power on clear channels, however, came not from FCC testimony but from the Senate. On the fourth day of the FCC hearings, Senator Burton K. Wheeler, a Democrat from Montana, introduced Senate Resolution 294, which contended that power in excess of 50,000 watts was "definitely against the public interest." It also spelled out specific arguments against superpower stations:

[S]uch operation would tend to concentrate political, social and economic power and influence in the hands of a very small group. ... [It] has been demonstrated to have adverse and injurious economic effects on other stations operating with less power ... and in limiting the ability of such stations to adequately or efficiently serve the social, religious, educational, civic and other like organizations and institutions [in their communities].

Wheeler had emerged in the preceding year as Congress' most vocal critic of the clear channel structure. Speaking before the NAB on Valentine's Day in 1938, he noted that superpower would definitely not be in the public interest. "With high power," Wheeler told the audience, "a station immediately loses its local or statewide status. It has no community to serve. The nation becomes its oyster."[53]

Senator Wheeler's ability to pass the resolution essentially without opposition was illustrative of the fact that the CCG had not yet established a lobbying presence in Congress. And although the resolution did not carry the force of law, it issued a strong message to the FCC. In June 1939, the commission decided to provide for 25 unduplicated Class I-A clear channels, but it retained the power limit of 50,000 watts. A report released by the Superpower Committee acknowledged increased power's potential "from a technical standpoint" to provide improved rural service, yet it termed data on superpower's effects "far too meager to warrant this Commission's advocating super power as the only means of improving service to the rural listeners of the nation." The commission, of course, had to consider Wheeler's senate resolution as well.[54]

Although the issue of regular superpower licenses was dead for the time being, the commission's new rules had no effect on WLW's experimental license, and Wheeler, too, had noted that his resolution did not affect existing superpower facilities. The FCC Superpower Committee heard testimony on whether WLW's 500,000-watt license should be renewed during the summer of 1938. Payne, whose decision to set WLW's application for a hearing had resulted in the proceedings, did not ask any questions, but the committee subpoenaed the owners of stations in Indianapolis and

Charleston who had had trouble selling advertising against WLW. A week after the conclusion of the hearings, the FCC extended WLW's superpower license until February 1, 1939, on "express condition that it is subject to whatever action may be taken by the commission." By October, the Superpower Committee had reached a decision. Crosley's application for an extension of WLW's 500,000-watt experimental license, the committee said, should be denied. While the committee acknowledged that WLW's increased power had improved rural service, it expressed concern that superpower operation would "render impossible the operation of [smaller] stations as media of local self expression." Despite oral testimony by Crosley's counsel before the commission in late December, the FCC—minus Commissioner Payne, who did not sit in on the decision—went along with the Superpower Committee's findings in February 1939. The commission's refusal to renew WLW's experimental license, observed *Business Week*, was the only way the FCC could "avoid a horrid fate" at the hands of Congress.[55]

The FCC denied a WLW request for a rehearing, and Crosley appealed the decision to the U.S. Court of Appeals. The court ruled against Crosley, chiding him for insisting on "a continuation of rights in disregard of its obligations to surrender them whenever the commission declared they were no longer necessary." Crosley also tried to get the Supreme Court to hear the case, but it refused; WLW returned to 50,000 watts daytime on March 1, 1939, although the station continued to experiment with 500,000 watts from midnight to 6 a.m. as W8XO until the end of 1942. As expected in the face of S. Res. 294, the FCC also rejected pending superpower applications from other clear channel stations. In a report released in April 1939, the commission said the possible benefits of superpower did not justify taking "speculative risks."[56]

In defeat, Crosley presented a far less boastful view of superpower. Although he had previously bragged of WLW's ability to "cover the world," he now downplayed superpower:

> The power output is only 680 horsepower. It is not as some would have us believe, a high-power trust, but it involves ... less than the power produced in eight Ford, Chevrolet or Plymouth engines

running wide open. The so-called "superpower" is a myth.

In Congress, debate on clear channels continued, and although clear channel proponents had now become more vocal, the damage of the Wheeler Resolution had already been done. Representative Martin L. Sweeney of Ohio contended that superpower "does nothing more than furnish radio parity to rural listeners" and said that the FCC's denial of WLW's superpower license "shuts the door to progress and serves notice that present conditions are satisfactory." Rural listeners, he said, would now be forced to turn to powerful Mexican stations for their radio listening and "be bombarded by a station that thrusts upon them not only the relative merits of goat glands but the machinations of crystal gazers, fortune tellers, astrologers, and the like." Interest in superpower culminated in a resolution introduced in the House by Indiana Democrat William Henry Larrabee in June 1939 asking the FCC to reconsider its superpower denials. The resolution, however, never emerged from the House Interstate and Foreign Commerce Committee.[57]

CONCLUSION

The WLW superpower era and the concurrent hearings on broadcast allocations established the outline of the debate over clear channels that would continue into the 1960s. The commercial broadcast industry, now firmly entrenched as in control of American broadcasting, had itself splintered into divergent interest groups. The clear channel discussion of the 1930s clearly illustrated this fact, as independent clear channel stations, regional stations, independent stations and networks each presented a unique point of view. Commercial interests, while holding widely differing opinions on issues, were able in this manner to ensure that those issues would be decided within the dominant commercial structure.

The terms of that debate would remain largely the same for the next three decades. Clear channel interests sought to preserve and enhance their position through power increases and the maintenance of nighttime exclusivity, arguing that high-powered clear channel stations were the only way to provide reliable radio service to isolated rural areas of the country. Smaller stations and their spokespersons in Congress argued that clear channels were a monopoly and that granting power increases would merely drown out weaker stations by siphoning away their listeners, advertisers and airspace. Networks, at least during the 1930s, were in a win-win situation; either way, they would be free to establish the most advantageous affiliate agreements with the most appropriate stations. Still, they sought to thwart any radical changes that might upset the balance of power that clearly favored them.

Ironically, the clear channel stations escaped the intense scrutiny placed on the networks as a result of the 1936 and 1938 hearings. In 1938, the FCC initiated an examination of the network structure, which resulted in 1941's *Report on Chain Broadcasting*, discussed in Chapter 4. The Clear Channel Group, which had taken great pains to separate itself from charges of a monolithic clear channel–network monopoly of the late 1920s and early 1930s, seemingly did so. Clear channel stations, at least as they operated with 50,000 watts, were affirmed by the FCC; the true monopoly concern seemed to lay with the dominance of the networks.

Of course, the future of clear channels was open to question. The victory for clear channels, such as it was, came by a narrow margin, and the calls for duplicating the clear channels, relocating clear channel stations or curbing their power continued. The congressional surprise in the form of the Wheeler Resolution also exposed the CCG's lack of a presence on Capitol Hill. The members of the Clear Channel Group, who after the 1936 hearings wondered if there was a need to continue their alliance, now knew for certain that they must. In fact, they realized that if they were to have a chance at thwarting the breakdown of clear channels, they would have to do more: they would have to be more organized, put together more resources, do more lobbying and work harder to convince the public and Congress of the value of clear channels. With the creation of the Clear Channel Broadcasting Service, they hoped to do all of these things.

NOTES

1. See "Radio Waves Played Tricks in WLW Super-Power Days," Cincinnati *Enquirer*, August 22, 1948; Lawrence W. Lichty, "The

Nation's Station: A History of Station WLW" (Ph.D. Diss., Ohio State University, 1964), 248; and "QRX," *Time*, May 23, 1938, 25.

2. FCC, *Annual Report* (Washington, D.C., 1936), 61.

3. See Report of Committee, October 17, 1938, Docket 5012, Docketed Case Files, RG 173, National Archives, College Park, Md. (hereafter referred to as NACP); "Cincinnati Giant on the Air: WLW 20 Years Old This Week," *Newsweek*, April 14, 1941, 66; Lichty, "The Nation's Station," 239, 275; and FCC, *In the Matter of the Application of the Crosley Corporation*, 6 FCC 798 (1939).

4. See CCBS, Bulletin No. 36, October 30, 1962, Box P-1130, Clear Channel Group Records, Wiley, Rein and Fielding, Washington, D.C. (hereafter referred to as WRF).

5. See FRC, *Second Annual Report* (Washington, D.C., 1928), 50–51; George Harry Rogers, "The History of the Clear Channel and Super Power Controversy in the Management of the Standard Broadcast Allocation Plan" (Ph.D. Diss., University of Utah, 1972), 103, 105; and Harold LaFount to Commission, February 23, 1929, 20-2 Memorandums, General Correspondence, 1927–1946, RG 173, NACP.

6. See Ellis A. Yost, Report, October 16, 1930, 7-0 General Orders, General Correspondence, 1927–1946, RG 173, NACP; "Nine Stations Given Maximum Power," *Broadcasting*, October 15, 1931, 8; and "More 50 Kw. Stations Are Seen as Commission Lifts Limitation," *Broadcasting*, October 1, 1933, 18.

7. See Crosley Corporation, Brief, January 9, 1948, Volume 1, Docket 6741, Docketed Case Files, RG 173, NACP; Report of Committee; William Diehl, Jr., "Crosley's Clear Channel Colossus," *Cincinnati*, March 1968, 26; and Erik Barnouw, *The Golden Web: A History of Broadcasting in the United States, Volume II—1933–1953* (New York: Oxford University Press, 1968), 131.

8. See Sol Taishoff, "WLW 500 kw Ruling Unlikely This Year," *Broadcasting*, August 1, 1938, 3; "RCA Victor Given WLW 500 kw Job," *Broadcasting*, February 15, 1933, 8; "First Regular Broadcast of New 500,000 Watt Radio Station WLW" (Advertisement), *Broadcasting*, May 15, 1934, 35; "More Power To You!" *Broadcasting*, May 15, 1934, 26; and "Largest Radio Transmitter on Air," *Literary Digest*, April 28, 1934, 18.

9. See FCC, *In the Matter of Crosley*; and "Notables at WLW Dedication," *Broadcasting*, May 15, 1934, 10.

10. See CCBS, *Summary History of Allocation in the Standard Broadcast Band* (Washington, D.C.: Press of Byron S. Adams, 1948), 35–37; and CCBS, Comments, August 15, 1958, Docket 6741, Docketed Case Files, RG 173, NACP.

11. See R. Russell Eagan to Reed T. Rollo, April 3, 1956, Box P-1130, WRF; and John H. DeWitt, telephone conversation with author, August 8, 1993.

12. Eagan to Rollo.

13. See Eagan to Rollo; and CCG, The Case for Clear Channels and High Power (Docket 5072-A), September 6, 1938, 17, Docket 5072-A, Docketed Case Files, RG-173, NACP.

14. See CCG, The Case for Clear Channels, 17; and Transcript, 116, Docket 4063, Docketed Case Files, RG 173, NACP.

15. See "Death of Louis G. Caldwell," *Journal of the Federal Communications Bar Association* 12 (Spring 1952): 60; and Louis G. Caldwell, "The Rules and Regulations of the FRC," *The Journal of Radio Law* 2 (January 1932): 80–81.

16. "16 Independent Stations Urge Clear Channel Inquiry by FCC," *Broadcasting*, August 15, 1934, 9; "FCC Orders an Investigation into Clear Channel Structure," *Broadcasting*, November 1, 1934, 13; Tracy F. Tyler to Hampson Gary, December 7, 1934, 194-3 Clear Channels, General Correspondence, 1927–1946, RG 173, NACP; Hampson Gary to Tracy F. Tyler, December 15, 1934, 194-3 Clear Channels, General Correspondence, 1927–1946, RG 173, NACP; "First Analysis of Rural Listening Habits," *Broadcasting*, September 15, 1936, 7; and "FCC Getting Data on Clear Channels," *Broadcasting*, February 1, 1935, 40.

17. See Allocation Survey Results, September 1, 1936, 194-3 Clear Channels, General Correspondence, 1927–1946, RG 173, NACP; FCC, *Annual Report* (Washington, D.C., 1935), 30–31, 65–66; and FCC, *Annual Report* (Washington, D.C., 1936), 61.

18. See FCC, *Annual Report* (Washington, D.C., 1937), 40; "Whys-Hows of Reallocation Hearings," *Broadcasting*, August 1, 1936, 11; House Committee on Interstate and Foreign Commerce, *Regulation of Broadcasting: Half a Century of Government Regulation of Broadcasting and the Need for Further Legislative Action*, 85th Cong., 1st Sess. (Washington, D.C., 1958), 17–18; FCC, *Annual Report* (1936), 58; "Davis Amendment Repeal Lifts Quota Bar," *Broadcasting*, June

15, 1936, 13; and FCC, Press Release, July 25, 1936, Docket 4063, Docketed Case Files, RG 173, NACP.

19. See Eagan to Rollo; CCG, Engineering Report, July 14, 1936, Box P-1130, WRF; CCG, Report No. 3, June 27, 1936, Box P-1130, WRF; and CCG, Report No. 8, September 18, 1936, Box P-1130, WRF.

20. See Transcript, 249, Docket 5072-A, Docketed Case Files, RG 173, NACP; and CCG, Report No. 4, July 14, 1936, Box P-1130, WRF.

21. See CCG, Report No. 4, July 1, 1936, Box P-1130, WRF; NARBS, Petition, August 8, 1936, Docket 4063, Docketed Case Files, RG 173, NACP; CCG, Report No. 6, August 11, 1936, Box P-1130, WRF; John Shepard III, Memorandum, August 7, 1936, Docket 4063, Docketed Case Files, RG 173, NACP; Transcript, 491, Docket 4063; and NARBS, Memorandum, August 10, 1936, Box P-1130, WRF.

22. See "NAB Faces Show down at Chicago Conclave," *Broadcasting*, July 1, 1936, 19; *The First 50 Years of Broadcasting* (Washington, D.C.: Broadcasting Publications, Inc., 1982), 26; "Big Independents Organizing Under Leadership of Crosley," *Broadcasting*, April 1, 1936, 20; "Political Fervor at High Heat as NAB Sets Convention Date," *Broadcasting*, May 1, 1936, 12; and Barnouw, *The Golden Web*, 110.

23. CCG, Report No. 11, September 23, 1936, Box P-1130, WRF; CCG, Report No. 9, September 18, 1936, Box P-1130, WRF.

24. See Sol Taishoff, "Policy Changes, Not Reallocation Foreseen," *Broadcasting*, October 15, 1936, 9; "WGY, KSL Apply for 500,000 Watts," *Broadcasting*, October 15, 1936, 64; and Transcript, 3–4, Docket 4063.

25. Transcript, 29–68, Docket 4063.

26. Transcript, 1631–36, Docket 4063.

27. See FCC, Engineering Department, *Report on Social and Economic Data Pursuant to the Informal Hearing on Broadcasting, Docket 4062, Beginning October 5, 1936* (Washington, D.C., 1938), 83–85; CCG, Report No. 10, September 19, 1936, Box P-1130, WRF; and Transcript, 104–11, Docket 4063.

28. Transcript, 115–18, 138, Docket 4063.

29. See FCC, *Report on Social*, 83–85; and Transcript, 199, Docket 4063.

30. See FCC, *Report on Social*, 87–89; and Transcript, 401, 443–44, Docket 4063.

31. See Transcript, 670–71, 674, 700, Docket 4063; and FCC, *Report on Social*, 91–96.

32. See Transcript, 988–99, 1363, 1372–73, Docket 4063; and FCC, *Report on Social*, 97–98.

33. See Transcript, 906, Docket 4063; and FCC, *Report on Social*, 99–103.

34. See "Superpower a Success, Says Crosley; Tilts with Payne," *Broadcasting*, October 15, 1936, 73–74; Lawrence W. Lichty, "The Impact of FRC and FCC Commissioners' Backgrounds on the Regulation of Broadcasting," *Journal of Broadcasting* 6 (Winter 1961–1962): 100–102; and Barnouw, *The Golden Web*, 119.

35. See Transcript, 1065–66, 1075, Docket 4063; and "Strange Interlude," *Broadcasting*, October 15, 1936, 50. Payne sued *Broadcasting* magazine for libel but eventually dropped the suit.

36. Lichty, "The Nation's Station," 288, 293–94.

37. Report of Committee.

38. See "Joint Hearing on Superpower May Result from 500 kw Pleas," *Broadcasting*, May 15, 1936, 16; "That Radio Channel Plan Is Here," *Business Week*, January 13, 1937, 38; FCC, *Report on Social*, 1; and FCC, *Annual Report* (1937), 41–42.

39. FCC, *Report on Social*, 1.

40. See "Creation of Economic Sections in the FCC Again Indicated," *Broadcasting*, January 1, 1937, 10; and CCG, Report No. 16, January 15, 1937, Box P-1130, WRF.

41. Preliminary Engineering Report to the Broadcast Division Concerning the October 5, 1936 Hearing—Docket 4063, January 11, 1937, Docket 4063, Docketed Case Files, RG 173, NACP.

42. FCC, *Report on Social*, 10.

43. See FCC, *Report on Social*, 15, 17, 25; and FCC, Press Release, January 20, 1938, Frequencies 66-7c, General Correspondence, 1927–1946, RG 173, NACP.

44. FCC, *Report on Social*, 24, 31, 43, 53, 56, 59, 61–62.

45. See "Approval of XER Stirs U.S. Stations," *Broadcasting*, November 15, 1931, 6; Erik Barnouw, *A Tower in Babel: A History of Broadcasting in the United States, Volume I—to 1933* (New York: Oxford University Press, 1968), 170, 258; "Brinkley's XER is Autho-

rized to Use 500,000 Watts Power," *Broadcasting*, October 15, 1932, 6; Ewell K. Jett and William Dempsey to Commission, May 5, 1939, Inter-Office Memorandums, General Correspondence, 1927–1946, RG 173, NACP; Sol Taishoff, "Cuba Looms as New Menace to U.S. Radio," *Broadcasting*, January 15, 1932, 5, 6; and CCG, Report No. 18, March 16, 1937, Box P-1130, WRF.

46. See CCG, Report No. 14, November 5, 1936, Box P-1130, WRF; CCG, Report No. 15, November 28, 1936, Box P-1130, WRF; CCG, Report No. 20, April 30, 1937, Box P-1130, WRF; CCG, Report No. 31, March 14, 1938, Box P-1130, WRF; and CCBS, *Summary History*, 52.

47. CCBS, *Summary History*, 52–54.

48. CCBS, *Summary History*, 52–54.

49. See "FCC Would Be Absorbed by Department of Commerce Under President's Plan," *Broadcasting*, January 15, 1937, 1; Carl J. Friedrich and Evelyn Sternberg, "Congress and the Control of Radio Broadcasting, Part I," *The American Political Science Review* 37 (October 1943): 810; and July 19, 1937, *Congressional Record*, 75th Cong., 1st Sess., 7280, 7282.

50. See Stanley High, "Not-So-Free-Air," *Saturday Evening Post*, February 11, 1939, 73; "Scandal in the Air," *The Nation*, April 27, 1937, 455; "Heading for Radio Investigation," *Business Week*, August 21, 1937, 17; Sol Taishoff, "New FCC Leadership to Start Cleanup," *Broadcasting*, September 1, 1937, 5; and "Starts FCC Cleanup," *Business Week*, October 23, 1937, 53.

51. See Transcript, 222–53, Docket 5072-A; and Oral Argument, 2201, Docket 5072-A, Docketed Case Files, RG 173, NACP.

52. See Transcript, 97, Docket 5072-A; and CCG, Report No. 44, July 1, 1938, Box P-1130, WRF.

53. See S. Res. 294, June 9, 1938, *Congressional Record*, 75th Cong., 3d. Sess., 8585; and "Avoid Monopoly, Improve Service: Wheeler," *Broadcasting*, February 15, 1938, 19.

54. Quoted in CCBS, *Summary History*, 47.

55. See Report of Committee; FCC, *In the Matter of Crosley*, 797; and "WLW Power Cut 90%," *Business Week*, February 18, 1939, 32.

56. See FCC, *Decision and Order on Petition for Rehearing*, 6 FCC 805 (1939); FCC, *In the Matter of Crosley Corporation*, 9 FCC 202

(1942); and "Vast Array of Data Compiled by the FCC," *Broadcasting*, April 15, 1939, 20.

57. See Lichty, "The Nation's Station," 275; October 26, 1939, *Congressional Record*, 76th Cong., 1st Sess., 2020–21, A514-16; Lewie V. Gilpin, "Superpower Issue Is Revived; House Votes Logan-Walter Bill," *Broadcasting*, May 1, 1940, 16.

CHAPTER FOUR

Meet Mr. Big

The new FCC allocation rules, adopted in August 1939, and the 1937 NARBA agreement had effected little change as far as clear channels and superpower were concerned. The five-year WLW experiment had shown the technical ability of higher power to provide rural service but also crystallized the social, economic and political arguments against superpower. While clear channel proponents took relief in the fact that the majority of clear channel frequencies maintained their nighttime exclusivity so far, their status was decidedly tenuous. Louis Caldwell's conversations with FCC personnel confirmed that the commission had given serious consideration to duplicating more—or perhaps all—clear frequencies. "The question is, therefore, not closed," he told CCG members in 1939.[1]

Members of the Clear Channel Group believed they had established beyond argument the technical effectiveness of high power and clear channels during the allocation hearings of the 1930s. However, they also knew that what they termed "the so-called economic and social issues" were keeping the commission from granting clear channel stations higher power. And it was becoming obvious that without higher power the clear channels were vulnerable to duplication, either individually or through broad future allocation changes. Thus, if the clear channels were to be preserved, clear channel stations would have to continue to show the engineering possibilities of higher power while simultaneously assuaging fears of monopoly power.[2]

It also was obvious to clear channel proponents that merely presenting testimony before the FCC was no longer enough to protect the position of clear channels. The high-profile WLW experiment had made clear channels a political issue transcending the engineering emphasis of the FCC; even steadfast engineers acknowledged that clear channel stations using half a million watts raised concerns beyond mere engineering questions. In fact, all of the engineering data presented by clear channel stations during the 1930s was essentially rendered moot by Senator Burton K. Wheeler's 1938 resolution, which cited superpower's negative social and economic effects. The fact that Wheeler was able to get the resolution passed with only a brief presentation on the floor of the Senate was both embarrassing and frightening to members of the Clear Channel Group. Obviously, proponents of clear channels would have to work to "educate" Congress to prevent similar actions in the future.

The formation of the Clear Channel Broadcasting Service (CCBS) in 1941 indicated a broadening of the independent clear channel stations' efforts to preserve and enhance their position. By buttressing the technical arguments established in the 1930s with a message of public service directed at radio-barren rural areas, the CCBS hoped not only to establish an effective engineering case for clear channels and higher power but to rebut monopoly charges. At the same time, the CCBS expanded its sphere of influence beyond the FCC to Congress and the general public as well. In so doing, it was a model not only for groups that formed to oppose it on the clear channel issue but for later groups that formed in response to other policy debates.

FORMATION OF THE CCBS

At the conclusion of the 1938 FCC allocation hearings, a CCG committee developed the idea of an "information office": in effect a public relations firm charged with promoting the value of clear channel stations to Congress and the public. The committee's plan called for a full-time director with public relations—but not necessarily radio—experience. It also called for Washington, D.C., office space to provide close proximity to Congress and the FCC. The CCG would continue to be the focal point for gathering engineering data and presenting testimony to the FCC, but the new group would help back up that data by eliciting public and congressional support as well. The name of the new group, Clear Channel Broadcasting Service, reflected the function group members had in mind: promoting clear channels as a means of providing reliable, quality broadcast service to rural listeners.[3]

The existing 14 members of the Clear Channel Group signed on for the new venture, as did the two Westinghouse-owned clear channel outlets, WCAU in Philadelphia and KDKA in Pittsburgh. Until 1940, the Westinghouse stations had been operated by NBC and were thus ineligible for membership in the CCG. Again, the clear channel alliance had signed on every eligible station except KSL. To run the office, leased in Washington's Shoreham Building, the group hired Victor A. Sholis, former public relations chief with the Department of Commerce under Secretary of Commerce Harry Hopkins. A native of Chicago, Sholis also had been a newspaper reporter with the Chicago *Times* before coming to Washington. In announcing the new organization, WSM's Edwin W. Craig presaged the group's message of looking out for the rural radio listener. "Without these [clear channel] stations," he said, "all the residents of this tremendous portion of our country would be living in a radio 'black-out.'"[4]

Originally, the clear channel stations had intended to maintain a separation between the work of the Clear Channel Group and the Clear Channel Broadcasting Service. But while on paper the two groups existed concurrently from 1941 to May 1944, in reality they had merged soon after the formation of the CCBS. The difference between the two groups, according to Ward Quaal, CCBS director in the late 1940s, was "merely a matter of semantics." By the end of 1941, legal and technical activities had been drawn under the CCBS umbrella, and in May 1944 the Clear Channel Group officially disbanded.[5]

NARBA SHIFTS AND
THE CHAIN INVESTIGATIONS

The results of the 1937 North American Regional Broadcasting Agreement (NARBA) finally came to the U.S. radio band in 1941. After much delay, Mexico ratified the agreement in 1940, the final signatory to do so. While the United States had substantively preserved its rights in the broadcast band, the terms of the agreement necessitated a massive reassignment of frequencies in order to make the hemispheric allocation plan operative. Thus, March 29, 1941, became known as "moving day," as more than 800 of the United States' 890 AM stations changed frequency to comply with the new agreement. Although the majority of clear channel stations maintained their existing assignments, it was for many stations the first time they had moved since the early 1920s; the frequency assignments in place after the move remain the basis of allocation in the standard broadcasting band to this day. While the mass migration of U.S. stations came off without serious incident, several Mexican and Cuban stations were slow to conform to the terms of the agreement. A few Mexican border stations, directing programming at the United States, for instance, took their proper assignment only after the U.S. State Department pressured the Mexican government to make them move.[6]

Meanwhile, there was something of a lull in FCC action pertaining to clear channels. The commission, under the guidance of Chairman James Lawrence Fly, had been taking a more aggressive stance toward monopoly implications in the broadcast industry, but so far the clear channels had escaped serious attention. Fly, nominated by Franklin D. Roosevelt in 1939, was far more interested in the network control situation; Roosevelt himself was more concerned with newspaper ownership of radio stations. Both issues, of course, affected the clear channel stations indirectly, but the pressure for mass duplications of clear channels was off, at least temporarily.[7]

Upon taking office, Fly aggressively pushed the commission's network investigation, which had begun in 1938. The result was the *Report on Chain Broadcasting,* issued in May 1941. The report blasted the networks' indirect control of affiliate stations and, to a lesser degree, their direct ownership of high-power clear channel stations. It recommended that NBC be forced to divest one of its two networks and that affiliation agreements lessen the networks' ability to usurp local programming time from affiliate stations. Immediately, Fly became the object of the industry's scorn, specifically through the National Association of Broadcasters, which spurred congressional investigations of Fly and the commission throughout the war years. The CCBS, however, held no particular animosity toward Fly, and Sholis—sharing the chairman's New Deal pedigree—had a friendly and rather informal relationship with him.[8]

Still, Fly was no particular fan of the clear channels, and he was definitely opposed to superpower. At hearings on the FCC's chain investigation before the Senate Committee on Interstate Commerce in June 1941, Fly noted that the clear channel situation deserved serious study. Clear channel stations, he felt, despite having the best wavelengths and access to the best and most lucrative markets, were doing a poor job of serving rural listeners. "I think there could have been a more orderly and effective system of allocations, and one that would have come nearer [to] meeting the needs of the listening public," he said.[9]

The CCBS did not participate in the 1941 Senate hearings, although Sholis attended as an observer. Since the hearings did not directly involve the clear channel issue, the group feared that it would merely draw anti-monopoly attention to itself if it testified. Sholis originally planned to maintain similar distance from hearings before the House Interstate Commerce Committee the following year, but he eventually changed his mind, concluding that the issues in the hearings had become broad and comprehensive enough that the CCBS could effectively tie in its arguments in favor of using powerful clear channels to provide improved rural radio service. Noting that he was neither a lawyer nor an engineer, Sholis told the committee that he wanted "to give in lay language the story of rural radio service and the dangers threatening it." The recent emphases on network domination and the economics of the radio industry, the CCBS chairman contended, had overlooked the fact that a substantial number of rural Americans received no radio service:

> To the families that can hear no radio, what does it matter who owns radio stations? To the millions of Americans whose radio reception is an uncertainty of here today and gone tomorrow, what does it matter whether stations take too many or too few network programs? To the millions of Americans whose radio reception is marred by static and interference, what does it matter how the economics of the industry are regulated?

The CCBS argument of the primacy of providing *service,* obviously, was a convenient way to sidestep nearly all of the nonengineering criticisms of high-power clear channel stations. Significantly, it also served to affirm the dominance of commercial interests in broadcasting by leaving programming issues completely to the free market system.[10]

In addition, the CCBS attempted to further distance itself from monopoly charges by tacitly supporting the FCC's efforts to regulate monopoly in the form of network dominance. Sholis told the House committee it was pointless to "simply howl criticism" at the FCC and defended the agency's ongoing efforts to rein in the networks. Still, the CCBS made no attempt to criticize the overall network structure and implicitly supported the notion that American listeners—urban and rural—wanted network programming. "I hope no one here feels that rural listening tastes are sharply different from those of city listeners," he said. "You don't entertain the American farmer by running off a batch of so-called hillbilly records. Today he wants and gets the best in entertainment that metropolitan talent can provide." Sholis also noted that American farmers were "the best informed people in the world" because clear channel radio delivered newscasts into their homes. Caldwell, appearing before the committee in his capacity as counsel for the Mutual Broadcasting System, also applauded FCC efforts to regulate the vastly more powerful NBC and CBS chains. Supporting Fly's tenure as chairman, he noted that the FCC had in the past few years "endeavored increasingly to bring its policies out into the open ... after full and fair hearing."[11]

Sholis' appearance before the House committee, his first such testimony as representative of the CCBS, illustrated the group's increased emphasis on "educating" Congress about the value of clear channels. He spoke in layman's terms, eschewing the arcane technical jargon that characterized the Clear Channel Group's presentations to the FCC during the 1930s. In describing how adding new stations to clear channels destroyed nighttime service, he said the skywave turned "from the Dr. Jekyll of service to the Mr. Hyde of interference." Using colorful maps and displays, Sholis portrayed the clear channel stations as the veterans of radio and devoted servants of farmers and the rural population. Although the clear channel stations still sought to frame the rural service problem as chiefly an engineering issue, Sholis' performance demonstrated an understanding that such technical arguments could best be made against the backdrop of public service, especially in a congressional venue. He closed his testimony by urging Congress to be cautious in re-allocating broadcast frequencies, as long as the FCC "gives evidence of doing the job itself."[12]

PIECEMEAL DUPLICATIONS IN THE EARLY 1940s

Although the CCG and CCBS had been able to stave off large-scale duplications of the clear channels, several individual duplications had taken place since the late 1920s. The 1939 allocation acknowledged the duplicated status of these formerly clear channels by designating them as I-B frequencies. And while the remaining clear channel license holders made little effort to restore the original 40 clear frequencies, they vigorously fought further reductions in the number of clear channels. With each clear channel duplicated, the clear channel interests correctly surmised, it became more difficult to defend those that remained.[13]

Thus, the CCBS was intensely concerned about efforts during the early 1940s to duplicate KOA's clear channel, despite the fact that the station was owned by NBC and so was not eligible for CCBS membership. Indeed, many observers saw the potential duplication of the Denver clear channel as the entering wedge toward the piecemeal breakdown of all clear channels by assigning one eastern and one western full-time station on each frequency.

Such a solution to the clear channel issue had been discussed by the commission during the allocation hearings of the 1930s but was not adopted as part of the 1939 allocation structure. Still, before that allocation plan even was implemented, the FCC, by allowing a daytime-only station in Boston to expand to full-time on KOA's frequency, appeared to be taking steps that would undermine the clear channels that plan had preserved.[14]

However, the FCC's actions become less mysterious when the makeup of the commission is examined. Throughout the middle 1930s, the commission was in effect balanced between proponents and opponents of clear channels (as it would be throughout the later 1940s and 1950s as well), but in 1939 and 1940, that balance tipped in favor of opponents of clear channels. Commissioners George Henry Payne, Paul A. Walker and Frederick I. Thompson supported the duplication of KOA's frequency, while Commissioners Craven and Case, longtime proponents of clear channels, opposed it. Fly, the new chairman, whose vote with Craven and Case could have deadlocked the shorthanded commission, chose not to participate in the case, citing his inadequate knowledge of the issues involved. A single clear channel duplication also was easier to push through than a mass duplication of clear channels because it gave the commission a chance to experiment with the effects of duplication without permanently eroding all of the clear channels. Still, *Broadcasting* magazine affirmed the fears of clear channel proponents by calling the duplication "the forerunner of an all-out crusade by the FCC's present anti-clear channel majority to duplicate clear-channel stations."[15]

The daytime station in question was WHDH, owned by Matheson Radio Company. In October 1938, the station applied to the FCC for an increase in power from one to five kilowatts and full-time operation. The application was clearly not in accordance with the commission's existing regulations, which designated 830 kHz as a clear channel on which only one station was permitted to operate full-time, and under existing regulations the application should have been returned to Matheson. However, the commission, against the recommendation of its engineering department, instead designated the application for a hearing, proposing to determine, among other things, if and to what extent KOA would be adversely affected and whether the public interest would be served by modifying the rules to authorize WHDH's request.[16]

The CCG petitioned the FCC for permission to intervene in the hearing, as did NBC and CBS. "It should not be possible for individual applicants constantly to bring the resulting rules into question by simply applying for something not permitted by the rules," Caldwell's petition noted. The FCC denied each petition, although it granted WEEU, another daytime-only station on 830 kHz, permission to participate in the hearing, which was held in January 1940. On the basis of testimony heard, the FCC's engineering department again advised against granting the WHDH application, noting that "many persons in different areas" who could now receive KOA's signal would lose their reception if WHDH went full-time. Engineers reiterated the importance of clear channels in the overall allocation plan. They stated that new services such as FM offered potential for improving urban radio service but "had no prospect whatsoever of augmenting broadcast service to ... rural areas." The FCC, however, recommended that WHDH's application be approved, noting that it would increase the station's coverage area by approximately 621,000 people and provide better service to metropolitan Boston and the fishing banks of the New England coast. In effect, the commission proposed making the 830 kHz clear channel (which would shift to 850 kHz under terms of the NARBA realignment) a Class I-B channel. The FCC declared that this would allow a "more efficient use of the frequency."[17]

Commissioners Case and Craven, for their part, issued a strong dissent. Writing that "no construction, interpretation or application" of the commission's allocation policy could allow 850 kHz to have more than one station operating at night, they doubted the legality of the FCC's decision and asserted that the present rules were the result of "a public hearing [that] considered the engineering opinion of the nation." They warned that allowing those rules to be subverted "is bound to result in repercussions against the entire radio industry." By not rejecting the application as in violation of existing rules, Case and Craven contended, the commission was inviting other applicants to seek authorizations without regard to the existing "rules" of the allocation structure.[18]

The commission continued to deny NBC and CCBS requests

for reconsideration of the WHDH grant; the FCC maintained that curtailing a station's service area did not modify its license to the extent that it could show economic loss and thus did not give a station the right to intervene. Although Fly continued to eschew direct participation in the WHDH matter, he pointed out that "I entertain no doubt as to its legality." He also attacked the clear channel structure in general and noted that "a studious, careful appraisal of this vital problem" was needed. "Great waste results from the fact that clear channel stations, whose *raison d'etre* is to serve over great distances and in vast rural areas of the country, have to a great extent been concentrated along the coasts and the borders of the country."[19]

NBC appealed the case to the U.S. Court of Appeals for the District of Columbia, arguing that the FCC's decision to grant WHDH's full-time license violated the commission's own regulations, the NARBA treaty and the due process clause of the Fifth Amendment. Meanwhile, following the FCC's final adoption of its WHDH decision in May, Case and Craven's prediction about other stations filing applications in violation of existing clear channel regulations was coming true. By September, 13 part-time stations had applied to the FCC to operate full-time on clear channels. Three stations each had applied for full-time operation on the clear channels of KFI and WEAF, while one station each had applied for full-time on the clear channels of WJZ, WCCO, WABC and KSL. In addition, three more stations applied for full-time operation on 850 kHz, which had in effect become a Class I-B channel pending the outcome of NBC's court case. In December 1942, the commission granted WNYC, the New York City municipal station, a "special service authorization" to operate from 6 a.m. to 10 p.m. on WCCO's clear channel. Although the authorization was granted only for the duration of WNYC's existing license, it was in effect another breakdown of a clear channel, and both CBS and the CCBS protested the action. Westinghouse's WBZ in Boston also went from I-A to I-B status when a New Mexico station, displaced by the NARBA changes, was assigned to its frequency.[20]

On September 12, 1942, the appeals court ruled that the FCC should allow KOA full participation in the WHDH hearings; the court noted that the commission's denial of participation based on the station's inability to demonstrate financial loss would prevent noncommercial and educational stations from ever filing appeals. Stopping short of saying that station licensees possessed a property right, the court nonetheless ruled that KOA had a right to be heard if its service area was going to be affected. In reversing the commission's decision and remanding the case back to the FCC, the court made no specific demands as to the nature and extent of participation KOA would be allowed. "[W]e may leave such matters to the commission's judgment, where they properly belong, subject only to compliance with the basic requirements of fair play and adequate opportunity to be heard," the court said.[21]

The FCC appealed the case to the Supreme Court, which in May 1943 affirmed the circuit court's decision. The high court rejected the FCC's assertion that the Matheson application involved only a modification of WHDH's license. "[T]he grant of WHDH's application, in the circumstances, necessarily involved the modification of KOA's outstanding license," the court said. "The Commission's order deprives KOA of freedom from interference in its night service over a large area lying east of the Mississippi River." The FCC dutifully scheduled hearings in the KOA-WHDH and WCCO-WNYC cases, and in a third case involving two local class stations. However, the commission continued to deny the Clear Channel Broadcasting Service's request to participate in the WCCO-WNYC hearings. Despite this fact, the Supreme Court's decision was potentially a two-fold victory for clear channel interests. The immediate duplications of KOA and WCCO would have to be revisited—with full participation afforded the individual clear channel stations to be affected—and the FCC's ability to break down individual clear channels through unilateral action on daytime-only licenses could now be stopped. As it would turn out, however, the decision had little effect on either the KOA or WNYC cases.[22]

By the time the Supreme Court rendered its decision in the KOA case, NBC was in a position where its interests would be better served by allowing 850 kHz to be duplicated. The FCC, as part of the regulations that resulted from its *Report on Chain Broadcasting*, now prohibited network ownership of broadcast stations in localities "where the existing broadcast stations are so few." Cleveland, Ohio, was considered such an area since it had only three full-time stations, one of them the NBC-owned clear channel WTAM. Thus, under existing conditions, NBC would not be able to renew its license for WTAM. However, if the WHDH application were permitted to stand and 850 kHz became a I-B frequency, Akron's WJW also would be allowed to move from its local channel to 850 kHz and broadcast full-time, thus adding another radio station to the Cleveland market and clearing the way for NBC to renew the WTAM license. In addition, both WHDH and WJW were affiliated with the NBC-Blue network, which, although being separated from NBC Red and prepared for divestiture under terms of the chain broadcasting regulations, was still a part of NBC's parent company, RCA.[23]

Initially, NBC asked the commission to delay a decision on the 850 kHz case until six months after the cessation of hostilities. When the FCC refused, the network said that it did not wish to take part in any further hearings on the proposed duplication. Thus, since the Supreme Court's decision played solely on KOA ownership's right to participate in hearings over the WHDH grant, not on the substantive issues involved in that grant, the FCC canceled further hearings it had scheduled on the matter. By the end of June 1943, both WHDH and WJW were authorized to broadcast full-time on 850 kHz with 5,000 watts. The commission similarly reinstated WNYC's extended hours after CBS, citing the benefits for the war effort, withdrew its opposition.[24]

CCBS IN THE WAR YEARS

For the members of the Clear Channel Broadcasting Service, the United States' entry into World War II presented a number of potential advantages. First, the war diverted the FCC's attention from any plans to change its rules to provide for mass duplication of the clear channels, which, judging by the KOA decision, was currently the dominant position at the commission. Second, the commission's 1942 freeze on new station construction to preserve material for the war effort temporarily lessened the demand to find channel space for additional stations. Third, the war provided the clear channel stations with an opportunity to tout their value for reliable, long-distance communications during times of national emergency. Finally, the industrial mobilization to produce war materiel meant thousands of factories were operating 24 hours a day, thus providing a large, eager audience for nighttime radio programming. The clear channel stations, of course, were in the best position to take advantage of what one WOR producer called the "army of insomniacs" seeking entertainment and war news at all hours of the night.[25]

The CCBS had already scheduled a meeting in Nashville for December 18, 1941, when the Japanese attack on Pearl Harbor drew the United States into the war. Sholis informed members that the meeting was still going to be held, in fact that the war made it even more important. Members drafted a letter to President Roosevelt affirming the group's support for the war effort and, of course, reiterating the value of clear channel stations:

> As the nation's independently owned clear channel stations, ours is a doubled responsibility in radio during this crisis. Our audiences comprise not only city listeners, but also the millions of Americans living on farms and in small towns across the country. The principal radio voice reaching some 50,000,000 rural and small town listeners must promote the unified effort needed to win this crucial struggle.

The letter added that the group had offered "all-out use of our facilities and personnel" to FCC chairman Fly and had also "considered specific proposals on how the radio voice of the clear channel stations can make the maximum contribution to our fight." "We have complete faith in you as our Commander-in-Chief," the letter concluded. "We are eager for the privilege of serving." Signed by Craig, a copy of the letter was sent to Fly as well.[26]

Believing concern for reliable communications during wartime provided an opportunity to tout the value of clear channels, the CCBS also focused attention on the Defense Communications Board (DCB). Formed in September 1940, the DCB, chaired by Fly, was charged with making the most efficient wartime use of radio, telegraph, telephone and cable communications facilities. Other members of the DCB included representatives from the branches of the armed forces, the State Department and the Department of the Treasury. The Committee on Domestic Broadcasting was one of five advisory committees made up of government and industry representatives, and although no one from the CCBS was appointed to the committee, Walter J. Damm and John Shepard III, operators of regional stations who opposed clear channels, were. Harold LaFount, the former FRC commissioner and now representative of National Independent Broadcasters, was also a member of the committee.[27]

CCBS engineers met in February 1942 to discuss a series of wartime broadcasting recommendations to Fly and the DCB. "We undertook this work without any public fanfare," Sholis wrote Fly, "and we do not intend to allow word of it to go out beyond our own group." The engineers made nine recommendations, most of them addressing concerns about enemy aircraft using broadcast signals to track American cities. The engineers suggested using mobile transmitters, exchanging frequencies among stations and examining other ways to keep enemy planes from homing in on broadcast signals. In areas where local stations were silenced during air raid warnings, the engineers suggested using "distant stations" to "disseminate information and entertainment so as to maintain morale." Other recommendations addressed preventing enemy takeovers of stations or transmitters; among them was a suggestion that no microphone equipment be kept at remote transmitters and that stations maintain the ability to turn off transmitters from several locations. Fly received the CCBS recommendations and then presented them for discussion at a meeting of the Domestic Broadcasting Committee in April. "Committee members attacked the report as containing 'Clear Channel Propaganda,'" Sholis reported, "and then in keeping with this attitude began sniping at individual recommendations." The minutes of the meeting contain no record of the discussion of the CCBS proposals, only that "They contain some commendable suggestions and indicate considerable time and thought were put into their preparation." The proposals on preventing enemy takeover of broadcasting facilities were referred to a subcommittee of Damm and Shepard, who recommended adopting them.[28]

The superpower issue was resurrected briefly during the war, mostly due to the efforts of WLW to resume higher-power operation. Although still experimenting at night with 500,000 watts as W8XO, the station applied for full-time operation with 650,000 watts in September 1942, but the FCC denied the request. Similarly, the commission rejected a later request by WLW to use 850,000 watts to provide coverage of the Normandy invasion. Instead, WLW's superpower transmitter was broken down into smaller units and used by the Office of War Information (OWI) to beam shortwave signals into Europe. The six 100- to 200-kilowatt transmitters of Powel Crosley, Jr., earned the scorn of Adolph Hitler, who reportedly called them "The Cincinnati Liars." The FCC continued to resist clear channel overtures for superpower in the standard broadcast band, although Chairman Fly was rumored to have asked Senator Wheeler if he would be willing to rescind his 1938 resolution against superpower to improve reception of war information. Wheeler reportedly replied emphatically in the negative.[29]

"THE BIG JOB" CAMPAIGN

Prior to the United States' entry into the war, Sholis had begun assembling what came to be known as "The Big Job," a campaign designed to increase listeners' awareness of the concept of clear channel broadcasting in an effort to build grassroots support for preservation of the clear channels. In the course of encouraging listener awareness, "The Big Job" also sought to provide evidence, in the form of correspondence from listeners, community businesses and government officials, that clear channel stations were doing a good job of serving their audiences. Early in 1941, the group published a seven-page informational booklet, "Meet Mr. Big," to publicize "how 25 American radio stations in the country do the big job of serving Rural America at night." The pamphlets were distributed to individual stations, which then imprinted them with their call letters.[30]

With the country at war, "The Big Job" took on added urgency. "[Clear channel] Broadcasting has a good story to tell!" Sholis told CCBS members. "In days of war with the Axis this story is EVEN BETTER." In 1942, "Meet Mr. Big" was supplemented by "The 25 American Radio Stations Hitler Likes Least," which emphasized clear channel efforts to "smash one of Hitler's pet strategies" by keeping Americans informed and unified in the war effort. Clear channel stations, the pamphlet claimed, drew Americans "into the very heart of our battle." Similarly, the CCBS publicized its member stations' programming contributions to the war effort. In January 1943, the group put out a press release on war activities, noting that clear channel stations had put "more showmanship and individual management" into war programming than any other group of stations, including 63,000 spot advertisements and 2,000 hours of live local war-related broadcasts. The total value of the time given to war programming, not counting talent and production costs, was $4.4 million, the CCBS said.[31]

A key element of the "The Big Job" campaign was on-air promotion, which clear channel stations undertook somewhat reluctantly. Early in 1941, the FCC had released its so-called "Mayflower Decision," named after a company that had challenged a Boston station's license on the basis of the licensee's editorial broadcasts. Although the FCC renewed the station's license, the commission cautioned broadcast stations not to engage in editorializing, noting that a station "cannot be used to advocate the causes of the licensee." Clearly, advocacy of the preservation of clear channels would have come under the Mayflower ruling, so "The Big Job" advised merely informing listeners about what clear channels were without expressly advocating a position.

"It [The Big Job] must be used *extensively* and *intensively* to convert *many listeners* into *AGGRESSIVE FRIENDS* of clear channel stations," Sholis urged. In this effort to build listener awareness of and loyalty to the concept of clear channels, stations were urged to promote not only their call letters and frequency but their clear channel status. "[The listener] must not merely be sold on the station," Sholis wrote. "He must be sold on *clear channels*. The term 'clear channel' must become a family byword with the listener." To do this, Sholis suggested working a brief "explanation" of the concept of clear channels into station identifications, as was done by WHO:

This is radio station WHO, the Central Broadcasting Company's clear channel radio station in Des Moines, Iowa. By a clear channel we mean that WHO is the only station in the United States broadcasting on this wave length. Radio station WHO is given this protection from interference by other stations, and is allowed to use more power so that its programs may reach a greater area without interruption or interference. At night, 80 percent of the United States is dependent upon WHO and 26 other stations with CLEAR CHANNELS. So keep this in mind: You can always depend on WHO, your CLEAR CHANNEL station at 1040 on your dial to give you the best in radio programs and radio reception.

A simpler station identification was used by Chicago's WGN, which said, "This is WGN, the Voice of the People, Chicago—a Clear Channel station at 720 kilocycles, broadcasting with 50,000 watts of power by authority of the Federal Communications Commission."[32]

WGN's ID notwithstanding, Sholis told stations to avoid using numbers and technical terms to describe clear channels. "The less we talk like Einstein," he said, "the more the average radio fan will understand us." The term "clear channel," for example, was to be emphasized, but "50,000 watts" was not; Sholis noted that the latter sounded too technical. He also explained that the wattage figure "sounds awfully big, and Small Town America isn't particularly fond of bigness." Stations also were urged to broadcast from rural areas whenever possible and to carry clear channel publicity to fairs and other community events, where "The 'Who's Who' of agriculture assembles." The CCBS office provided stations with sample copies of rural radio coverage maps to use at fair displays and in community meetings and recommended that stations give out clear channel souvenirs. Whenever possible, stations were told to publicize remote broadcasts from outlying towns as events. "Country [newspaper] editors, in general, don't like radio," Sholis observed. "But they can't ignore a big broadcast from their home town."[33]

Stations were urged to keep a file of listeners' letters, incorporating them into on-air promotions whenever possible. Sholis gave one example from Atlanta's WSB, in which part of a letter from a woman in "faraway" Illinois was read. "Just a letter of gratitude for this station and its programs," she wrote. "I always bring you dear people into my living room and sit back, relax and enjoy some real restful programs." After reading the letter, WSB said that it was pleased it could serve such distant listeners and noted that it could do so only because it was a clear channel station "protected by the government against interference" from other stations. "For many of these rural people," the station continued, "*clear channel* broadcasts are their only radio pleasure."[34]

The CCBS continued such attempts to promote the concept of clear channels throughout the early 1940s and—to a lesser degree—in the 1950s and 1960s. For a brief time in the 1960s, in fact, the CCBS considered bringing suit against a number of daytime stations on clear channels that used the term "clear channel" in their own promotions. The group's attorney, however, advised it that such action was "not likely to win much good will from the Commission," instead recommending that the CCBS send a "mildly worded and friendly" letter to the station. The group did so and similarly sent a letter to a Dayton, Ohio, daytime station that signed off each night by noting that "due to an archaic law governing broadcasting we are required to make way for a Philadelphia station which in no way serves the Dayton area." According to Quaal, the CCBS never went beyond "informational" discussions of the clear channel issue, although he said some stations occasionally advocated the CCBS point of view. It is, of course, difficult to assess how successful the group's sporadic attempts at building public awareness of clear channels were.[35]

From its inception, the CCBS also acted as a clearinghouse for programming, although these efforts, too, were sporadic; perhaps most enduring were the group's efforts to gather and distribute news of farm conventions, as discussed in Chapter 7. From the beginning, Sholis urged stations to place greater emphasis on rural programming in an attempt to demonstrate to the FCC that clear channel stations' rural service rhetoric was more than just that. Attempts to encourage clear channel stations to program to the rural audience, however, became increasingly futile in the 1950s and 1960s as more clear channel stations began emphasizing audiences in the cities and the growing suburban areas. During the 1950s, Quaal also made regular efforts to record and distribute to CCBS members messages from members of Congress. "They all had more exposure at home than they ever had before," Quaal later boasted. Such exposure, of course, was likely to engender support for the CCBS among legislators. Quaal also set up pooling arrangements, offering live reports and taping facilities, for CCBS members covering the 1952 Republican and Democratic conventions.[36]

EARLY CCBS LOBBYING ACTIVITY

The formation of the CCBS also allowed clear channel interests to create and maintain informal contact with FCC commissioners and commission personnel. Such off-the-record contacts, known as ex parte meetings, were and are a staple of the policy-making process, as well as the frequent focus of criticism of regulatory agencies. While administrative agencies are ostensibly supposed to conduct business fairly and in the open, ex parte contacts are suspect because they potentially undermine both the fairness and openness of administrative procedure. In a 1977 opinion the U.S. Court of Appeals for the District of Columbia said that ex parte contacts "violate fundamental notions of fairness implicit in due process" and place hearings and public discussions conducted by administrative agencies in jeopardy of being "a sham and a fiction." Still, throughout the 1930s, 1940s and most of the 1950s, ex parte contacts were commonplace at agencies such as the FCC. The Administrative Procedure Act (APA), passed in 1946 in response to criticism of the conduct of administrative agencies, contained no prohibitions on ex parte contacts in rule-making proceedings. In fact, the attorney general's manual on the APA supported ex parte contacts such as "informal hearings (with or without a stenographed transcript), conferences, consultation with industry committees, submission of written views, or any combination of these."[37]

Thus, until 1959's *Sangamon Valley Television Corporation v. United States* case, discussed in Chapter 6, placed restrictions on ex parte contacts in rule-making proceedings, industry representatives and politicians had free reign to meet with commission personnel informally to discuss pending (and other) issues. William B. Ray, formerly with the commission's Broadcast Bureau, recalled the hospitality suites provided to commissioners during a 1931 licensing conflict involving WWL and KWKH, in which each station provided food, drink and even bootleg liquor. A 1940 report by the attorney general's Committee on Administrative Procedure decried the "constant external pressure" exerted by members of Congress on FCC personnel in support of license applications. There are frequent references in CCBS internal documents to off-the-record meetings with commission personnel, and it is recognized that one of the chief reasons the CCBS established a Washington, D.C., office was to have close proximity to FCC commissioners. Until at least the mid-1950s, in fact, each incoming FCC commissioner received a visit from a CCBS representative soon after taking office. Using charts and diagrams, the CCBS representative would then "explain the clear channel situation" to the new commissioner. Hollis Seavey, CCBS director from 1953 to 1959, recalls playing a lot of golf with FCC personnel, and CCBS expense accounts show frequent meals with commission personnel. "It was common for the Commissioners to be wined and dined," said attorney William Potts, who began practicing before the FCC in the 1950s. "They didn't send White House helicopters to take them to the golf club, but big black limousines would do just as good." Such contacts are, of course, difficult to chronicle from a historical perspective except anecdotally, and their influence—or lack thereof—is nearly impossible to assess. Still, maintaining the ability to have such "unofficial" contact was clearly important to organized commercial interests and is, indeed, a fundamental part of the lobbying process.[38]

Another reason for the formation of the new group was the perception—held chiefly by Caldwell—that a number of regional and local stations were unfairly criticizing clear channels and in turn drumming up congressional support for anticlear channel legislation. The chief protagonist in these efforts, in the eyes of Caldwell, was Edward B. Craney, a regional station operator based in Butte, Montana. Craney either owned outright or had financial interest in several regional and local stations in Montana, Washington and Oregon, and he had established himself as something of a gadfly in the network-dominated radio industry. Since the mid-1930s, he had agitated for an independent alternative to the National Association of Broadcasters, and *Broadcasting* magazine noted in 1941 that he had been involved "in practically every major controversy in the craft for a dozen years." Although he was not a high-profile figure in the allocation hearings of the 1930s, his influence on his home state's Senator Wheeler sparked the 1938 anti-superpower resolution, and in 1941, he unsuccessfully attempted to have the FCC move WEAF's clear channel frequency to Butte. Thus, Craney became a bogeyman to clear channel interests, who at various times in the late 1940s and early 1950s implied that the Montanan was behind a sinister "plot" against clear channel stations.[39]

The other half of what Caldwell referred to as the "Wheeler-Craney axis" continued to work in opposition to clear channels as well. As chairman of the Senate Interstate Commerce Committee, Wheeler introduced several bills that sought to curb the dominance of networks and clear channel stations. "The 23 high-power clear channel stations are mostly located in the eastern United States," he wrote in a 1944 article in *The Progressive.* "So the programs they originate ... bear unmistakably the stamp and feeling of only one section of our country." In 1946, however, Wheeler was defeated in the Democratic primary, thus bringing to an end his Senate career, which began in 1922. He continued to be associated with Craney, with several members of his family co-owning stations in Craney's "XL Network."[40]

Throughout the war years, the FCC recognized that a comprehensive study of the clear channel issue would have to be one of its highest priorities at the conclusion of hostilities. With the exception of the KOA decision, the FCC promoted the status quo for the duration of the war, resisting congressional pressure, chiefly from Senator Wheeler, to duplicate the clear channels. "If we are impetuous in breaking down clear channels today we may start something most difficult to unscramble," Craven told a House committee in 1942. "Basically the clear channel problem is an engineering problem," Fly told the same committee, "and a very interesting one indeed." However, during the war the commission lacked the engineers and other personnel to devote to the required comprehensive examination.[41]

There also was uncertainty over how the development of FM broadcasting, which offered the promise of a static-free signal with higher fidelity than AM could offer, would affect the overall broadcast structure. In the late 1930s, Shepard's Yankee Network established a series of stations in New England, and by the middle of 1940, there were about 20 experimental FM stations operating in the United States. In January 1941, the FCC approved the commercial development of FM by allocating a band of frequencies for the new service. Unfortunately, FM's development was stunted initially by the fact that many broadcasters—especially NBC—saw it as a potential threat to AM and, of course, by wartime restrictions on material. Still, FM's potential for providing improved radio service was acknowledged to be quite significant.[42]

But while some feared FM, the CCBS saw the new service's development as a potential boon to clear channel broadcasting. One drawback to FM was its limited service area; FM signals can travel only in "line of sight," up to a maximum of about 60 miles. Thus, the CCBS envisioned many local and regional broadcasters moving to the FM band, leaving AM for high-power, clear channel broadcasting directed at rural areas. This vision also was forwarded by FCC engineers, who wondered in the late 1930s "whether local and regional broadcasting stations should be encouraged to continue [in the AM band]." "While it is perhaps a bit fantastic at the present time to visualize a future broadcast band which might consist entirely of clear channels," Caldwell told clear channel stations in 1940, "it is apparent that there now exists some unanimity of opinion on the subject of rural service as delivered by clear channel stations." Obviously, moving local and regional broadcasters out of the AM band held great appeal for clear channel stations, which then possessed the only means of providing long-range broadcast service.[43]

CONCLUSION

The formation of the Clear Channel Broadcasting Service represented far more than a mere name change for the clear channels' interest group. It was an acknowledgement that success in achieving favorable regulatory policies required more than presenting engineering studies to the FCC. The CCBS had a much broader charge, one that emphasized public and congressional education, as both were crucial elements in the broadcast policy-making process. The clear channels recognized that they had to

convince Congress that they provided crucial service to rural listeners and to make the listeners themselves aware of clear channel broadcasting.

The early 1940s also saw the beginnings of a schism between the
independent clear channel stations and the networks. Each, of
course, depended on the other to a significant degree, yet there
were also factors that increasingly pulled them in different direc-
tions. The CCBS, for instance, believed it could lessen scrutiny of
the clear channels by raising no objection to investigations of the
networks' monopoly power. The networks, as demonstrated in the
KOA case, showed that they had no particular interest in preserving clear channels if it was not advantageous to them. This animosity would increase in the postwar years.

Most importantly, there had been a significant change in the
way interest groups would approach the policy-making process,
and the CCBS led this change. After the war, the CCBS mobilized
not only its engineering expertise to show that clear channels were
an effective technical solution to the White Area problem but its
public information forces as well. Opposing groups quickly followed suit, recognizing that FCC policy would emerge not merely
from the commission itself but from grassroots pressure, Congress
and the courts as well.

NOTES

1. CCG, Report No. 53, June 23, 1939, Box P-1130, Clear Channel
Group Records, Wiley, Rein and Fielding, Washington, D.C. (hereafter referred to as WRF).

2. CCG, Report No. 44, July 1, 1938, Box P-1130, WRF.

3. See "Information Service Formed for Clear-Channel Promotion," *Broadcasting*, February 10, 1941, 16, 45; and R. Russell Eagan
to Reed T. Rollo, April 3, 1956, Box P-1130, WRF.

4. See FCC, *Report on Chain Broadcasting* (Washington, D.C.,
1941), 16; and "Clear Channel Members Sign All but One Outlet,"
Broadcasting, April 21, 1941, 10.

5. See Eagan to Rollo; and Ward Quaal, telephone conversation
with author, April 27, 1994.

6. See "Continent Allocation Shifts 1,300 Stations," *Broadcasting*,
March 24, 1941, 10; Ewell K. Jett to Commission, April 14, 1941,

Broadcast Memorandums, RG 173, National Archives, College Park, Md. (hereafter referred to as NACP); Ewell K. Jett to Commission, November 4, 1941, Broadcast Memorandums, RG 173, NACP; and Ewell K. Jett to Commission, November 10, 1941, Broadcast Memorandums, RG 173, NACP.

7. See Joon-Mann Kang, "Franklin D. Roosevelt and James L. Fly: The Politics of Broadcast Regulation, 1941–1944," *Journal of American Culture* 10 (1987): 23; and Erik Barnouw, *The Golden Web: A History of Broadcasting in the United States, Volume II—1933–1953* (New York: Oxford University Press, 1968), 169–70.

8. See Barnouw, *The Golden Web*, 170–73; Fran DeLaun and Gerald V. Flannery, "James L. Fly," in Gerald V. Flannery, ed., *Commissioners of the FCC, 1927–1994* (Lanham, Md.: University Press of America, 1995), 60–62; FCC, *Report on Chain Broadcasting*, 91–92; James Lawrence Fly to Victor A. Sholis, December 20, 1941, Box P-1130, WRF; and Victor A. Sholis to James Lawrence Fly, December 22, 1941, Box P-1130, WRF.

9. Senate Committee on Interstate Commerce, *Hearings on S. Res. 113*, 77th Cong., 1st Sess. (Washington, D.C., 1941), 25, 75.

10. See Victor A. Sholis to CCBS Members, n.d., Box P-1130, WRF; and CCBS, *Radio Service for Rural and Small Town Listeners*, 3, Box P-1130, WRF.

11. See CCBS, *Radio Service for Rural and Small Town Listeners*, 16–17, 20; "Probe to Hear Chairman Fly in June," *Broadcasting*, May 25, 1942, 52–53; "Fly Opens FCC Case Against Sanders Bill," *Broadcasting*, June 15, 1942, 14; and "Running Account of House Hearings on Sanders Bill," *Broadcasting*, June 15, 1942, 48.

12. CCBS, *Radio Service for Rural and Small Town Listeners*, 1, 6, 35.

13. CCBS, *Radio Service for Rural and Small Town Listeners*, 1, 6.

14. "FCC Starts Drive to Divide Clears," *Broadcasting*, December 15, 1940, 24.

15. See CCG, Report No. 53; and "FCC Starts Drive to Divide Clears."

16. See A.D. Ring, Memorandum, July 15, 1938, 20-10 Broadcast Division, General Correspondence, 1927–1946, RG 173, NACP; and CCG, Report No. 55, September 28, 1939, Box P-1130, WRF.

17. See CCG, Report No. 56, October 13, 1939, Box P-1130, WRF;

FCC, *In the Matter of Matheson Radio Company*, 8 FCC 397 (1940); and A.D. Ring, Memorandum, May 7, 1940, 20-10 Broadcast Division, General Correspondence, 1927–1946, RG 173, NACP.

18. FCC, *In the Matter of Matheson*, 403, 406, 411.

19. See "Clears Lose Plea in Grant to WHDH," *Broadcasting*, January 13, 1941, 68; FCC, *In the Matter of Matheson*, 420, 433.

20. See "Clear Breakdown by FCC Opposed in Appeal by NBC," *Broadcasting*, June 16, 1941, 35; "Court Upholds Stations' Right to Hearing," *Broadcasting*, September 21, 1942, 70; "Appellate Tribunal Holds Clears' Fate," *Broadcasting*, June 22, 1942, 62; "Half-Dozen Clears Would Be Duplicated in Applications Filed by 13 Stations," *Broadcasting*, September 22, 1941, 28; "WNYC Granted Added Hours on Clear Channel of WCCO," *Broadcasting*, December 7, 1942, 22; "Clear Channel Group Protests WNYC Grant as Detriment to Rural Areas," *Broadcasting*, December 28, 1942, 40; and FCC, *In the Matter of Clear Channel Broadcasting in the Standard Broadcast Band*, 31 FCC 594–95 (1961). WBZ's frequency was restored to Class I-A status in 1951.

21. NBC v. FCC, 132 F. 2d. 545, 547 (D.C. Cir., 1942).

22. See FCC v. NBC, 319 U.S. 239, 243, 244 (1943); and "Obeying Highest Court, FCC to Rehear WCCO and WMT Interference Pleas," *Broadcasting*, June 7, 1943, 28.

23. See "NBC Defaults Hearing, Allowing WJW and WHDH to Break down 850 kc. Wave," *Broadcasting*, June 14, 1943, 18; and Barnouw, *The Golden Web*, 187–88.

24. See NBC, Petition, June 4, 1943, Docket 5453, Box 1634, RG 173, NACP; WJW, Petition, June 7, 1943, Docket 5453, Box 1634, RG 173, NACP; WHDH, Petition, June 7, 1943, Docket 5453, Box 1634, RG 173, NACP; FCC, *In Re Applications of Matheson Radio Company, Inc. and WJW, Inc.*, 10 FCC 128 (1943); NBC, Petition, June 10, 1943, Docket 5453, Box 1634, RG 173, NACP; "850 kc. Fight Over; Others Eye Wave," *Broadcasting*, June 28, 1943, 24; "CBS in Compromise Petition on WNYC Night Operation," *Broadcasting*, August 30, 1942, 22; and "FCC Okays WNYC Operation at Night," *Broadcasting*, September 20, 1943, 10.

25. Jerry Lawrence, "The Night is Long—and Cheerful," *Broadcasting*, July 27, 1942, 16.

26. See Victor A. Sholis to CCBS Members, December 15, 1941, Box

P-1130, WRF; and CCBS to Franklin D. Roosevelt, December 18, 1941, Box P-1130, WRF.

27. DCB, Minutes, April 8, 1942, E-14 Special Planning Committees, RG-259, NACP.

28. See Victor A. Sholis to James Lawrence Fly, February 27, 1942, Box 1700, WRF; CCBS to Members, April 20, 1942, Box P-1130, WRF; and DCB, Minutes.

29. See R.J. Rockwell, Memorandum, n.d., MSS 944, Box 1, Folder 9, William B. Robbins Papers, Cincinnati Historical Society; "Authority to Operate 500-kw Daytime by License Change Is Asked by WLW," *Broadcasting*, September 14, 1942, 10; "WLW Denied Higher Wattage for Invasion," *Broadcasting*, June 12, 1944, 26; "WLW's 500 kw. Transmitter Slated for Psychological War," *Broadcasting*, December 7, 1942, 14; "750 kw Authorized for WLW Adjunct at Request of OWI," *Broadcasting*, February 1, 1943, 10; "Most Powerful Shortwave Transmitters Built by WLW Are Formally Opened," *Broadcasting*, September 25, 1944, 18; and "Plan to Permit Superpower as Defense Measure Studied," *Broadcasting*, October 15, 1940, 32.

30. See CCBS to Members, March 20, 1942, Box P-1130, WRF; and "Clear Channel Service Is Explained in Booklet," *Broadcasting*, September 29, 1941, 76.

31. See CCBS to Members, March 20, 1942, Box P-1130, WRF; CCBS, Making the Listener a Member of the CLEAR CHANNEL Family, Box P-1141, WRF; "Clears Described as Hitler Enemy," *Broadcasting*, August 3, 1942, 28; and "War Broadcasting Extended by CCBS," *Broadcasting*, January 11, 1943, 44.

32. CCBS, Making the Listener.

33. CCBS, Making the Listener.

34. CCBS, Making the Listener.

35. See Roy Battles to R. Russell Eagan, April 20, 1966, Box P-1145, WRF; JLB, Memorandum, November 20, 1967, Box P-1145, WRF; Ward Quaal to Roy Battles, December 22, 1968, Box P-1145, WRF; and Roy Battles to R. Russell Eagan, March 2, 1967, Box P-1127, WRF; and Ward Quaal, telephone conversation with author, November 12, 1998.

36. See Ward Quaal, telephone conversation with author, January 5, 1994; and "The Chicago Political Show Is About Under Way," *Broadcasting*, June 30, 1952, 25.

37. See Home Box Office v. FCC, 567 F. 2d. 9, 15 (1977); and Michael E. Ornoff, "Ex Parte Communication in Informal Rulemaking: Judicial Intervention in Administrative Procedures," *University of Richmond Law Review,* 15 (1980): 80.

38. See William B. Ray, *FCC: The Ups and Downs of Radio-TV Regulation* (Ames: Iowa State University Press, 1990), 35; "Discourage Lobbying of FCC Federal Committee Suggests," *Broadcasting,* February 15, 1940, 15; Telford Taylor to Commission, April 16, 1941, Broadcast Memorandums, RG 173, NACP; Eric F. Brown, "Nighttime Radio for the Nation: A History of the Clear Channel Proceeding, 1945–1972" (Ph.D. Diss., Ohio University, 1975), 164–65; John H. DeWitt, telephone conversation with author, August 8, 1993; Hollis Seavey, telephone conversation with author, May 12, 1994; and William Potts, telephone conversation with author, June 1, 1994.

39. See E.B. Craney, "Wanted—An Industry-Wide Trade Group," *Broadcasting,* February 28, 1944, 11; and George P. Adair to Commission, December 19, 1941, 61–26 Broadcasting Frequencies, General Correspondence, 1927–1946, RG 173, NACP.

40. See CCBS, Memorandum No. 7, May 5, 1948, Box P-1142, WRF; Burton K. Wheeler, "The Shocking Truth About Radio," *The Progressive,* November 6, 1944, 1, 10; "Wheeler Defeated," *Broadcasting,* July 22, 1946, 10, 88; Memorandum on Interests of Edward B. Craney, n.d., Box P-1133, WRF; and "Sen. Wheeler's Son Becomes Broadcaster with KFPY Sale," *Broadcasting,* July 30, 1945, 80.

41. See Memorandum Concerning Clear Channel Broadcasting Stations, n.d., 61-26 Broadcasting Frequencies, General Correspondence, 1927–1946, RG 173, NACP; Ewell K. Jett to Commission, October 8, 1941, 66-4 Allocation, General Correspondence, 1927–1946, RG 173, NACP; CCBS to Members, July 2, 1942, Box P-1130, WRF.

42. Christopher H. Sterling and John M. Kittross, *Stay Tuned: A Concise History of American Broadcasting* (Belmont, Calif.: Wadsworth Publishing Company, 1990), 142–45.

43. See Ewell K. Jett to Commission, December 4, 1939, 20-10 Engineering Memos, General Correspondence, 1927–1946, RG 173, NACP; Memorandum Concerning Clear Channel Broadcasting Stations; and CCG, Report No. 64, April 1, 1940, Box P-1130, WRF.

CHAPTER FIVE

The Clear Channels Are on Trial

With the conclusion of World War II imminent, the Federal Communications Commission in early 1945 announced its intention to begin a comprehensive examination of clear channels. It would be the first time since the implementation of the broadcast allocation structure in the 1920s that the clear channels would be singled out for study. In theory, at least, everything would be under consideration, including superpower, mass duplication, relocation and even programming.

The clear channel study was, of course, of great interest to the independent clear channel operators, for it could have a substantial direct impact on them. And yet the examination of the clear channels took on even greater significance because resolution of the long-debated issue was seen as a crucial element in establishing the postwar order of the rapidly changing broadcasting industry. Not only did the clear channel debate have significant ramifications for the AM allocation structure, it also could have an impact on developing broadcast services such as FM and television.

The status of AM radio was more uncertain at the conclusion of

World War II than it had been at any time since the mid-1920s. The medium remained profitable as advertising revenues, unabated by the war, continued their steady climb, but many wondered whether AM radio could survive the coming challenge of FM and television. Major networks and manufacturers thus wanted not only to preserve their place in AM but also put themselves in position to profit from new technologies as well. Thus, the resolution of the clear channel issue—which was so crucial to establishing the overall character of AM broadcasting—would also have substantial influence on how new services would develop. Would, for example, FM become the dominant service for local and regional stations, with AM used only for clear channel operation? Would networks abandon FM completely, maintain the status quo on AM and pursue the development of television? The answer to these and other questions depended to a significant degree on the resolution of the clear channel conflict. For that reason, industry groups in the clear channel debate jockeyed for position not only in the AM band but also for future prosperity in FM and television as well. The clear channel debate, then, was about far more than whether clear channel frequencies would be duplicated and how much power clear channel stations would use.[1]

This fact also was illustrated by the continuing congressional interest in the clear channel question. Ultimately, in fact, a congressional inquiry would once again narrow the FCC's options in resolving the issue, just as Senator Wheeler's anti-superpower resolution had done in 1938. Meanwhile, renegotiation of NARBA was complicated not only by the increasing demands of other countries for channel space but by the conflicting positions of various factions of the United States' broadcasting industry. Frequently, these areas of contention focused on clear channels.

This chapter examines the debate over clear channels from 1945 to 1948 as carried out in hearings before the FCC and the Senate Interstate and Foreign Commerce Committee; it also discusses the disputes over renegotiating the NARBA treaty in the mid-1940s. Throughout, the chapter concentrates on the positions of various industry factions, most notably the Clear Channel Broadcasting Service. Along with Chapter 7, it chronicles the FCC's long-running clear channel inquiry, an inquiry that was not completed until 1963.

DOCKET 6741 OPENED

After nearly two decades of fragmentary consideration, the commission on February 20, 1945, finally announced the long-promised comprehensive examination of the clear channels. The day of reckoning came not only because the end of the war was in sight but because domestic and international pressure was building to resolve the issue. The end of the wartime freeze on station modification and new station construction was imminent, and the commission had pending applications both from the clear channel stations for power increases and from stations wishing to duplicate clear channels. In addition, the NARBA treaty was set to expire on March 29, 1946, and the commission wanted to resolve the domestic clear channel situation before entering international negotiations. Thus, the clear channel inquiry, given the FCC designation Docket 6741, seemingly would be both wide-ranging and relatively brief.

The commission listed 11 issues to be resolved by Docket 6741, among them the familiar questions of power levels, the number of clear channels to be reserved and the regulation of daytime stations on clear frequencies. However, the commission also said it would consider relocating clear channel stations, program duplication and whether clear channel programming was "particularly suited to the needs of listeners in rural areas." In fact, the commission seemed to indicate that it intended to consider all options for resolving the clear channel issue. "The order itself is enough to cause broadcasters to wince," *Broadcasting* magazine mused, "for the topics run the gauntlet of social and economic as well as technical principles." The magazine also predicted that the hearings would "go into the whole underlying philosophy of broadcast allocations and service," with the likely result that they would be "the most comprehensive ever conducted."[2]

It was clear to the CCBS that it would have to present a strong engineering case for the clear channels as an effective way—indeed as the *only* way—to serve the rural population, while at the same time rebutting proposals to relocate clear channel stations geographically, which seemed to provide an even more compelling engineering alternative. The CCBS, of course, opposed any relocation of clear channel outlets but welcomed the promised comprehensive inquiry into the clear channel issue. Indeed, since the 1930s, clear channel proponents had believed that if they were given a chance to present their case—technically, socially and economically—the FCC would be compelled to stop piecemeal deterioration of the clear channels and in fact would be likely to enhance their position with power increases. "Anyone who studied [our] information would realize that our data spoke for itself," Ward Quaal, chairman of the group from 1949 to 1952, later said.[3]

Unlike the clear channel stations, which had remained organized and active during the prewar and war years, the regional group that opposed clear channels disintegrated soon after the conclusion of the 1938 allocation hearings. But with the announcement of Docket 6741, regional stations sprung to action, with Edward B. Craney once again playing a central role. By the end of 1945, he and John Shepard III had revived the National Association of Regional Broadcast Stations (NARBS), now renamed the Regional Broadcasters Committee (RBC). Shepard was elected chairman of the new group, and Craney became a member of its executive committee. Ironically, the group's choice for vice-chairman was former FCC commissioner and longtime defender of clear channels T.A.M. Craven. But now Craven, having left the commission in 1944 to become a vice president with Cowles Broadcasting Company, the owner of several regional stations, endorsed the breakdown of clear channel frequencies. Eventually, the RBC organized 99 stations: three Class I-Bs, 12 Class IIs, two Class IVs and 82 Class IIIs. A handful of RBC members were limited-time stations on I-A clear channels and thus stood to benefit directly from duplication of the clear channels; more commonly, however, the impetus for RBC membership was the fear of economic harm that would accompany increased power for clear channel stations. Also, regional stations saw the preservation of clear channel frequencies as a waste of channel space, thus leading to overcrowding on the regional and local frequencies, a problem likely to worsen once the wartime freeze was lifted.[4]

For the networks, the issues were much broader. Neither NBC

nor CBS had any particular interest in the resolution of the clear channel issue apart from preserving its own affiliations and coverage. Thus, although both networks owned clear channel stations in large markets, they were at best indifferent to power increases above 50,000 watts. Far more important to the networks were preserving their current status in the profitable AM broadcast band and establishing a foothold for profitability in new broadcast services. Here, however, the two networks' strategies diverged, as each had a different idea of how FM and television should be developed. These differences would underlie each network's position in the Docket 6741 proceedings.

As television and FM radio paralleled each other in their development, it is not surprising that they in many ways became rivals. Both needed spectrum space in the high-frequency bands, and both would require significant commitments of money for developmental work. Thus many organizations, from manufacturers to networks to individual stations, would have to choose which new technology to emphasize. RCA, parent company of NBC, initially embraced FM, giving its inventor, Edwin Howard Armstrong, space in its New York City headquarters to conduct tests in 1933. But when it became clear that Armstrong envisioned FM radio as a replacement for AM, RCA, wanting to protect its significant investment, parted ways with the inventor. In May 1935, after evicting Armstrong from its building, RCA threw its support behind television. The company's president, David Sarnoff, vowed to spend $1 million to develop a complete television system, and by 1941 RCA had emerged with the patents crucial to making television operational. CBS, however, opposed the RCA system, encouraging the commission to wait until a color system—such as the one CBS engineers were working on—could be developed. Nonetheless, the commission approved commercial use of television in the spring of 1941, only to halt station construction a year later to conserve material. Finally, in 1945, the commission again endorsed the television system developed by RCA and others before the war. CBS, fearing that television would usurp both AM and FM and at the same time fatten RCA with patent royalties, continued to oppose the RCA television standard, pushing instead for full-scale deployment of FM and a color television system.[5]

ABC, the network formed by NBC's forced divestiture of its Blue network in 1943, saw the clear channel hearing as a potential opportunity to bring itself to parity with CBS and NBC. While both CBS and NBC had substantial daytime and nighttime coverage of the country through their network-owned clear channel stations and affiliate outlets, ABC was in a significantly weaker position. Weaker still was Mutual, which was organized in 1934 by four stations—Chicago's WGN, Newark's WOR, Cincinnati's WLW and Detroit's WXYZ—in an attempt to provide an alternative to the established networks. While programs such as WXYZ's *The Lone Ranger* brought limited success to the new network, eventually WXYZ and WLW pulled out of the venture because they feared losing their lucrative NBC affiliations. By the mid-1940s, Mutual had signed on nearly 200 affiliates, but most of them were regional and local outlets; WGN and WOR remained the network's only clear channel affiliates. Like ABC, Mutual lagged behind NBC and CBS not only in coverage but in advertising sales and profitability of affiliated stations. Mutual, however, took no part in the Docket 6741 proceedings.[6]

The broad scope of the clear channel inquiry required the acquisition of a voluminous amount of technical data. Having made radio service to rural areas the primary benchmark for the clear channel solution, the commission needed first to establish modern engineering definitions for satisfactory signals, objectionable interference and signal propagation. Lacking the resources and, to a large extent, the expertise to gather such data itself, the commission instead set up four so-called industry-government committees, each chaired by a commission engineer. The committees were largely populated by representatives of the organized interests—the networks, the CCBS and the RBC—as well as a few "independent" broadcasters.[7]

The FCC's reliance on the industry to gather and provide interpretation for data continued throughout the Docket 6741 proceedings. While such reliance would assure the commission that it would receive a variety of viewpoints and interpretations from the fractured industry, it also would once again assure that radical solutions to the clear channel issue would not be considered. The industry, for all its differences, was not about to suggest alternatives that would call into question the commercial broadcast structure. Early in 1946, for example, the industry eagerly agreed to help finance a rural survey of radio listeners to gauge the quality of radio service, then promptly and unanimously pulled its support when the FCC insisted on gathering data on programming preferences. The various factions of the industry were happy to provide support for data that was likely to help them make their case but were unwilling to finance inquiries that held the possibility of exposing listeners' distaste for advertising or advertiser-supported entertainment.

NARBA RENEGOTIATION

Extended delays in gathering preliminary data made it impossible for the FCC to complete the clear channel inquiry before the expiration of the NARBA treaty in March 1946. Certainly, however, renegotiating the pact would not be an easy process regardless of the status of Docket 6741. Cuba had already made it known that it wanted to increase its radio presence on U.S. clear channels and to this end authorized additional stations on the frequencies occupied by WGN and WMAQ in 1945. This squatting was clearly a violation of the existing NARBA agreement. However, facing the prospect of having Cuba not bound by any treaty after the expiration of NARBA, the State Department decided to negotiate bilaterally with the Cubans.[8]

The resulting agreement between the United States and Cuba became part of the NARBA "Interim Agreement," negotiated in Washington, D.C., in February 1946. The new pact essentially extended the existing NARBA for three years while giving Cuba the right to put Class II stations on five U.S. clear channels and to increase station power on eight U.S. regional channels. It also waived NARBA's so-called 650-mile rule that prohibited nighttime broadcasting by Class II stations on another country's clear channel within 650 miles of that country's border. Obviously, this rule would have applied to any Cuban station operating on a U.S. clear channel, as the island is only 90 miles from the United States. *Broadcasting* magazine termed the agreement "a complete capitulation," and Commissioner Ewell K. Jett, who headed the U.S. delegation, admitted that it was "a victory for the Cubans." Still, the commissioner stressed the importance of extending the hemispheric treaty to prevent further encroachments on U.S. frequencies, despite the fact that the new treaty had in effect legalized Cuba's violations of the old one.[9]

While the RBC approved of the interim pact, calling it the best agreement possible under the circumstances, the CCBS vehemently opposed it. At an off-the-record meeting called by Jett two days before the agreement was signed, the commissioner maintained that the concessions to Cuba were inevitable. Victor A. Sholis and Louis Caldwell disagreed and later met with Francis Colt de Wolf, chief of the State Department's Telecommunications Division, and "outlined in detail the ... threat to American radio service," and the "'sellout' of the American listener." Edwin W. Craig of WSM publicly condemned the treaty for the CCBS, noting its adverse effects on rural listeners in the United States. "It is ironic that this abject surrender to Cuba upon these clear channels hits hardest that portion of the American radio audience which now enjoys least the pleasures and services of radio," he asserted.[10]

The fallout from the new NARBA agreement also spilled over into the National Association of Broadcasters, with the CCBS charging that the NAB had taken sides against the clear channel stations. Craven, NAB director-at-large for regional stations, attended the negotiations as an observer and indicated that he favored granting the Cuban demands for U.S. clear channels as a way to decrease its demands on U.S. regional channels. The former FCC engineer, who had helped draft the original NARBA treaty in 1937, was in fact instrumental in arranging late-night meetings between members of the Cuban and the Bahaman delegations that cleared the way for Cuba to secure rights on the 640 kHz clear channel. Craven's actions infuriated CCBS representatives, who publicly protested the former commissioner's role in the NARBA "sellout." "We do not wish to again find NAB in support of any group or individual in their efforts to break down Clear Channel broadcasting," Craig wrote to NAB president Justin Miller. In a reply, also released publicly through the trade press, Miller denied Craven had done anything wrong. The confusion, of course, arose over the dual roles of Craven, who was acting as both an NAB representative and a representative of the regional group.

Just as the line between government and industry was often blurred in the clear channel dispute, in this case the line between industry groups was blurred as well.[11]

DOCKET 6741 HEARINGS BEGIN

Between January 14, 1946, and January 21, 1948, the FCC held 40 days of hearings on Docket 6741. During that time, the commission heard testimony from farm groups, representatives of state and local governments, individual stations and the National Association of Educational Broadcasters (NAEB). Still, the organized industry representatives—the CCBS, the RBC and the networks— clearly held sway over the proceedings, as their legal counsel were permitted to question and cross-examine all witnesses. The commission's preference for comprehensive "plans" of coverage also served to exclude noncommercial groups from serious participation as they lacked the financial and technical resources to produce such plans.

In the first series of hearings, held during January 1946, the commission heard testimony on the status of farm and rural programming on clear channels. At these hearings, as will be discussed in Chapter 7, the clear channels were unanimously criticized by government and private farm organizations for their inadequate farm programming. While the consideration of the overall commercial programming structure was anathema to the nearly all industry factions, groups opposing the clear channels were happy to allow criticism of the clear channels' specific programming. Thus, Paul D.P. Spearman and the networks' counsel remained largely silent throughout this testimony, while Caldwell meticulously cross-examined every witness who had something critical to say about clear channel programming. From the beginning, the clear channel interests sensed that the burden was upon them to justify their exclusivity, a suspicion confirmed by Commissioner Charles R. Denny in April 1946 when he announced that any daytime or limited-time stations on clear channels wishing to argue for improved facilities would be allowed to testify at the hearings. Caldwell objected, contending that the clear channel docket was a rule-making proceeding, designed for the purpose of enacting broad legislation, not for making comparative decisions between individual licensees. Denny, however, replied that it was both, as one of the issues in the hearing notice referred to possible changes to existing clear channel assignments. The FCC chairman had thus declared, *Broadcasting* magazine said, that the clear channels were on trial.[12]

More broadly, Caldwell questioned the commission's authority to even consider programming issues, citing Section 326 of the Communications Act's prohibition on censorship. "The commission has no jurisdiction to take programs or program performance into consideration in making any determination under the Communications Act," Caldwell argued early in the Docket 6741 proceedings. Months later, a large portion of the industry would echo this argument regarding the commission's *Public Service Responsibility of Broadcast Licensees*—the so-called Blue Book—which outlined programming practices that the FCC considered in the public interest. Most important among these were a balance of sustaining (noncommercial) programs, providing "reasonable provision for self-expression," airing discussions of public issues and maintaining "a reasonable relationship" between time devoted to advertising and programming. Caldwell called these criteria for judging programming in license renewal and competing license situations the "most effective and most dangerous method of censoring."[13]

The entire issue of programming was a thorny one for clear channel stations, for although they wished to portray themselves as providing the most favored programs for farmers and rural listeners, the programming on clear channel stations was not all that different from what other stations offered, especially in light of the fact that most stations turned over a substantial portion of their nighttime schedule to the networks. Thus, while the CCBS vaguely touted the clear channels' allegedly superior rural programming, it also was forced to fall back on a contention that what farmers wanted was not all that different from what other listeners wanted, namely, popular network and big-city entertainment and news programming. For the CCBS, the most important issue was ensuring that *a signal* reached rural listeners, and the group was intent on showing that the only practical way to do that over a large portion of the White Area was by using powerful clear channel stations. The introduction of concerns about programming, the CCBS contended, merely distracted from the real engineering issues. "We have found it difficult to see what relation [programming] had to the basic problem of inadequate radio service," Sholis testified. "Certainly the Commission didn't contemplate depriving farmers of a station's service because the 'gittah'—in its judgment—didn't twang often enough on Saturday night programs."[14]

Despite the group's aversion to the commission's consideration of programming, individual CCBS member stations hedged their bets by making great effort to emphasize their farm and rural broadcasts. Each CCBS member presented individual testimony and supplied exhibits touting its programming, and a number of stations, such as Los Angeles' KFI, brought along local farm group representatives to affirm the stations' value to local farmers. Louisville's WHAS supplemented its testimony with that of the president of the Committee for Kentucky, who praised the station's role in helping "to change Kentucky from a backward to a progressive state."[15]

The next stage of the hearings emphasized engineering plans designed to improve rural service. Three such plans were offered between April 1946 and October 1947: one by CBS, one by the RBC and one by the CCBS. Not surprisingly, each plan proposed a radically different solution to the White Area problem, and each plan was generally opposed by the other two presenters. NBC, for its part, opposed all major changes in the AM band, arguing instead for maintenance of the status quo, while ABC offered selective support for the portions of each plan that would potentially bring it to parity with NBC and CBS.

The first plan, offered by CBS, proposed providing rural coverage through the use of a combination of FM and AM stations. Under its plan, 200 FM stations would be strategically located, mostly in metropolitan areas near the East and West Coasts but in a few rural locations as well. Those stations, according to CBS's proposal, would provide day and night coverage for a substantial portion of the land area east of the Mississippi and on the West Coast. The rest of the country would be served by four 50,000-watt AM stations and a pair of million-watt clear channel AM stations, one located in eastern Colorado and the other in northern

Kentucky. Apart from its two high-power stations, however, the network opposed any further reallocation of the AM band, citing the possible threat to the development of FM. Clearly, the main intent of the CBS proposal was to tout the potential of FM at the expense, CBS hoped, of television.[16]

The CBS plan, called a "seemingly sensational proposal" by *Broadcasting* magazine, caused something of a panic within the CCBS. While the CCBS had long mused that FM's development as a metropolitan service would free up the AM band to provide clear channel rural service, CBS's plan called for relocating existing clear channel stations; it also proposed ownership of the stations in the system by the networks in an effort to balance the significant start-up costs. Caldwell doubted the sincerity of the CBS plan, calling it a red herring to divert the FCC's attention from making improvements to the AM band, yet the CCBS still had to prepare a rebuttal. Thus, Jack DeWitt assembled a committee made up of CCBS members that manufactured radio receivers (Westinghouse, Stromberg-Carlson and Crosley Corporation) to assess the CBS FM plan. The engineers focused their attention on CBS's assertion that the 200 FM stations could provide signals of usable strength to such a large portion of the country; DeWitt believed that the coverage claimed by CBS would be possible only with expensive receivers using outdoor antennas. "At present our best weapon seems to be one of cost," he wrote. "Radio advertising is built on the mass market. ... Anything which increases the cost to the general public will tend to reduce mass listening."[17]

The signal strength criteria used in the CBS plan was of particular concern to the CCBS because, if valid, it made FM viable as a means of providing coverage to large portions of the White Areas. The CCBS wanted FM to flourish for short-range local and metropolitan coverage in order to lessen the demand for local and regional AM stations, but the CBS plan forwarded FM as a means of covering many rural areas as well. Using CBS's data, DeWitt noted, the majority of the northeast section of the United States, where Shepard operated his Yankee Network, already received four to five suitable FM signals. "It may be that FM will ultimately supplant AM in the Eastern part of the country," he noted. "If this is true I am sure that the members of the CCBS would want to know it now." The CCBS's fear that the FCC might entertain FM-based alternatives to the clear channel structure was heightened by Chairman Denny's championing of the nascent service. He told the 1946 National Association of Broadcasters convention that every square inch of the country from Kansas to the East Coast and the Pacific Northwest would be covered night and day by FM signals. In the remaining areas, Denny said, a "revamped AM service" would "fill in the gaps."[18]

The CCBS's vigorous protests of the CBS plan led to criticism that the group was trying to thwart the growth of FM. To deflect these charges, Sholis in September 1946 released a report outlining group members' involvement in FM broadcasting. According to Sholis, 12 of the 16 members of CCBS had FM stations on the air, including WSM, which "sold one program to a candy sponsor for a dollar" to become the first commercial FM licensee in May 1941. "[T]he clear channel stations, which would be most directly involved in improving rural service by going to higher power, are in the forefront of those promoting FM," Sholis noted.[19]

But by the fall of 1947, the commission's enthusiasm for considering FM as part of the clear channel proceeding was waning. This was in large part due to the fact that Chairman Denny, who was the driving force in fostering the development of FM, had accepted a job as general counsel with NBC. The CCBS forced the issue by pressuring the commission to release its receiver data so that the CCBS could use it to argue against the CBS plan. On October 20, Commissioner Rosel Hyde opened the hearing session by saying that information that had been offered previously on FM would be excluded from the record. In late December, the commission formally denied the CCBS request for the FM data and noted that "necessities of administrative convenience require that any such consideration of FM be deferred for possible consideration in future, separate proceedings." While acknowledging the future potential of FM, the commission said it would be inappropriate to consider the nascent service as part of the AM clear channel proceeding:

Whatever may have been the possible advantages of securing a record which included exhaustive testimony concerning ... collat-

eral broadcast services, they are clearly outweighed by the need to
bring the extensive hearings to a speedy conclusion and to have a
definitive policy with respect to clear channel broadcasting ... as
soon as possible.

The decision to exclude FM was particularly significant, for it once
again confirmed the commission's unwillingness to effect substantial changes to the existing broadcast structure. While it is likely
that a coverage solution using a combination of AM and FM service was feasible, such a solution would have required a substantial realignment of the AM band.[20]

CBS, not surprisingly, vigorously protested the FCC's decision.
The network's general counsel said that making changes in AM
allocation without considering the potential service of FM would
be perceived by the industry as "official assurance from the commission that FM can be forgotten for the next several years, at
least." The CCBS protested the decision as well, although its sincerity was decidedly questionable. "We accepted this ruling with
regret and under protest," Caldwell said in closing arguments.
"We had not expected to say anything derogatory to FM, but simply what everyone knows, namely, that no matter how successful
it is it will not obviate the need for clear channels and high power."
But the FCC's decision to exclude FM from consideration allowed
the CCBS to continue to vaguely acknowledge its value as a separate service. At the same time the CCBS did not have to address
the issue of FM's potential value as an alternative to higher power
on the AM clear channels. The exclusion of FM data, of course,
also effectively eliminated the CBS allocation plan from consideration.[21]

The Regional Broadcasters Committee called its clear channel
plan a demonstration and noted that it was designed to show "not
necessarily what the commission ought to do, but one way it can
be done." It proposed duplicating 14 clear channels, creating an
allocation plan that it said would offer at least three signals—and
as many as four signals—to nearly all of the White Area. All but
one of the existing clear channel stations would be required to
directionalize their signals, thus allowing from one to five new stations to be added to each channel. On cross-examination, Caldwell

implied that the plan had been designed to enhance the facilities of the dominant members of the Regional Broadcasters Committee, notably Craney, Cowles Broadcasting and the Yankee Network. Paul Godley, RBC's engineer, replied that it was purely accidental that the RBC plan proposed enhanced stations in the cities where RBC members held licenses. "But you have got every member of the Regional Broadcasters Committee fixed up, haven't you?" Caldwell taunted. The exchange between Godley and Caldwell was disingenuous on both sides; it was obvious the RBC plan sought to enhance the facilities of RBC member stations, and Caldwell knew that the upcoming CCBS proposal would significantly enhance the license of every CCBS member.[22]

To demonstrate the inadequacy of the present clear channel structure, in which many areas of the country were forced to rely on distant stations for radio service, the RBC also arranged for several Montana politicians to appear at the hearings. Montana was one of several states in which listeners had few in-state choices for radio service, especially at night. Governor Lester C. Hunt called radio service in his state "totally inadequate" and complained that Montana listeners had to rely on distant clear channel stations that did not provide relevant programming. The governor called for at least one high-powered station in Montana, which at the time did not have any stations above 1,000 watts, noting that KFBC, a 250-watt station in Cheyenne, had volunteered to increase its power to 50,000 watts. Democratic senator Joseph C. O'Mahoney echoed the governor's call for more radio facilities for the state. On cross-examination, Caldwell showed deference to both men, avoiding the mention of any conspiracy involving Craney, Wheeler or members of the RBC. Instead, he merely tried to get both men to commit to whether they would support increased facilities at the expense of stations such as the clear channel outlets heard in the state. The CCBS also contended that Cheyenne was not a large enough city to have a 50,000-watt radio station, noting that nearly every American city large enough to support that powerful a station already had one. Spearman disputed this assertion: he said he would invest his own money in a start-up clear channel outlet in any number of cities that did not have one. "Brother, I will go ... there and swing an axe and dig ditches myself," he told the commission.[23]

THE CCBS'S TWENTY-STATION PLAN

The CCBS's clear channel plan was certainly the most controversial. The group's so-called Twenty-Station Plan would have
authorized 750,000 watts for 20 clear channel stations, thus providing, it said, four reliable signals to nearly every portion of the
White Area. It was certainly a radical change for the group, which
during the late 1930s had been reluctant to pursue mass superpower authorization for its members. Now, however, there was
consensus that power increases for clear channel stations should
be pursued. But as the group prepared for the Docket 6741 hearings, members still debated whether higher power was best proposed by demonstrating the improved coverage of individual stations or by devising a national plan to provide coverage as nearly
as possible to the entire country. The FCC's duplications of KOA
and—to a lesser extent—WCCO relied on isolated instances of
coverage rather than any overall national scheme; thus Caldwell
believed that the clear channels' best argument lay in proposing a
national system of coverage. The overall allocation scheme, he
argued, encompassed "an intricate and complex set of questions
which ... must be considered as a whole and not piecemeal." Still,
some CCBS members were concerned that if the group proposed a
national coverage plan it would open itself to monopoly charges.[24]

However, in meetings with CCBS representatives during 1946,
Commissioners Denny and Jett both expressed a desire for an
"ideal plan" that could then be "worked down to the best practical application." These meetings were enough to convince a majority of CCBS members that its engineers should work out a co-
herent application of superpower on clear channels to provide
service to the entire country. Further debate, however, focused
on the number of signals the group's plan should provide. "As
much [*sic*] as four seem necessary since one of the most [common]
sources of pressure on the commission for new stations, both from
applicants and the public, is to make available the programs of a
network not having an outlet in a given city," CCBS engineers contended. Thus, by the middle of 1946, the engineers were concentrating on a plan that would provide four nighttime radio signals

to the entire country. A multiple-signal plan also would provide the group with additional defense against monopoly charges, as listeners would not be dependent on a single station. During the plan's development, the CCBS attempted to keep it a secret, telling members that the group intended to use "surprise tactics on the opposition." However, word of the plan was leaked at the 1946 NAB convention, where, according to *Broadcasting* magazine, it "became a topic of corridor conversation."[25]

DeWitt began the CCBS's presentation of the Twenty-Station Plan, concentrating on its technical aspects; Sholis' testimony, which followed, addressed economic and social issues. The emphasis, however, was clearly on what the CCBS regarded as the indisputable technical evidence presented by DeWitt. The WSM engineer began by noting that despite the fact that the commission had added more than 800 new stations to the broadcast band since the end of World War II, the improvement in the White Area problem had been minimal. "The broadcast band is so crowded with stations at present that it is virtually impossible to add a station without reducing to some extent the areas covered by existing stations," he said. "[T]he addition of more stations within the broadcast band has not solved, and offers no possibility of solving, the coverage problem."[26]

DeWitt also sought to deflect criticism that the existing clear channel stations were illogically located to provide rural service. "Under the American system of broadcasting," he said, "the location of stations and coverage are directly tied in with and dependent upon the concentration of population per square mile. It is no accident that there is a concentration of radio service in the thickly-populated east and along the west coast of the United States." According to DeWitt, these economic realities had to be taken into account when considering the merits of any coverage plan. Similarly, he noted, economic realities prohibited large-scale changes in the broadcast structure, including moving into another band or substantially altering the existing allocation. On FM, DeWitt declared that the group had "made every possible effort" to study its potential before the FCC excluded FM evidence from the hearing. While saying he regretted that decision, he assured commissioners that the CCBS would have been able to show that

FM offered no hope of solving the White Area problem. Having exhausted these alternative options, DeWitt testified, the group arrived at the high-power Twenty-Station Plan as the only reasonable way of improving radio service to the White Areas. Above all, DeWitt asserted, the CCBS plan was based on engineering facts, and thus "out of the realm of opinion."[27]

The plan divided the country into five regions—Northeastern, Southern, Great Lakes, Western and Pacific—and within each of those regions called for four high-power clear channel outlets. Each of the 20 stations would broadcast with 750,000 watts day and night, while some would be equipped with directional antennas—designed to restrict signal flow in a particular direction—to lessen interference to other stations. The "new" definition of higher power as 750,000 rather than 500,000 watts, DeWitt said, was necessitated by increasing amounts interference from electrical appliances, neon signs and other man-made sources.[28]

Not surprisingly, CCBS member stations would form the core of the Twenty-Station Plan; 15 of the 20 clear frequencies would be occupied by the group's 16 members (WBAP and WFAA continued to share 820 kHz). Apart from an acknowledged "legitimate self-interest," DeWitt argued that CCBS member stations were favorably distributed geographically, located in cities of sufficient size to support high-power operation, independently owned by experienced management and "focal points of large and important areas which look to them as centers of information, culture, business and entertainment." The remaining five stations, DeWitt noted, were chosen for illustrative purposes only. One of them, Salt Lake City's KSL, was an independent I-A station not affiliated with CCBS, while the other four—KPO and KGO in San Francisco, KOA in Denver, and WBZ in Boston—were presently I-B channels. (See Table 5.1 for the stations proposed under the CCBS plan.)[29]

DeWitt admitted that the Twenty-Station Plan did not "achieve perfection" but said it demonstrated a significant improvement in coverage to the White Areas, especially at night. During the day, the CCBS plan still would leave a large number of people in the West without daytime service. Still, he argued that power increases on the clear channels would significantly improve coverage to these

TABLE 5.1   Members of the Twenty-Station Plan

Station	Location	Network
Northeast Region		
WHAM[a]	Rochester, NY	NBC
KDKA[a]	Pittsburgh, PA	NBC
WCAU[a]	Philadelphia, PA	CBS
WBZ	Boston, MA	NBC
Southern Region		
WSB[a]	Atlanta, GA	NBC
WHAS[a]	Louisville, KY	CBS
WSM[a]	Nashville, TN	NBC
WWL[a]	New Orleans, LA	CBS
Great Lakes Region		
WLS[a]	Chicago, IL	ABC
WLW[a]	Cincinnati, OH	NBC
WJR[a]	Detroit, MI	CBS
WGN[a]	Chicago, IL	Mutual
Western Region		
KOA	Denver, CO	NBC
WBAP[a]/WFAA[a]	Fort Worth/Dallas, TX	NBC
WHO[a]	Des Moines, IA	NBC
WOAI[a]	San Antonio, TX	NBC
Pacific Region		
KFI[a]	Los Angeles, CA	NBC
KPO	San Francisco, CA	NBC
KGO	San Francisco, CA	ABC
KSL	Salt Lake City, UT	CBS

[a] CCBS member.

areas. At night, the CCBS plan would provide at least four signals to all of the White Area. "It is most fortunate that the benefits of high power on clear channels are greatest at this time," he noted.[30]

The most significant aspect of the CCBS plan, however, was its potential for substantially altering the network-affiliate dynamic of the AM band. By making four powerful signals available in each region of the country, the plan would give two weaker networks (ABC and, most likely, Mutual) an opportunity to substantially increase their coverage. This, naturally, meant that a number of clear channel stations would have to change their network affiliations. The CCBS, however, suggested that this process would happen naturally through "the normal process of economic competition" and that whatever upheaval might occur in the AM band would be the networks' problem. Still, CCBS members' agreement to make these affiliation changes was in itself no small commitment, especially for those stations holding lucrative NBC affiliations (Table 5.1). But while a 750,000-watt station giving up NBC affiliation for, say, Mutual, would likely experience short-term revenue loss, the CCBS believed that its plan would eventually equalize the power and profitability of the four networks. The group maintained that such a dispersion would benefit the entire radio industry. "[T]he way to keep this radio industry independent of centralized control is to allow as many independent broadcasters as possible to become strong," Caldwell testified.[31]

The CCBS anticipated that the potential network affiliation shifts brought about by its plan would spark heated opposition from both NBC and CBS, especially NBC. Both networks, of course, opposed the CCBS plan, with NBC pursuing the most aggressive cross-examination of DeWitt. "Why else would they have $300,000 worth of vice-presidents present?" Caldwell asked after DeWitt's testimony. The network's criticism centered on the fact that the Twenty-Station Plan had conveniently granted significant power increases only to members of the Clear Channel Broadcasting Service. NBC also contended that in some cases reliable groundwave service of NBC programming would be replaced by unreliable skywave service from 750,000-watt clear channel stations, especially in the Northeast and West, where at least seven clear channel stations would be forced to give up their NBC affiliation. The network also dismissed the RBC plan for similar reasons and in the end argued that the existing allocation provided the greatest benefit to the listening public.[32]

Opposition to the plan also emerged from within the CCBS soon after the group presented it to the FCC. Westinghouse, licensee of KDKA and WBZ, broke ranks over the Twenty-Station Plan at

the beginning of 1948, saying that it "will not adequately or economically solve the issues announced in this proceeding." In truth,
Westinghouse was more concerned with the possibility of interference between KDKA on 1020 kHz and WBZ on 1030 kHz, both of
which were slated for 750,000-watt operation under the CCBS
plan. Beyond that, the company balked at having to give up NBC
affiliation on at least one of the two stations. Westinghouse said it
did not oppose power increases for clear channel stations, but it
maintained that the commission should do so on an individual
basis. The company chose to fall back on its Stratovision plan,
which proposed a series of airplanes equipped with FM transmitters to provide rural radio—and eventually television—service.
Westinghouse engineers maintained that a fleet of 14 planes could
provide nine different program services to 80 percent of the United
States' population. At the beginning of 1948, the company also
pulled out of the CCBS.[33]

ABC, from the beginning of the hearings seeking a way to achieve
coverage parity with NBC and CBS, welcomed the CCBS plan.
The network called clear channels' willingness to change network
affiliations "one of the most significant developments of the hearing" but urged them to keep that commitment even if the higher-
power plan was not approved. ABC said that such a change would
"be to the mass transmissions of intelligence by radio what the
Kingsbury commitment was to the transmission of intelligence by
wire," referring to the 1913 agreement in which American Telephone and Telegraph consented to provide interconnection for
independent telephone companies. The network called the monopoly of CBS and NBC a far greater danger than any potential
monopoly of 750,000-watt stations; however, it proposed altering
the CCBS plan to provide 750,000-watt licenses for its I-A stations KGO, WJZ and WENR.[34]

DOCKET 6741 CLOSING ARGUMENTS

With the presentation of the CCBS plan completed, the commission then scheduled three days of final arguments on Docket
6741. Caldwell, hoping to put one final engineering spin on the
hearings, requested that CCBS engineers as well as counsel be
permitted to give testimony. Spearman, however, objected, not-

ing it would cause "a retrial of issues already presented." The commission agreed, allowing only legal counsel to present closing arguments.[35]

Caldwell began by arguing that the FCC should not let the powerful network interests obstruct the CCBS's plans to improve rural coverage. Continually revisiting the issue as one of engineering principles, Caldwell said that with a power increase from 50,000 to 750,000 watts "good signals become better, fair signals become good, poor signals become fair and a certain amount of service is made available in regions which have never had it before." Such results were "axiomatic," just as "speedier trains, boats and airplanes" provided "more comfortable facilities for transportation," according to Caldwell. "750,000 watts is not very much power," he said, recalling the soothing metaphors Powel Crosley, Jr., in the 1930s. "It is not even enough to run a motor on a B-29 airplane. No signal becomes so strong that it electrocutes the listener, or burns the receiving set, or does any damage to life, property and the pursuit of happiness." Finally, Caldwell argued that the licensees of the independent clear channel stations were willing to take significant risks in order to unselfishly improve rural service:

> Here are people, the broadcasters of the clear channel group, proposing to be allowed to spend huge sums of money, so large that it may use up a large portion of the profits, men willing to take the risk involved to serve sparsely-settled areas and provide a sort of rural free delivery.[36]

Spearman presented closing arguments for the RBC and focused on the harm that clear channel stations with higher power would do to the regional—as well as to the local—stations. He once again emphasized the long-cited danger of "too much power in the hands of too few":

> I don't believe you ought to put up the possibility of the leaders of those stations, 25 or 30 years from now, coming together in a smoke-filled room and deciding who they are going to make President of the United States, and gentlemen, that is a possibility.

He also emphasized the inadequacy of programming on clear channel stations, noting that the clears "almost without exception firmly lock their network lines in place and present an uninterrupted schedule of national network programs" at night.[37]

The concluding testimony of NBC and CBS once again called for the maintenance of the status quo. NBC opposed the plans offered by CCBS and RBC, as well as the plan—now no longer under consideration—offered by CBS, but said that it might not oppose higher power for a small number of individual clear channel stations. This, of course, had been the argument offered by NBC since the 1930s. CBS continued to protest the FCC's exclusion of FM, while ABC supported the broad outlines of the CCBS plan but called for its stations to be given superpower as well. The National Association of Educational Broadcasters stopped short of mandating a complete breakdown of the clear channels but asked the FCC to consider the diversity of service that could result by duplicating some clear channels. "[A]ll we are asking for is a hearing on each particular problem as it arises," said Marcus Cohn of WOI of Ames, Iowa, "and for you to weigh the pros and cons in the public interest in each individual case." The existing allocation plan that preserved cleared frequencies without regard to program service kept many rural and small town listeners from hearing programming of "unique and local interest" at night, the group said. Representatives of several daytime stations appeared as well, asking the commission to take into consideration their unique local programming contributions.[38]

The FCC closed the record on Docket 6741 in January 1948, hoping to have a decision in time for the next NARBA engineering conference, tentatively scheduled for May 1. The commission had collected more than 22,000 pages of exhibits, and by the beginning of 1948, the FCC engineering staff was working on three different plans to resolve the clear channel issue. The first plan, which had been under study since the beginning of 1947 at the request of then-chairman Denny, would have given power increases of 750,000 watts to 22 stations: 15 I-As, two existing I-Bs and five new I-Bs. A second plan would have created 18 750,000-watt stations: 13 I-As and five new I-Bs, with none of the network-owned stations tapped for higher power, and several network clears to be reduced to I-B status. The final plan, which proposed duplicating all 24 I-A channels, was requested by the commission at the beginning of 1948. Under this plan, 50,000 watts would remain the power limitation on all clear channels, and new stations would be added to clear channels where they could provide service to White Areas.[39]

SENATE HEARINGS ON THE JOHNSON BILL

News of the impending FCC resolution of the long-debated clear channel issue—and especially the rumors that higher power was under consideration—again attracted congressional attention. On February 26, 1948, Senator Edwin Johnson, a Democrat from Colorado, introduced a bill (S. 2231) to duplicate the clear channels and limit their power to 50,000 watts. "For the Congress to permit the commission to decide the all-important questions of super-power and clear channels without a formal or informal expression of the views held by the Senate is nonfeasance," Johnson told the Senate. "Such failure may result in the tail wagging the dog." He called the existing allocation structure arbitrary and discriminatory, saying that the reservation of clear channels was "wasteful of frequencies and uneconomic." The next day, Republican senator Charles Tobey of New Hampshire, acting chairman of the Senate Interstate and Foreign Commerce Committee in the absence of longtime radio authority Wallace H. White, wrote to FCC chairman Wayne Coy requesting that the commission delay a decision in the clear channel case pending the outcome of Senate hearings on S. 2231. Tobey also sent letters to all AM stations and broadcast groups and invited "full and frank comments" on the proposal. The invitation, however, was clearly slanted against the clear channels and particularly the CCBS's Twenty-Station Plan. Tobey claimed that the CCBS plan would force many, if not most, smaller stations out of business.[40]

The hearings on the Johnson Bill prompted the first full-scale mobilization of CCBS forces on Capitol Hill. This bill was potentially more significant than the Senate's 1938 resolution against superpower, for it would actually amend the Communications Act to prohibit power increases and mandate the duplication of clear channels. Senator Johnson quickly became the chief political nemesis of the CCBS—he took the place Senator Wheeler had occupied for nearly a decade. "Big Ed [Johnson] was our number one opponent," Quaal later said. The CCBS was convinced, however, that Craney and Wheeler still lurked behind the bill, as Wheeler's son, Edward, a lawyer who represented Craney's stations, had made a presentation to the Senate committee earlier in 1948. Caldwell described Johnson as a close political associate of the former Montana senator and also speculated that Edwin Howard Armstrong had been a substantial influence on Tobey. A final connection was made to the Commerce Committee's secretary, Ed Cooper, who formerly worked for Senator Wheeler.[41]

As the CCBS began to prepare its case for the hearings, Caldwell instructed DeWitt to produce an abbreviated technical description in lay language of the group's Docket 6741 presentation. CCBS stations were encouraged to write letters to their local representatives and senators as well as members of the Interstate and Foreign Commerce Committee to promote the value of clear channels and encourage the Senate to leave such technically complicated issues in the hands of the FCC. In addressing the latter topic, stations were warned that letters "should be phrased in diplomatic terms" to avoid the appearance of questioning the Senate's authority. "Unquestionably Congress has the right to enact such a bill as the Johnson Bill," Caldwell wrote, "the only question is as to the wisdom and justice of doing so." The CCBS also considered taking its argument against the Johnson Bill to the airwaves on individual clear channel stations, which caused intense disagreement among members. The group finally decided that doing so would merely antagonize members of the Interstate and Foreign Commerce Committee, as well as provide fodder for opponents who cited the dangers of the clear channels' persuasive powers.[42]

In the two weeks leading up to the hearings, Caldwell's communications with group members took on an increasingly urgent tone. He had been in regular contact with Cooper, and he called his conversations with the committee secretary "disturbing." "[A]rrangements for the hearing are being made more with an eye to staging a demonstration against clear channels than for the purpose of ascertaining the facts," he wrote. Cooper was vague about the agenda of the hearings, but he indicated that the committee would likely allot a block of time for each station that wanted to testify. Caldwell pointed out that this would favor stations supportive of the bill since there were more of them. Cooper noted that nearly 300 replies to Tobey's original letter had been received, most of them "vigorously upholding" its assertions, and made it clear that the committee would not welcome an extended technical presentation from the CCBS because there was no need for a "repetition of the testimony heard by the FCC." Caldwell told CCBS members that Cooper termed the CCBS's proposal for making a comprehensive presentation "crazy" and more generally viewed as "intemperate" any criticisms of the Johnson Bill. "Otherwise the conversation was entirely amicable," Caldwell sarcastically noted.[43]

After meeting with Cooper, Caldwell advised stations to step up their efforts to contact members of the Interstate and Foreign Commerce Committee and that all stations should send letters to each member of the committee and all members of the FCC. He enclosed a sample letter in which individual stations could simply fill in the blanks. The letter took pains to point out that CCBS members were affiliated with—but not owned by—networks and that the danger of clear channel stations causing economic ruin for smaller stations was a "worn-out and discredited fallacy." It also urged the committee to let the FCC decide "intricate technical subjects":

> The Commission has spent over three years in a full and impartial hearing of the issues. … I fear that your committee will not have either the time or the facilities for a thorough study of the matter. Do you think it wise to deprive the Commission of the authority which Congress delegated to it for just such matters?

Caldwell also enclosed copies of a recent resolution passed by the American Farm Bureau Federation asking for improvements in rural radio service. "[A]ttention is called to the fact that the CCBS plan attempted to do just that," Caldwell reminded stations. Meanwhile, he urged individual CCBS members to continue to work on securing the support of state and local farm organizations.[44]

Sholis, who had left his position as CCBS director to take a job at WHAS, wrote his own letter to Tobey but eschewed Caldwell's reserve for a more strident tone. "[T]he committee's announcement of hearings reveals it has been misinformed and is working on the basis of false premises," he wrote. "Throughout the memorandum filed by Senator Johnson run [*sic*] the same string of myths which have blocked improvement of radio service to farmers for many years." Sholis told Tobey WHAS intended not just to provide "a simple presentation of station testimony" but to bring "a series of witnesses representing our rural and small town audience. ... We do hope you will earmark ample time for us to present our case."[45]

The senator's reply was equally caustic, noting that the committee had received several hundred letters from radio stations that indicated the committee was not as misinformed as Sholis had implied. "Are we to assume that all of these people are wrong while only you and the other clear channel people are right?" Tobey asked. "I do not believe it is fair to charge 'false premises' to the committee simply because some members of the committee have a viewpoint different from your's [*sic*]." As for Sholis's indication that WHAS planned to make an extensive presentation, Tobey warned that the committee would not condone "a Roman holiday with a protracted hearing during which those best equipped financially can put on the best show."[46]

Such confrontational exchanges with representatives of the Interstate and Foreign Commerce Committee merely fueled the CCBS's fears that the hearings would be biased against it. "The situation is becoming worse than critical," Caldwell warned member stations the week before the hearings. "A high pressure campaign is being conducted by the regional group, masterminded by Ed Craney and the Wheelers. They are succeeding in getting commitments in favor of the Johnson Bill to an alarming degree." Worse still for the CCBS, Cooper informed Caldwell that opponents of the bill would be forced to testify first, the reverse of normal procedure. Caldwell told CCBS members this was an outrage.[47]

Broadcasting magazine was not far off in calling the Johnson hearings "a ten-day version of the FCC's three-year clear-channel proceeding." However, during the Johnson Bill testimony there was less discussion of technical issues and a greater emphasis on personalities, especially the CCBS's conflict with Craney, former senator Wheeler and Senator Johnson. There also appeared to be tension among members of the Interstate and Foreign Commerce Committee, some of whom believed the hearings were being conducted in a biased fashion; only five of the 13 members of the committee attended the sessions regularly. Clear channel proponents found themselves on the defensive from nearly the first sentence of testimony; as Caldwell began his presentation, Tobey protested the attorney's intention to read a prepared statement. After some argument, Ernest McFarland, a Democrat from Arizona, asserted that Caldwell should be allowed to present his case in any manner he saw fit. Tobey said he agreed but noted that "to sit and listen to 80 pages of stuff read out here is going to be torture all along the line." Senators Tobey and McFarland also immediately challenged Caldwell's assertion of the existence of White Areas, with McFarland maintaining that he had been on "practically every highway between here and Arizona" and never had trouble picking up stations. Senator Homer Capehart of Indiana defended Caldwell, noting that most towns in southern Illinois and central Illinois lacked adequate radio service.[48]

For the most part, the clear channel proponents echoed the arguments they had forwarded during Docket 6741 testimony. James Shouse of WLW defended his station's superpower operation during the 1930s and said the voluminous record in Docket 6741 had contained no proof that WLW's high power harmed any other stations. "We put nobody out of business," he said. The CCBS also organized the testimony of 11 local and regional farm groups and persuaded numerous others to write letters to the committee. There was no organized group testifying in favor of the bill, but several individual station representatives did. Throughout the hearings, the CCBS insinuated that Craney was the major force behind the bill and behind broader efforts to break down the clear channels, yet Caldwell said he could guarantee that Craney would not appear at the hearings. "He never does [testify] in these hearings," Caldwell said. "He does all his work elsewhere." "I see," Tobey replied. "Get set."[49]

Later, Craney did testify, and his demeanor belied CCBS portrayals of him as a radical antagonist. Craney's testimony was re-markably subdued, and the Montanan made little effort to attack the clear channels beyond saying that they were not doing a good job of serving rural residents and that the CCBS was merely inter-ested in maintaining the privileged position of the clear channel stations. Johnson also rebutted CCBS charges that Craney was responsible for the bill. "You are accused of being entirely respon-sible for this legislation," he said. "If so, you must have some method of remote control over me because I never discussed the matter with you or talked with you or anybody representing you." Still, Tobey's earlier confidence that Craney would appear at the hearings implied at least some contact between the committee and Craney, and he was not in the list of witnesses released on the Friday before the hearings began. It is doubtful that, as Caldwell contended, Craney was solely responsible for the Johnson Bill, but it seems certain that his contact with the committee—either directly or indirectly—was greater than either Tobey or Johnson admitted.[50]

Former senator Wheeler also testified, denying any sinister al-liance with Craney against the clear channels. In reality, he said, it was the clear channel interests that "have carried on a propa-ganda campaign from the beginning down to the present moment" through their lobbying activities. He tied the clear channel sta-tions and chains together as monopolistic influences in radio and noted that every FCC lawyer "is looking forward to the time when they will step off the Commission and be employed by one of the chains or a clear-channel station." Johnson also criticized the clear channel public interest efforts. "[They] parade pictures of bare-foot girls and everyone else trying to prove the point that they are philanthropically inclined and patriotically inclined also, and that the great burden of their interest was the rural listener," he said. In rebuttal testimony, Caldwell downplayed CCBS lobbying ac-tivities, saying the group had never attempted to initiate any legis-lation. "To the best of our ability, we have opposed the Johnson Bill and an earlier attempt to prohibit higher power and to break down clear channels back in 1944," he said. "I am sure you can-not blame us for that."[51]

Representatives of NBC, CBS, ABC and Mutual testified against the bill. Even though the networks presented divergent viewpoints before the FCC, they were unanimously opposed to congressional intervention in allocation matters. The networks, having greater influence at the commission than in Congress, wanted to keep allocation decisionmaking at the FCC, at least as long as the FCC did not propose radical changes. Raymond F. Guy of NBC's allocation and engineering department even went so far as to call the clear channels sacred. "I might say, sirs, the Lord made AM clear channels for long distance rural transmission, and I don't think the committee wants to go against the Lord," he said. Craven testified against the bill as well, although he admitted that as vice-chairman of the RBC he sought the same aim: preventing the monopolistic use of radio channels. But he warned against passing the Johnson Bill. He noted that "in a fast-developing scientific art such as radio it seems unwise to legislate specific limits upon future technical developments." He said that both the CCBS and the RBC were ultimately looking out for their own interests, the members of the CCBS were "shrewd businessmen," and RBC stations were "not in business for charity."[52]

Soon after the conclusion of the hearings, it seemed clear that the Johnson Bill would not make it out of committee. Nonetheless, Caldwell urged CCBS members not to relax, noting that the result could be "a photographic finish." Wheeler and Craney, Caldwell asserted, were making strenuous last-minute efforts. The ideal outcome for the CCBS would have been for the Interstate and Foreign Commerce Committee to vote down the Johnson Bill, as Caldwell feared the FCC would view the issue as undecided by the Senate if the committee did not vote on it. At its meetings in May and June, however, the committee did not address the bill, and Johnson himself seemed to acknowledge that it had little chance of making it out of committee, much less being voted on by the full Senate. On May 19, he introduced a resolution (S. Res. 240) urging the FCC to take no action on Docket 6741 until a new NARBA had been ratified by the Senate, but it, too, failed to win support of the Interstate and Foreign Commerce Committee. On June 1, Johnson introduced another resolution (S. Res. 246). The resolution noted that the Communications Act of 1934 should not be construed as limiting the power of the FCC to consider program content when making license renewal decisions and prohibited the FCC from granting power in excess of 50,000 watts unless authorized by NARBA.[53]

Caldwell viewed Johnson's series of resolutions as merely an effort to "confuse things," but on June 9, the Interstate and Foreign Commerce Committee reported out a version of the White Bill (S. 1333) that included the language from Johnson's S. Res. 246. Caldwell called the development an "unexpected bad blow," and was equally apprehensive about Senator White's formation of a Subcommittee on Communications made up of Johnson, Tobey and McFarland. White's order, dated June 19, said that the subcommittee's mission would be to gather "additional information ... concerning certain aspects of the operations of the Federal Communications Commission." Under such a mandate, the clear channel structure would certainly fall under the subcommittee's scrutiny, and the three members of the subcommittee were decidedly not fans of the clear channels.[54]

Congress adjourned before action was taken on S. 1333 or any of Johnson's proposals, but the CCBS knew it had only dodged another in a continuing series of bullets. "This last time we were aided by time limitations," Caldwell wrote the following summer. "This will not be true of the next session." The Subcommittee on Communications was ordered to begin its work as soon as the Senate reconvened in January 1949. "Everything possible should be done, therefore, between now and next January to enlist support," Caldwell wrote.[55]

CONCLUSION

Docket 6741 could have been one of the most significant rule-making proceedings ever to come before the FCC. One need only look at the intense interest in the hearings—from individual station groups, networks and others—to understand that the docket was seen as extremely important to the future of broadcasting. In vowing to make a comprehensive examination of the clear channel structure, the FCC also was seemingly opening up the entire broadcast structure—past, present and future—to inquiry. This, of course, could have affected not only the clear channels but the entire AM band and new services such as FM and television.

The FCC's decision to throw out consideration of FM, however, provided the first indication that it would not radically restructure the broadcast structure through Docket 6741. Instead of considering an overall broadcast system including AM, FM and television, the commission considered each individually, largely because it was administratively convenient to do so. But that did not mean that Docket 6741 could no longer effect great change in the AM band; thus, station groups and networks jostled to maintain and enhance their positions in AM. The CCBS's Twenty-Station Plan was the most radical proposal offered during the hearings, and it served to illustrate the divisions within the broadcast industry. Strong networks—NBC and CBS—opposed it, while weaker networks such as ABC supported its potential to provide parity. Regional and local stations, of course, opposed the plan as well.

In the overall view of the clear channel issue, which had been debated for more than 20 years, the additional six months of delay brought about by the Johnson Bill would seem to be a minor issue. But those six months—and the additional delay caused by FCC uncertainty over where the Senate stood on the clear channel issue—made the FCC's initial intention to resolve the issue by May 1948 impossible. It would have to wait for a new NARBA agreement, and then the FCC would find itself consumed by other tasks, most notably the allocation of television frequencies. Another 13 years would pass before the FCC ultimately resolved Docket 6741. By then, the context of the issues had changed dramatically, and both the Golden Age of radio and the dominance of the clear channels were a distant memory.

NOTES

1. Christopher H. Sterling, *Electronic Media: A Guide to Trends in Broadcasting and Newer Technologies, 1920–1983* (New York: Praeger, 1984), 83–84.

2. See FCC, Order, Docket 6741, February 20, 1945, Volume 1, Docket 6741, Docketed Case Files, RG 173, National Archives, College Park, Md. (hereafter referred to as NACP); "All's Unclear Ahead," *Broadcasting*, February 26, 1945, 38; and Sol Taishoff, "Clear Channel Parley May Alter All Radio," *Broadcasting*, April 9, 1945, 15.

3. See CCG, Report No. 22, September 21, 1937, Box P-1130, Clear Channel Group Records, Wiley, Rein and Fielding, Washington, D.C. (hereafter referred to as WRF); Taishoff, "Clear Channel Parley May Alter All Radio"; "Probe to Hear Chairman Fly in June," *Broadcasting*, May 25, 1942, 53; and Ward Quaal, telephone conversation with author, January 5, 1994.

4. See "Shepard, Damm, Craney Seek to Revive Regional Stations," *Broadcasting*, March 5, 1945, 16; Jack Levy, "FCC Will Probe Clear Channel Issues," *Broadcasting*, December 10, 1945, 18; R. Russell Eagan to Louis Caldwell, n.d., Box P-1133, WRF; Brenda Trahan and Gerald V. Flannery, "Craven, Tunis A.M.," in Gerald V. Flannery, ed., *Commissioners of the FCC, 1927–1994* (Lanham, Md.: University Press of America, 1995), 52–53; and RBC Member Stations, November 18, 1947, Volume 1, Docket 6741, Docketed Case Files, RG 173, NACP.

5. See Joseph H. Udelson, *The Great Television Race: A History of the American Television Industry, 1925–1941* (Tuscaloosa: University of Alabama Press, 1982), 91–92, 150–58; and Christopher H. Sterling and John M. Kittross, *Stay Tuned: A Concise History of American Broadcasting* (Belmont, Calif.: Wadsworth Publishing Company, 1990), 233–34.

6. See ABC, Brief, January 12, 1948, Volume 2, Docket 6741, Docketed Case Files, RG 173, NACP; House Interstate Commerce Committee, *Proposed Changes in the Communications Act of 1934 (HR-5497)*, 77th Cong., 2d Sess. (Washington, D.C., 1942), 439–42; William J. Norfleet to Commission, February 21, 1944, Broadcast Memorandums, RG 173, NACP; Sterling and Kittross, *Stay Tuned*, 156–58; and John H. DeWitt to Chief Engineers, September 13, 1946, Box P-1130, WRF.

7. George P. Adair to August G. Hiebert, April 6, 1945, Volume 1, Docket 6741, Docketed Case Files, RG 173, NACP.

8. See "State Department Protests to Cuba over Clear Channel 'Squatting,'" *Broadcasting*, February 19, 1945, 13; and Confidential Memo on Cuban Conference, February 23, 1946, Box P-1130, WRF.

9. The clear channels in question were 640 kHz (KFI), 670 (WMAQ), 830 (WCCO), 850 (WHAS) and 890 (WLS). See CCBS, *Summary History of Allocation in the Standard Broadcast Band* (Washington, D.C.: Press of Byron S. Adams, 1948), 53, 56.

10. See Confidential Memo on Cuban Conference; and Edwin W. Craig, "NARBA Views of Clears, Regionals," *Broadcasting*, March 4, 1946, 17, 78.

11. See "NAB Will Keep Its Hands off When Clear Hearings Resume," *Broadcasting*, November 18, 1946, 102; and Bill Bailey, "Cuba's NARBA Victory Portends U.S. Row," *Broadcasting*, March 4, 1946, 17, 78.

12. See Transcript, 1907–1908, Volume 16, Docket 6741, Docketed Case Files, RG 173, NACP; Jack Levy and Rufus Crater, "Denny Indicates Breakdown of More Clears," *Broadcasting*, April 29, 1946, 17; and Jack Levy and Rufus Crater, "Clears' Fate Debated; Resume April 15," *Broadcasting*, January 21, 1946, 15.

13. See Transcript, 56, Docket 6741, Docketed Case Files, RG 173, NACP; Louis G. Caldwell, "Censorship Is Censorship .. Regardless," *Broadcasting*, April 1, 1946, 25.

14. Transcript, 6175, Docket 6741.

15. Rufus Crater and Jack Levy, "Duplication of 10 to 12 Clear Channels Is Indicated," *Broadcasting*, May 6, 1946, 18.

16. Levy and Crater, "Denny Indicates Breakdown," 17, 95.

17. See Jack Levy and Rufus Crater, "CBS FM-AM Plan Would Cost 10 Million," *Broadcasting*, May 13, 1946, 17; Transcript, 3432, 3460, 3474, Docket 6741; and Jack DeWitt, Report on Meeting Called to Discuss FM Coverage, January 20, 1947, Box P-1130, WRF.

18. See DeWitt, Report on Meeting; John H. DeWitt to Garrard Mountjoy, August 27, 1947, Box P-1130, WRF; and Letter, n.d., Box P-1130, WRF.

19. See "Sholis Cites CCBS Efforts for FM," *Broadcasting*, September 16, 1946, 18.

20. See John H. DeWitt to John M. Reid, August 12, 1947, Box P-1141, WRF; Michael A. Konczal and Gerald V. Flannery, "Charles R. Denny," in Flannery, ed., *Commissioners of the FCC*, 80; Victor A. Sholis to CCBS Members, October 27, 1947, Box P-1130, WRF; Rufus Crater, "CCBS Offers 750-kw Station Plan," *Broadcasting*, October 27, 1947, 90; FCC, *In the Matter of Clear Channel Broadcasting in the Standard Broadcast Band*, 12 FCC 587 (1947); FCC, *Memorandum Opinion and Order*, December 30, 1947, Volume 1, Docket 6741, RG 173, NACP.

21. Oral Argument, 79-80, Volume 3, Docket 6741, Docketed Case

Files, RG 173, NACP.

22. See Rufus Crater, "Regionals Chart Breakdown of Clears," *Broadcasting*, July 22, 1946, 20, 86–87; Rufus Crater, "Clears Emphasize Need for Higher Power," *Broadcasting*, July 29, 1946, 28, 32; and Transcript, 4251, Docket 6741.

23. See "Breakdown of Clear Channels Urged," *Broadcasting*, July 15, 1946, 16, 91–92; and Oral Argument, 320–1, Docket 6741.

24. See Louis Caldwell to CCBS Members, April 12, 1945, Box P-1130, WRF; CCBS, Bulletin Number 2, April 25, 1945, Box P-1130, WRF; and CCBS, Brief, January 27, 1941, Box P-1130, WRF.

25. See Louis Caldwell to CCBS Members, April 12, 1945, Box P-1130, WRF; Minutes, June 14, 1945, Box P-1130, WRF; Preparation for FCC Hearing on Clear Channel Broadcasting, March 1945, Box P-1130, WRF; John S. Campbell to CCBS Engineers, June 21, 1946, Box P-1130, WRF; Oral Argument, 10, Docket 6741; and "Clears Develop Revolutionary Plan," *Broadcasting*, October 28, 1946, 13, 100.

26. John H. DeWitt, Testimony, 1, 3, 14, Box P-1130, WRF.

27. DeWitt, Testimony, 2, 3, 18, 24.

28. DeWitt, Testimony, 46, 47, 50.

29. See DeWitt, Testimony, 48–50; and NBC, Brief, January 12, 1948, Volume 1, Docket 6741, Docketed Case Files, RG 173, NACP.

30. DeWitt, Testimony, 53–54.

31. See CCBS, Outline of Case for High Power, n.d., Box P-1130, WRF; and Oral Argument, 140, Docket 6741.

32. See CCBS to Members, August 25, 1947, Box P-1130, WRF; CCBS to Members, October 27, 1947, Box P-1130, WRF; NBC, Brief, January 12, 1948; and Transcript, 5078, Docket 6741.

33. See Westinghouse Radio Stations, Brief, January 8, 1946, Volume 1, Docket 6741, Docketed Case Files, RG 173, NACP; Ward Quaal, telephone conversation with author, May 12, 1994; and "Westinghouse Veers from CCBS Plan," *Broadcasting*, January 12, 1948, 18, 101.

34. See ABC, Brief, January 12, 1948, Volume 2, Docket 6741, Docketed Case Files, RG 173, NACP; and Oral Argument, 170, Docket 6741.

35. See Louis Caldwell to FCC, November 1, 1947, Volume 1, Docket 6741, Docketed Case Files, RG 173, NACP; Paul D.P. Spearman to FCC, November 6, 1947, Volume 1, Docket 6741,

Docketed Case Files, RG 173, NACP; and T.J. Slowie to Louis
Caldwell, December 23, 1947, Volume 1, Docket 6741, Docketed Case
Files, RG 173, NACP.

36. Oral Argument, 8, 16, 59, 112, Docket 6741.

37. See Oral Argument, 319, 417, Docket 6741; and RBC, Brief,
January 12, 1948, Volume 2, Docket 6741, Docketed Case Files, RG
173, NACP.

38. See Oral Argument, 170–76, 228–29, 244–48, 446–51; 459–61,
Volume 3, Docket 6741, Docketed Case Files, RG 173, NACP; and
NAEB, Memorandum Brief, January 9, 1948, Volume 1, Docket 6741,
Docketed Case Files, RG 173, NACP.

39. See Rufus Crater, "Record Closed in Clear Channel Case,"
Broadcasting, January 26, 1948, 17, 87; and George Harry Rogers,
"The History of the Clear Channel and Super Power Controversy in
the Management of the Standard Broadcast Allocation Plan" (Ph.D.
Diss., University of Utah, 1972), 51–52.

40. See Senate Interstate and Foreign Commerce Committee, *To
Limit the Power of Radio Broadcast Stations*, 80th Cong., 2d Sess.
(Washington, D.C., 1948), 3, 4; and Rufus Crater, "Clears Blasted,"
Broadcasting, March 1, 1948, 13, 85.

41. Ward Quaal, telephone conversation with author, May 5, 1994;
Louis Caldwell, Memorandum on Johnson Bill, n.d., Box P-1142,
WRF; and Louis Caldwell, Memorandum No. 2, n.d., Box P-1142,
WRF.

42. Louis Caldwell, Tentative Modus Operandi in Preparation for
Hearing on Johnson Bill, n.d., Box P-1142, WRF; and Louis Caldwell,
Memorandum No. 2.

43. Louis Caldwell, Memorandum No. 4, March 17, 1948, Box P-
1142, WRF.

44. Louis Caldwell, Memorandum No. 3, n.d., Box P-1142, WRF.

45. Victor A. Sholis to Charles Tobey, March 15, 1948, Box P-1142,
WRF.

46. Charles Tobey to Victor A. Sholis, March 17, 1948, Box P-1142,
WRF.

47. Louis Caldwell, Memorandum No. 6, March 23, 1948, Box P-
1142, WRF.

48. Senate, *To Limit*, 17–19, 22–25.

49. See Rufus Crater, "Clear Channels' Fate," *Broadcasting*,

March 22, 1948, 13; and Senate, *To Limit*, 45.

50. See Senate, *To Limit*, 684; and Rufus Crater, "Clear Channels at Cross Roads," *Broadcasting*, April 5, 1948, 21.

51. Senate, *To Limit*, 675, 825, 1063.

52. Senate, *To Limit*, 572–675.

53. See Louis Caldwell, Memorandum No. 7, May 5, 1948, Box P-1142, WRF; R. Russell Eagan, Memorandum No. 8, May 20, 1948, Box P-1142, WRF; Louis Caldwell, Memorandum No. 9, May 29, 1948, Box P-1142, WRF; and Louis Caldwell, Memorandum No. 10, June 2, 1948, Box P-1142, WRF.

54. See Caldwell, Memorandum No. 9; Louis Caldwell, Memorandum No. 11, June 9, 1948, Box P-1142, WRF; Louis Caldwell, Memorandum No. 13, June 25, 1948, Box P-1142, WRF; and Wallace H. White, *Order Appointing Subcommittee on Communications*, June 19, 1948, Box P-1142, WRF.

55. Caldwell, Memorandum No. 13.

CHAPTER SIX

Heads It's Clear Channels,
Tails It's Regionals

A cartoon in the September 5, 1948, issue of *Broadcasting* magazine perhaps best summed up the continuing clear channel controversy. A few weeks earlier Congress had passed a law forbidding the broadcast of lottery results, finally bringing to a conclusion another drawn-out regulatory debate. Now, the cartoon showed six FCC commissioners sitting at a conference table, watching as the seventh commissioner flips a coin into the air. "Now that lotteries are settled," the commissioner is saying, "heads it's clear channels, tails it's regionals." The solution to the issue was, of course, not that simple, as evidenced by the thousands of pages of testimony and exhibits collected by the FCC during the Docket 6741 proceedings, yet nearly everyone expected that resolution of the issue was imminent. In reality, more than 13 years would pass before the commission resolved Docket 6741, and even then—by the FCC's own admission—it had not achieved a complete solution.[1]

Although the years between the conclusion of the Johnson Bill hearings and the FCC's final termination of the clear channel proceedings were largely uneventful from the perspective of direct FCC action, other factors had a bearing on the clear channel issue. As was the case in 1946, the renegotiation of the North American Regional Broadcasting Agreement (NARBA) once again divided the U.S. radio industry. Disagreement frequently centered on issues involving clear channels: while opponents of U.S. clears saw NARBA as a wedge to force the breakdown of the frequencies without FCC action, the Clear Channel Broadcasting Service vigorously framed the NARBA issues in nationalist terms by urging the United States not to squander its natural resources (the clear channels) to foreign concerns.

The CCBS also kept up the domestic pressure, producing engineering studies for the FCC and plying the halls of Congress both to squelch anti-clear channel legislation and to persuade friendly members of the House and Senate to pressure the FCC to "do the right thing by America's rural listeners." The group continued to orchestrate public relations campaigns as well, frequently relying on its contacts with major farm organizations, as will be discussed in Chapter 7. But at the same time, opposition to the CCBS position was becoming more diversified and better organized. Where during the 1930s and 1940s groups such as the National Association of Regional Broadcast Stations (NARBS) and the Regional Broadcasters Committee (RBC) existed only informally and for as long as the current set of FCC hearings, now anti-clear interests were taking a cue from the CCBS and establishing a more permanent and organized presence in the capital. Perhaps most adept was the Daytime Broadcasters Association (DBA), which arose among daytime licensees during the 1950s to oppose CCBS efforts to restrict subordinate stations on clear channels.

Most importantly, however, the 1950s brought changes to the radio industry that transcended existing interest groups. Television, the long-promised replacement for radio, finally came to prominence, and although AM radio was now so entrenched that few believed it really would be subsumed by television, the new medium significantly altered radio's commercial structure, stealing away important national advertisers and eroding the massive evening listening audience. With the advent of commercial television, network advertising on AM began a rather precipitous decline, falling from a high of $211 million in 1948 to only $43 million by 1962. All the while, of course, television's national advertising and network revenue were rising. AM radio, then, shifted toward local advertising, and in 1948 local revenue surpassed national revenue for the first time. FM, too, was becoming a significant factor, with its improved fidelity, resistance to static and ability to provide radio service over limited areas without blanketing interference over a much wider area. By the time the FCC finally decided the clear channel issue, the economic landscape of AM radio looked significantly different than it did when Docket 6741 hearings commenced.[2]

CONGRESSIONAL INTEREST

Senator Edwin Johnson resumed his agitation for breaking down the clear channels in the 1949 session of Congress. His 1948 hearings had effectively halted FCC action on Docket 6741, and now the senator from Colorado continued to pressure the FCC against any inclination it might have to grant higher power to clear channel stations. He introduced another bill, S. 491, which was largely the same as the anti-clear channel measure he had sponsored the year before. Now, however, in the newly Democratic Senate, Johnson had ascended to chair of the Interstate and Foreign Commerce Committee, and *Broadcasting* magazine mused that he would "cause more anxiety in the clears' camp" than he had in 1948. The Subcommittee on Communications, created in 1948, became his primary forum for examining the clear channel structure, and the senator, of course, left no doubt as to where he stood. Not only did he portray the clear channel stations as monopolies, he criticized the Clear Channel Broadcasting Service for its lobbying activities in Congress and at the FCC. Characterizing the CCBS as "a well-entrenched, well financed, well staffed group who are determined to have radio control in the United States," Johnson said the clear channel stations, "the kingpins of the radio world," were as monopolistic as the major radio networks.[3]

In addition to his public work, Johnson also applied private pressure to the members of the FCC. The senator wrote several letters to commissioners during 1949, offering to "render a valuable public service" by dispelling what he said were untrue notions about the clear channel issue. Foremost among these was the existence of White Areas, upon which, he said, the CCBS based its entire case. "I am unable to find convincing testimony regarding these alleged unserved or underserved areas," he wrote. "[W]e must be alert not to accept fantastic claims frequently put forth so blandly and with such a volume of technical detail as to delude even the engineers." He invited the commission to explain how it established that White Areas existed and whether any "actual on-the-ground surveys of listeners" had been done. Commissioner Rosel Hyde sent Johnson a long letter of reply, in which he recounted efforts since the 1930s to gauge rural radio reception and attempted to explain the commission's often-conflicting objectives of providing signal choices and additional local stations at the same time. There was no definition of White Area, Hyde explained, but the term had over the past two decades "acquired a certain accepted meaning." Johnson obviously was not satisfied. "Your letter leaves me completely confused," he wrote. "I thought we were considering a very simple matter which could be disposed of by a very simple answer." If the FCC chairman could not provide a precise definition of the White Area, Johnson asked, how could the commission consider policy based on it? "May I respectfully urge the Commission not to let the cart get ahead of the horse?"[4]

Johnson was not, however, the only member of Congress pressuring the FCC to resolve the clear channel case. Several other senators and representatives sent letters to Chairman Wayne Coy, usually demanding a report on why the commission had yet to act, while calling attention to local licensees who sought to improve their broadcasting facilities but were being held in limbo by the clear channel proceeding. One senator enclosed a letter from a local station owner who complained that the FCC was placing too much emphasis on television while "a billion dollar back-bone-of-the-nation radio industry wallows in the mire of delay, confusion, interference and restraint and suffers severe economic hardship." Most of these letters received a courteous reply from the chairman, in which he cited the immense volume and complexity of the clear channel issue and noted that a decision was not imminent.[5]

At least some of the pressure from Congress was likely the result of the renewed efforts of longtime CCBS opponent Edward B.

Craney to organize nonclear stations. In a letter to potential member stations, Craney said that they needed to band together to oppose the CCBS. "You should know by the efforts they put forth on the Johnson Bill that the clear channel boys will be on the job every day during the coming session of Congress trying to convince its members that there should be a continued waste of facilities by use of clear channels," he warned. At the beginning of 1949, Craney said he had more than 100 stations signed on for the new organization, called the Independent Broadcasters Protective League, which planned to set up a permanent Washington, D.C., office. At the group's first official meeting in January 1941, Craney unanimously was elected chairman.[6]

Senator Johnson also was on hand at that inaugural meeting, where he urged stations to organize themselves to fight the "shrewd, carefully calculated, well financed" clear channel stations. "Intelligent, hard-hitting action is imperative," Johnson said. The senator noted that the 1948 Senate hearings had delayed the imminent FCC action on the clear channel matter, thus giving smaller stations time to mobilize:

> I say in all kindness that you have not yet gotten over to Congress the fact that the overwhelming majority of the radio stations in this country oppose superpower and clear-channel operation. ... The defeatist viewpoint echoed by some of the independent broadcasters is exactly the viewpoint that the big stations and the networks want you to have. They want you to quietly fold up your AM and FM operations so that when they are ready they, and only they, will be in position to take over television.

Johnson also warned the group that if it did not take action there would soon be no "middle class" in radio. "Either radio will be big and powerful or small and strictly local," he said. Despite the senator's fiery rhetoric and Craney's continuing work, however, attempts to establish a permanent organization ultimately failed.[7]

But during the early part of 1949, Craney's organizing efforts, combined with Johnson's ascendancy to head of the Senate Interstate and Foreign Commerce Committee, alarmed members of the CCBS. The group knew that an FCC decision in Docket 6741 was not imminent but worried that Congress might usurp the FCC's authority and pass anti-clear channel legislation itself. The CCBS did not have to wait long for Johnson to act in the Senate, as he invited Craney to appear at hearings on a modified version of the original White Bill in early 1949. This bill contained no provision against clear channels, however, and the CCBS did not want to become involved in legislation that did not impinge on the clear channels. In fact, if Congress did pass any radio legislation that did not reiterate a stance against higher power, the CCBS was prepared to argue that the Senate no longer believed in the 1938 Wheeler Resolution. But after Craney's testimony, Ward Quaal, who had taken over as CCBS director after Victor A. Sholis' departure, attended the next day's hearing and requested an opportunity to testify. A confrontational atmosphere was established immediately as Johnson ordered that Quaal be sworn before testifying, despite the fact that none of the other witnesses had been. Several committee members objected, but Johnson insisted.[8]

Before Quaal could begin his prepared statement, Johnson interrupted to ask him if he was a registered lobbyist, to which Quaal applied in the affirmative. Johnson then began to ask the acting CCBS director questions about his expense account, and Quaal confirmed that he used it for, among other things, entertaining members of Congress. Quaal denied, however, paying to have material read into the record; instead he said he merely spoke to members of Congress, informed them about the clear channel issue, then left them a written statement. Sometimes, Quaal said, this led to members of Congress placing favorable statements in the record. Quaal maintained that there was no difference between what he did as director of the CCBS and what Craney did except that he "had enough respect for the gentlemen in this honorable body" to register as a lobbyist. Later, when recalled to the stand, Craney—after being sworn at the insistence of another member of the committee—said he was not a lobbyist and had come to Washington, D.C., merely to represent his own private interests. Although no bills containing any limitations on clear channel broadcasting in the House or Senate came to a vote, the continuing attention to clear channel allocations in Congress further muddled the issue and made it even less likely that the FCC would reach a decision.[9]

NARBA NEGOTIATIONS

Another factor was the necessity of renegotiating the NARBA treaty, a task that became still more challenging as foreign countries' radio systems developed and their demands for channel space became more aggressive. The "sellout" to Cuba in the 1946 interim agreement was still fresh on the minds of clear channel stations, as was the continual squatting by Mexican and Cuban stations on unauthorized frequencies. Cuba's undersecretary of communications, Carlos Maristany, however, indicated that his country had no intention of being satisfied with its 1946 victory, much less relinquishing any of the assignments it had won, warning the "American industry lords" that they must "awake from their 1937 dream."[10]

The CCBS, of course, had always objected to concessions to other countries on U.S. clear channels and consistently portrayed Mexico and Cuba as menaces threatening the United States' rural radio listeners. Clear channel stations, of course, had the greater stake in international agreements because of their long-distance skywave service, which could be significantly impacted by the presence of foreign stations. Local and regional stations, in contrast, were happy to allow concessions to foreign countries if it lessened the chances of U.S. clear channel stations getting superpower or if it prevented concessions on other channels. Once again—as it had during the 1946 negotiations—the CCBS warned the National Association of Broadcasters not take any stance in NARBA negotiations that would lead to concessions on clear channels. In 1949, Sholis even threatened to pull CCBS members out of the broadcasters' association if it did not comply, noting that "if we resigned, the NAB would collapse."[11]

After numerous delays, a third NARBA agreement was signed in Washington, D.C., on November 15, 1950. While it continued in large part the overall allocation of frequencies among the signatory countries, it also granted to Cuba the use of two additional U.S. clear channel frequencies. Although the treaty required Cuban stations to use directional antennas to minimize signals toward the United States, the CCBS vehemently objected to the concessions. NBC and CBS also objected—although less strenuously—because the two new frequencies to be used by Cuba were occupied by CBS's WBBM in Chicago and NBC's WNBC in New York. The CCBS's major opposition to the treaty, however, arose from the fact that Mexico had pulled out of the conference because of conflicts with Cuba. Having a NARBA agreement without Mexico was wholly unacceptable to the CCBS, especially in light of the long history of interference to CCBS members caused by rogue Mexican stations.[12]

The CCBS thus attempted to build industry opposition against the NARBA agreement, as the issue of Mexican nonparticipation was one it believed should be of concern to all classes of radio stations. In a letter sent to all broadcasters, Quaal outlined why the CCBS was not supporting ratification of NARBA and why other stations should not either and attempted to frame the NARBA issues as transcendent to differences of opinion among U.S. stations. He wrote that the proposed pact would not even benefit those who opposed the CCBS in the clear channel proceedings and called on the industry to put its differences aside in order to prevent the derogation of American broadcasting by foreign countries. "If our governmental representatives can only shake off their defeatist attitude and their willingness to appease at great cost," Quaal wrote, "a satisfactory agreement can be achieved." Similarly, the CCBS worked vigorously to block ratification of NARBA by the Senate and rallied farm groups and rural listeners to oppose the pact. The group's effectiveness in this regard was acknowledged by the FCC in its 1959 *Annual Report,* and although the Senate held hearings on NARBA in 1953, it took no action on the treaty. One year later, the United States entered bilateral talks with Mexico.[13]

The CCBS sent three observers to the negotiations in Mexico City. Hollis Seavey, a former lobbyist with Mutual Broadcasting System who had taken over as director of the CCBS after Quaal accepted a job with the Crosley Corporation, led the CCBS contingent. R. Russell Eagan, who became the group's lead counsel after the death of Louis Caldwell in 1951, accompanied him, as did George Curran, KFI's chief engineer. The CCBS representatives had little direct involvement in the negotiating process but were kept informed of the progress—or lack thereof—through frequent meetings with new FCC chairman Hyde, who led the U.S.

delegation. The negotiations were anything but hospitable, with Mexico alternately refusing to agree to anything until it ironed out differences with Cuba and expressing demands to split additional U.S. clear channels. Hyde, according to Eagan, "was really burned up" and "ready to give up and come home," which, essentially, the U.S. delegation did in December, recessing with an agreement that Mexico would not immediately do anything inconsistent with the existing NARBA. Before leaving, however, the U.S. delegation toured a series of Mexican broadcast facilities. CCBS members, long boastful of their engineering quality and expertise, had always viewed Mexican and Latin American broadcast operations with more than a little scorn, believing that foreign station operators lacked the knowledge to run stations properly and that foreign governments did a poor job of controlling broadcasters in their countries. Eagan affirmed these perceptions, reporting that even Mexico's largest stations maintained poor technical standards and that station operators boasted of their freedom to change frequency and power "without fear of reprisals from the government."[14]

THE DAYTIME SKYWAVE CASE

By this time, the domestic clear channel debate had in fact severed into two separate docket proceedings. Docket 6741, of course, had been started before the end of World War II, but in 1947 the commission was compelled to open a separate proceeding to examine the existence of skywave signals during daytime hours. The latter proceeding traced its origin to the lifting of the wartime freeze, when the FCC began assigning daytime stations on Class I-A and I-B frequencies using standards developed under the 1939 rules, which recognized skywave signals only between sunset and sunrise. The commission assigned numerous new daytime outlets, including 11 stations on Class I-A frequencies, but in June 1946, in an effort to prevent adding further complexity to the Docket 6741 proceeding, it began refusing any new daytime requests on clear channels unless the proposed new station was within 750 miles of the dominant station. The operators of stations farther away than that, the commission assumed, would eventually want full-time operation; operators of stations located in close proximity to a 50,000-watt station, however, knew they could never reasonably expect to operate full-time barring a substantial change in the allocation structure.[15]

In October 1946, the CCBS petitioned the FCC to place a freeze on all daytime grants on clear channel frequencies and on frequencies adjacent to clear channels because it feared that such new stations "may have the effect of making more difficult the grant of increased power to clear channel stations." The FCC denied the petition; it noted that the freeze would prohibit new stations on nearly the entire broadcast band. "The net result would be to preclude the Commission to a very large extent from exercising its licensing functions," it stated. The clear channel stations then began to protest daytime grants individually, with WJR, WGN and WSM arguing that newly authorized daytime stations on their frequencies would interfere with their signals in the hours just after sunrise and just before sunset. When the FCC rejected these protests, several stations sought relief in the courts. Eventually, the U.S. Court of Appeals for the District of Columbia ruled that one Class I-B station was entitled to a hearing before the FCC could place an additional daytime station on its frequency, but in May 1947 the FCC took preemptive action by opening Docket 8333, the so-called Daytime Skywave Case. The crucial issue in the new proceeding was whether FCC regulations should recognize the existence of skywave radiation in the hours after sunrise and before sunset.[16]

Engineering opinion in Docket 8333 was nearly unanimous that a daytime skywave did in fact exist in what came to be called the "transitional" two-hour periods after sunrise and before sunset. The CCBS thus called for the FCC to reassign all daytime stations located within 750 miles of the I-A station on their frequency in order to prevent them from interfering with clear channel stations' skywave service during these transitional periods. The FCC took no action, but in December 1947 it combined Docket 8333 with Docket 6741. In August 1953, with the drawn-out NARBA proceedings allowing little hope of resolving the clear channel studies in their entirety any time soon, the FCC severed Docket 8333 from Docket 6741. Since Docket 8333 dealt chiefly with the technical criteria for the operation of daytime stations on Class I-A and I-B channels, and not the broader issue of whether Class I-A frequencies should be duplicated at night, the FCC hoped to at least clarify policy on daytime assignments by rendering a decision on Docket 8333.

The FCC's announcement that it was ready to consider the daytime skywave issue separately, combined with the CCBS's high-visibility lobbying against NARBA and further daytime assignments, compelled daytime licensees to organize themselves. By the beginning of 1954, more than 100 stations had joined the Daytime Broadcasters Association, which grew out of a group of 10 daytime stations that had petitioned the FCC in 1948 to allow longer hours for daytime stations on clear channels. Daytime stations, the group noted, were prepared to render important and much needed nighttime service, especially in small and medium sized cities, but found their hours "reduced to pitiful proportions." At the time of the DBA's formation, there were more than 750 daytime licensees in the United States; their numbers, of course, had been growing steadily since the conclusion of World War II. The majority of those licensees operated on U.S. Class III channels and channels designated as foreign clear channels under NARBA; only 117 daytime stations operated on U.S. Class I-A and I-B channels. But as many daytimers sought additional operating time, especially for lucrative evening hours, they were concerned that the FCC's recognition of a daytime skywave on clear channels would portend further restriction of broadcast hours for all daytime stations. The DBA's first formal participation in Docket 8333 came in the form of a petition filed with the FCC in February 1954. Responding to the commission's announced intention to sever Docket 8333 from Docket 6741, the DBA called on the commission to dismiss Docket 8333 entirely or—alternately—to leave the dockets connected and relocate clear channel stations to allow "more efficient use" of clear channel frequencies.[17]

In March, the FCC released a proposed Report and Order to resolve Docket 8333. The FCC acknowledged the transitional period skywave and noted that clear channel stations should receive protection during these hours. Although the commission said that existing daytime stations would not have to comply with any new standards at that time, it did propose to cease the so-called bonus operation of some daytime stations located east of the dominant clear channel stations. These bonus hours were given to Western daytime stations during evening hours after full-time stations signed off. Additionally, the FCC proposed to retain the freeze on new daytime applications on clear channel frequencies "in order not to prejudice the outcome of the clear channel proceeding."[18]

The proposed order prompted the DBA to take its case to Congress, a venue in which the group would have considerable success. Since the DBA had a large number of members that were scattered throughout the country, it was able to win a significant number of congressional allies. Certainly, far more members of Congress had a DBA-affiliated station in their district than a clear channel station; thus, the DBA position resonated for many of them. The FCC immediately received numerous letters from members of Congress, warning the commission not to sacrifice the rights of daytime stations in order to protect powerful clear channel outlets. South Carolina congressman William Jennings Bryan Dorn, for example, noted that the proposed Docket 8333 decision had small broadcasters in his state "very much alarmed."[19]

The DBA once again called for the FCC to terminate the Docket 8333 proceeding and to end the freeze on new daytime stations. A brief filed by several college daytime stations and the National Association of Educational Broadcasters agreed with the DBA petition but asked the FCC to consider the unique programming offered by educational institutions' daytime stations. "[T]he Commission's report is based upon ... only a small portion of the whole story," the brief noted. "It deals exclusively with engineering standards and completely ignores consideration of program content." The brief argued that public interest dictated that the commission "cannot substitute a theoretical and abstract electrical interference engineering formula for the human interests and needs of people who listen to radio in all the cities and communities of the United States." CBS also filed a brief opposing the proposed order, while NBC remained silent.[20]

After oral arguments in June 1954, the commission reiterated its belief that its proposal was superior to any alternatives offered in evidence. However, the commission elected to withhold final adoption of its orders pending comments on how and if they should be applied to existing stations. The DBA responded by calling for uniform minimum hours for daytime stations of 5 a.m. or sunrise (whichever is earlier) until sunset or 7 p.m. (whichever is later). Ironically, as 1957 began, the DBA would assume the CCBS's former role in opposing ratification of the NARBA agreement. After the United States and Mexico finally signed a bilateral agreement in January, the CCBS supported ratification of NARBA since it preserved its members' clear frequencies and provided no insurmountable obstacles to superpower operation. Now, however, the DBA (which came into existence after the overall NARBA framework had already been developed) opposed the agreement because the preservation of Mexican clear channels would substantially limit U.S. daytime operation and would maintain what the group called "the ridiculous protection" for U.S. and foreign clear channels. While NARBA allowed U.S. stations more than 650 miles from the Canadian border to operate at night on Canadian clear channels, the bilateral Mexican agreement prohibited all U.S. nighttime broadcasting on Mexican clear channels. Nearly 250 U.S. daytime stations were assigned to Mexican clear channels, so such a concession would mean that these stations could never increase their hours. Ray Livesay, DBA president, told the Senate in 1959 that the Mexican restrictions were "unjust, inequitable, discriminatory and contrary to the best interests of this country." "We think the daytimers are taking a very narrow attitude," the CCBS's Jack DeWitt told the same hearing, without a hint of irony. The United States finally ratified the bilateral Mexican agreement and NARBA in 1960.[21]

DAYTIME STATIONS ORGANIZE

The formation of the Daytime Broadcasters Association substantially altered the character of the long-running clear channel debate. Until the 1950s, the discussion had essentially involved two sides: the clear channel stations and the regional stations. Now, there were three points of view. In addition, the DBA's aggressive push for increased—or at least uniform—hours of operation for daytime stations placed it in conflict not only with clear channel operators but with regional stations as well. In fact, the DBA push for more hours had potential impact on many more regional stations than clear channel stations, and some of the most strident opposition to the DBA came from these regional stations. For once, the CCBS did not stand alone against seemingly all other station operators, and the group took pains to point out the adverse effects of the daytimers' demands not only on clear channel stations but on other stations as well.

The DBA, however, had considerable success in portraying the daytime stations as small businesses being subsumed by richer interests and victimized by unsympathetic regulators. This was most clearly evident in hearings held before a subcommittee of the Senate's Committee on Small Business in April 1957. Senator Wayne Morse, a Democrat from Oregon, headed the subcommittee, and it was clear that the DBA's portrayal of daytime operators as the small businessmen held down by the monopoly power of clear channel stations was being embraced by at least some members of the subcommittee. Morse spoke to a DBA meeting three weeks before the hearings were scheduled to begin and decried the FCC's delay in lifting the daytime freeze, noting that its continuation merely worked "to the detriment of the small fellow" while helping clear channel stations. "It is increasingly my view from all outward appearances that the FCC shall never be found guilty of partiality toward small business," he said.[22]

Not surprisingly, the same framing of the daytime broadcasting issue as one of big versus small business carried throughout the hearings, although the FCC—not the clear channel stations—bore the brunt of criticism. Several operators of daytime stations testified about their local programming services and how continually changing hours of operation caused hardship on them and their listeners. Station operators stressed the local information they broadcast, such as school closings and weather alerts, that stations located outside the community could not provide. A farmer from North Carolina testified as to his reliance on the programming of a nearby daytime station, while a bank president from Gainesville, Texas, said it was difficult to purchase advertising on the local daytime station at times when people were listening. When the local daytime station signed off, he said, listeners could only listen to large city advertisers "who prove to be the biggest thorn of competition to our local merchants."[23]

Livesay testified for the Daytime Broadcasters Association, the members of which he said "constitute the core of small business in this industry." He criticized both the FCC and the Clear Channel Broadcasting Service for what he called "a history of stumbling, fumbling and lethargy":

> It is a history which forcefully shows how powerful interests repre-senting a handful of stations in this country have been able with their tremendous resources, to use every tactic not merely to per-petuate the status quo and preserve their entrenched favored posi-tion but to obtain additional privileges at the expense of needed service to the public in many parts of the country and to the great detriment of the small operators in this business.[24]

Seavey testified for the CCBS and restated the group's conten-tion that extending the hours of operation of daytime stations with-out damaging service to a large number of listeners was an engi-neering impossibility. Two operators of full-time regional stations also testified against the DBA proposal; they noted that extended hours for daytime stations would reduce the coverage of full-time stations. Leroy Kilpatrick of WSAZ, a full-time regional station in Huntington, West Virginia, submitted a letter in opposition to the DBA, signed by 167 other regional broadcasters. "This DBA pro-posal in its essence is contrary to the spirit in which the daytime broadcasting authorizations were made in the first place," he wrote, adding that it would create an advantage for daytime broad-casters "which is not rightfully theirs." Archer S. Taylor, a con-sulting engineer who had testified for the National Association of Regional Broadcast Stations in the Docket 6741 proceedings, also opposed the DBA proposal:

> Daytime stations applied for their permit with full knowledge that the FCC rules and regulations would necessitate signoff at sunset. On the other hand, full-time operators, most of whom are also small businesses, understood when applying for their permit that they would be accorded freedom from interference. ... It is a mat-ter of one section of small business men desiring an advantage they were unwilling or unable to pay for, and which can only be ob-tained by causing injury to other small-business men who did make the considerable added investment.

Taylor did, however, say that the demand for increased facilities could be eased if "big, monopolistic clear-channel operators" stopped blocking development of clear channel frequencies. Representatives of the FCC, including Commissioners Craven and Hyde, also testified, noting that the DBA proposal could not be considered separately from the complicated clear channel issue and that the commission was presently consumed with television allocations.[25]

The subcommittee's final report echoed the context of the hearings, emphasizing the FCC's inaction and demonstrated preference for "big" business. The report chided the FCC for what it called a policy of "ignoring it and hoping it will go away" and termed the FCC's inaction "unwarranted and inexcusable." The report recommended that the FCC give immediate attention to resolving the longstanding clear channel and daytime broadcasting disputes and threatened congressional action if the issues were drawn out further.[26]

Immediately after the Senate released its report, the FCC issued a Proposed Rule Making granting the DBA request for a decision in the daytime skywave case but denying its request for dismissal of the clear channel case and the removal of the application freeze. In September 1959, the commission concluded Docket 8333 by affirming in large part the 1954 report that recognized the existence of skywaves during transitional periods. However, the commission more definitively stated its intention not to apply the new standards to existing daytime stations. It noted that "listeners have become accustomed [to] and [have] come to rely upon" these stations. "We must also take into account the undoubted value of adequate service of local origin," the commission noted. In a departure from the 1954 report, the commission left intact existing bonus hours for daytime stations and lifted the application freeze on six Class I-B frequencies that were not involved in the clear channel proceeding.[27]

DOCKET 6741 RECONSIDERED

The attention from Congress also had prompted the FCC to begin to refocus attention on the Docket 6741 case, which, after being delayed by the Johnson hearings in 1948, fell in priority in the face of the commission's work on television assignments. Although the clear channel issue had been essentially dormant since 1948, in 1956 the commission redirected efforts toward a resolution by appointing an internal task force of staff members to examine the voluminous Docket 6741 record. The task force, citing the outdated nature of much of the information in the record and the expense of updating it, recommended dismissing the proceedings. The FCC commissioners, however, rejected the recommendation, as they simply could not ignore the growing pressure to resolve the long-running dispute.[28]

Further proposals, including one that would have increased the power of 12 Class I-A stations to between 500,000 and 750,000 watts and opened seven others to duplication, also were rejected, but in April 1958 the commission released a Further Notice of Proposed Rule Making. It contained the commission's first public conclusions in the 13-year-old Docket 6741 proceedings and the first official assessment of the clear channel structure since 1938. The notice also attempted to rein in the scope of the proceeding by dispensing with several of the original issues set forth in 1945. Some of these issues, including what recommendations to make for NARBA negotiations, were now moot points, the commission noted, while others involving the use of higher power on clear channels could be deferred. On three of the issues the commission presented conclusions, noting that it was economically unfeasible to relocate clear channel stations, that the number of clear channel frequencies should not be changed and that congressional action was not required to make the needed allocation changes.[29]

The commission once again affirmed the basic structure of the broadcast allocation plan, including the use of clear channel frequencies to render rural and wide-area service. However, it contended that the present implementation of that structure, with a 50,000-watt power limitation and no nighttime duplication, was not justifiable. The commission proposed that changes—encompassing a judicious combination of both higher power and duplication—would represent a more efficient use of clear channel frequencies.[30]

To that end, the commission divided the existing 24 clear channels into two groups: those to be duplicated and those that it believed were most suitable for higher power. The channels selected for duplication were largely in the Northeast, including all of the New York and Chicago clear channel frequencies. The commission noted that these frequencies held the least potential for expanding White Area service through higher power and that stations on them could be directionalized to allow new assignments in the West—where White Area service was most needed—without destroying any area's primary service. On five of the channels to be duplicated, the commission proposed that both the existing Class I-A station and the Class I station to be added use directional antennas in order to avoid interference. On the remaining seven frequencies, the commission would add unlimited-time Class II stations, with all new stations to be located in areas where they would provide significant new White Area service. The commission, however, proposed to address only the issues of duplication, leaving higher power for later consideration.[31]

Industry reaction to the proposal was nearly unanimously negative, with some factions objecting to duplicating clear channels and some objecting to the possibility of higher power for clear channel stations, but nearly all opposing a piecemeal approach to the problem. The CCBS, individual clear channel stations, NBC, CBS and ABC all objected to duplicating some clear channels without also granting higher power, while DBA objected to the limitations to be placed on new assignments, including requiring expensive directional antennas. In September 1959, the FCC issued a Third Notice of Proposed Rule Making; it discarded the piecemeal approach for a proposal to duplicate each of the clear channel frequencies with one Class II station of at least 10,000 watts. The commission acknowledged arguments that the 1958 plan would have created substantial new White Areas yet said it did not believe that counterproposals offered by industry representatives would achieve any substantial White Area reductions either. Now, the FCC asked for views on both the plan to duplicate all clear channels and the possible use of higher power. The commission noted that it was not persuaded on the basis of the existing record that higher power would be in the public interest but said it would defer a final decision until it had a chance to examine an updated record.[32]

Predictably, the reaction to the proposal was mixed: regional and daytime stations seeking better assignments supported the plan, while clear channel stations individually and through the CCBS opposed duplication and argued for higher power. ABC supported the plan's intention to duplicate clear channels but suggested providing service to sparsely populated Rocky Mountain areas via stations on the West Coast by duplicating Eastern clear channels. NBC opposed the duplications, arguing that they would destroy substantial areas of clear channel skywave service while providing little new coverage of White Areas. CBS did not oppose the concept of clear channel duplications but asked the FCC to make a thorough study of the use of clear channels before implementing any new plan. The National Association of Educational Broadcasters (NAEB) reiterated its call for the reservation of channels for education, calling the FCC disregard for educational assignments "unthinkable."[33]

The CCBS offered the most voluminous brief in support of its contentions that the only way to improve service to the White Areas was through the use of higher power. The result of more than 4,000 hours of work in a three-month period between December 1959 and March 1960, the brief showed that the group viewed this as perhaps its final opportunity to make arguments in the clear channel proceedings. Presenting engineering studies on several of the proposed duplications, CCBS argued that the improvement in White Area coverage would be negligible, and at the same time it cast doubt upon the ability of the communities proposed for new Class II stations to support them. Citing the increase in interference from man-made sources such as television and other electrical appliances, the CCBS contended that higher power was needed to merely preserve existing coverage areas. "The standard broadcast band is more underpowered today than it was when the Clear Channel hearing opened in 1947," the group argued. The CCBS once again offered its Twenty-Station Plan as a relevant solution but noted that the specific details of the plan need not be implemented. Once again downplaying the possibility of adverse economic impact on other stations, the CCBS said that the addition of new stations since World War II had not damaged existing stations' revenues.[34]

The spurt of activity on the clear channel issue in the late 1950s had seemingly not moved the commission any closer to a resolution by the beginning of the 1960s. The commission was obviously wavering, as evidenced by its Notices of Proposed Rulemaking released in the past two years, each of them followed by industry legal and technical briefs that merely added to the already voluminous stack of data. The commissioners, as they had been since the early 1940s, were divided on the question: T.A.M. Craven (who rejoined the commission in 1956), Robert Bartley and John Cross favored the duplication of all clear channels, and Hyde, Robert E. Lee and Frederick Ford opposed mass duplication. The final commissioner, Charles King, was undecided but left the commission in March 1961 after serving only seven months. His replacement was Newton H. Minow, who became chairman. Minow made resolving the clear channel issue a top priority, instructing his staff in June 1961 to draw up a plan to duplicate half of the existing clear channels.[35]

THE DOCKET 6741 DECISION

In June, the FCC, agreeing with Minow, announced its intention to resolve the Docket 6741 matter by duplicating half of the clear channels. As this was happening, the CCBS was without a director in Washington, D.C.; Seavey had resigned in 1959 and his replacement, Gayle Gupton, left at the end of 1960. Still, the group mobilized its lobbying efforts in Congress, and by the end of the summer four bills were introduced in the House and one in the Senate that would, if passed, prohibit the FCC from duplicating any clear channels. Ironically, the CCBS, which in 1948 had protested congressional intrusion into broadcast regulation during the Johnson Bill hearings, now found itself calling for congressional intervention.[36]

The group's closest allies in Congress were Democrat John Dingell and Republican John Bennett, both representatives from Michigan and both close associates of WJR vice president and general manager James Quello. Dingell had brought the clear channel issue before the House Interstate and Foreign Commerce Committee, and his presentation piqued the committee's interest. In September, the committee's chairman, Oren Harris, wrote to

Chairman Minow requesting that the FCC delay implementing its decision until Congress reconvened in 1962 and could hold hearings on the matter. Minow refused to delay the final adoption of the Docket 6741 decision. He noted that the commission "has reached a result which a substantial majority of its members consider to be the very best possible solution to the very difficult problems involved." He stated, however, that it would be at least six months before any new stations were actually authorized on the clear channels. Thus, Congress would have time to hold hearings if it desired.[37]

By the time the Docket 6741 decision was released, the D.C. Circuit Court of Appeals had, through its decision in the case of *Sangamon Valley Television Corporation v. United States,* placed new restrictions on ex parte contacts with commissioners. Prior to *Sangamon Valley,* as discussed in Chapter 4, parties involved in rule-making matters before the FCC were allowed more latitude in meeting with commission personnel than parties involved in judicial matters (i.e., contested licenses). The prevailing notion was that in rule-making proceedings, the commission needed to gather as much information as possible from all sources, and it did not matter if some of that information was gleaned from off-the-record private contacts. On the other hand, it was recognized that in proceedings placing the specific, direct interests of one licensee in conflict with those of another, such off-the-record contacts should be prohibited to avoid "fixing" the commissioners who were acting as judge and jury.[38]

Sangamon Valley effectively negated the distinction between rule-making decisions and judicial actions in any matter involving "resolution of conflicting private claims to a valuable privilege." In the *Sangamon Valley* case, the FCC had instituted a rule making to amend the table of television channel assignments. Eventually, a desirable VHF channel was shifted from Springfield, Illinois, to St. Louis, Missouri, and the Signal Hill Television Company was given authority to operate on the channel. After this decision, the president of Signal Hill admitted that he had spoken to commissioners individually "in the privacy of their own offices, not while they were sitting in a body as the Commission," about his desire to receive the VHF assignment. He also had entertained each of the commissioners as luncheon guests, and in 1955 and 1956 he had sent Thanksgiving turkeys to each commissioner. The court vacated the FCC's decision, in large part because of the ex parte contacts. The *Sangamon Valley* case became a watershed decision in the conduct of proceedings before the FCC and other regulatory agencies. Although the ruling did not prohibit all contact with commissioners, the CCBS recognized that the decision meant it would have to concentrate its efforts in preventing the implementation of the unfavorable Docket 6741 decision on Capitol Hill and in the courts.[39]

On September 13, 1961, the FCC released its formal decision in Docket 6741. Thirteen channels were set for duplication by one full-time Class II station each, with the commission designating in which state or states each Class II station could be located (Table 6.1). On 750 kHz and 760 kHz, the commission proposed assigning two existing stations that had been dislocated by the new United States–Mexico broadcasting agreement. In addition, 1030 kHz was changed from a Class I-B channel to a Class I-A channel, thus bringing the total number of Class I-A stations to 25. This move required no physical changes, since WBZ had been operating exclusively on that frequency at night anyway. The commission specified that each new Class II station had to protect the dominant station's service area for approximately 700 miles, thus not requiring existing I-A stations to directionalize their signals, and also mandated that each station's service area include at least 25 percent White Area. The question of superpower was left to further study, but regulations restricted new assignments on channels adjacent to clear channels in order to preserve the possibility of higher power in the future. The decision noted, however, that due consideration was given to the Senate's 1938 resolution against power in excess of 50,000 watts.[40]

The commission vote was 5–1, with Lee issuing a strong dissent. He began by decrying what he felt was an arbitrary resolution to the long-standing conflict. "After sixteen years of spasmodic consideration," he wrote, "it has now been decided to cut the baby in half." Lee believed that all clear channel stations should be allowed to use up to 750,000 watts, and those that did not file superpower applications within a year should be duplicated. "I lack the

TABLE 6.1   Channels to be duplicated by Class II stations according to Docket 6741.

Frequency	Station	Location(s) of new station
670	WMAQ, Chicago	Idaho
720	WGN, Chicago[a]	Nevada or Idaho
750	WSB, Atlanta[a]	KFQD, Anchorage, Alaska
760	WJR, Detroit[a]	KFMB, San Diego, California
780	WBBM, Chicago	Nevada
880	WCBS, New York	North Dakota, South Dakota or Nebraska
890	WLS, Chicago	Utah
1020	KDKA, Pittsburgh	New Mexico
1030	WBZ, Boston	Wyoming
1100	KYW, Cleveland	Colorado
1120	KMOX, St. Louis	California or Oregon
1180	WHAM, Rochester[a]	Montana
1210	WCAU, Philadelphia	Kansas, Nebraska or Oklahoma

[a] CCBS Member

confidence of the majority that its decision will result in any substantive consequence," he wrote. "I submit that it imposes an unwarranted freeze to foster eleven peanut whistles which may never be constructed." Commissioner Cross also issued a statement, concurring in part and dissenting in part. He, too, criticized the commission's decision, calling it only a half solution. His preference, however, was to open all 25 channels to duplication in a "controlled" manner, with the merits of each case considered individually. He noted that the engineering reasons for duplicating 13 of the clear channels also applied to the remaining 12 channels.[41]

REACTION TO THE DOCKET 6741 DECISION

With the FCC's formal decision in Docket 6741, the CCBS accelerated plans to hire a new Washington, D.C., director. The group's attorneys said that they were able to handle the legal work but needed help in mobilizing congressional and farm group support. The group's choice for the job was Roy Battles, assistant to the master at the National Grange and former WLW farm director and president of the National Association of Television and

Radio Farm Directors. Battles wasted no time getting started in his new position; by the end of his first week on the job, he had already established both short-term and long-term plans for the group's activities. "[W]e are fighting with our back to the wall," he told stations. "The stakes—both now and in the future—are staggering." In brainstorming particular efforts the CCBS could make, Battles came up with some bold ideas. He stopped short of suggesting that the group try to have a hand in selecting replacements for Commissioners Cross and Craven, whose terms would expire within the next two years, but he wondered if it might be feasible. He also noted that tacking a clear channel amendment onto the commission's budget appropriation would be likely to "'persuade' the FCC to do the right thing." However, the CCBS never pursued these ideas and in fact, according to Quaal, never made contributions to political candidates.[42]

Battles brought together station managers at the beginning of 1962 and encouraged them to meet with their local members of Congress before they returned home from Washington, D.C. "It should be remembered," he wrote, "that, as a rule, there is nothing [that] takes the place of personal contact, especially if made by the right person and properly followed up." He said that the organization's greatest task was to "dispel the notion that clear channels are a privileged group." He also encouraged DeWitt to pursue defense applications of clear channel stations and noted that "it is promising and may well spell the difference between full success or something less desirable in the months ahead."[43]

DeWitt, president of Nashville's WSM and former chief engineer of the CCBS, had been working on a way to pass information between clear channel stations since the 1950s. He developed a system in which stations could transmit teletype information to one another as part of their regular broadcasting without disturbing the audio portion of the signal. The Air Force, meanwhile, wanted a backup to its high-frequency radio system that could send presidential attack orders from the Joint Communications Agency in Ft. Ritchie, Maryland, to Offutt Air Force Base near Omaha, Nebraska. Ken Miller, an engineer at the FCC, urged DeWitt to tell the Air Force about his system, which he did in the summer of 1961. Soon after, DeWitt began working with Air Force personnel on the system, which came to be known as BRECOM (BRoadcast Emergency COMmunications). DeWitt, of course, acknowledged the system's positive implications for the CCBS. "This is the finest cooperative effort which we have ever undertaken," he told members, "and if successful it will do much to stabilize the allocation picture with respect to duplication and further daytime operators."[44]

Work continued on BRECOM throughout the early 1960s, and DeWitt found that WGN in Chicago and WSM in Nashville could exchange information during the day with only 50,000 watts. The Air Force remained interested, and in mid-1962 a link was established from Washington, D.C., to Omaha using KDKA Pittsburgh, WJR Detroit, WGN Chicago and WHO Des Moines. In 1963, DeWitt showed his BRECOM system to representatives of RCA, who expressed interest in pursuing it for other defense applications.[45]

In the end, however, BRECOM was doomed by the CCBS's desire to use it as a tool to protect the clear channels and the fact that the signals were susceptible to atmospheric interference. The FCC and Air Force wanted a system that was not based solely on clear channel stations, but the CCBS maintained that it would not be possible to do it any other way. Miller, who had become the driving force in pushing BRECOM, wanted to separate the system's development from the controversial clear channel issue, and the Air Force wanted a minimum of industry involvement. DeWitt complained to Eagan after a meeting with Miller and others at the FCC that the clear channels' investment in BRECOM was going to waste. The death knell for BRECOM, however, finally came in the mid-1960s when the Air Force scheduled a test of the system during a Midwest summer thunderstorm. BRECOM failed the test miserably, and according to DeWitt, "that killed it right there." Despite BRECOM's failure, the CCBS continued to tout the value of clear channel stations for national defense. During the Cuban Missile Crisis in October 1962, 10 radio stations, including CCBS member WSB in Atlanta, began dusk to dawn broadcasts to Cuba of Voice of America programming. Battles offered the U.S. Information Agency use of all CCBS member stations for this purpose, but the agency declined, noting that the present configuration seemed to be working. Still, the gesture was in keeping with the continuing CCBS efforts to demonstrate the value of long-distance AM broadcasting during times of emergency.[46]

In February 1962, the Subcommittee on Communications and Power of the House Committee on Interstate and Foreign Commerce held hearings on the four pending bills to stop implementation of the FCC's Docket 6471 decision. The hearings became essentially a show and tell session for the clear channels, as there was no organized opposition. The DBA was more interested in securing increased operating hours for existing daytime stations and thus had little interest in efforts to block the commission's Docket 6741 decision. The Regional Broadcasters Committee had fallen apart in the late 1940s and since that time had not been involved in the proceedings. In stark contrast to the adversarial nature of the 1948 hearings before the Senate Committee on Interstate and Foreign Commerce, the conduct of the 1962 hearings was largely friendly to the CCBS.[47]

The CCBS and its allies presented very little at the hearings that was new. Battles and DeWitt testified for the group, with the former handling the economic and social questions and the latter presenting technical data. In his testimony, Battles alluded to the value of clear channels for keeping listeners informed in emergencies: "Duplicating any of the remaining clear channels will 'congest' our only remaining superhighways of the air, and block the only existing routes for fast, reliable nighttime communications to sparsely settled areas by overcrowding them." DeWitt also testified about his work on BRECOM, as did Major General John B. Bestec, the Air Force director of telecommunications. He said he favored higher power for clear channel stations and noted that nuclear attacks could more easily knock out telephone lines or high-frequency radio units than the clear channel stations. "Considering this," Bestec told the committee, "we must exploit every means of communicating which may survive." He also noted that clear channel stations—and especially the CCBS—had been extremely helpful in developing emergency communications. The Department of Defense submitted a letter to the committee indicating that the bills in question could have advantages to the national defense.[48]

FCC commissioners also testified at the House hearings, and—with the exception of Lee—defended the Docket 6741 decision. All pointed out, however, that it was a confusing issue in which each side could easily support its cause. "Our view here of the majority represents a lot of adjusting of views just within the commission so that we could reach a conclusion," Minow said. "This is such a technical, complicated subject that we could not satisfy everybody's view on it." The commissioners also said that they felt inhibited by the 1938 Senate Resolution, and when asked if it would be helpful if Congress enacted some sort of general policy on the matter, Chairman Minow said yes.[49]

When the hearings concluded, the CCBS kept in continual contact with the members of the Interstate and Foreign Commerce Committee. In a telephone conversation with Battles, Dingell said the key was overcoming the sympathy in Congress for small station operators, and to that end both Dingell and Bennett sent letters to all of the members of the House Committee on Interstate and Foreign Commerce after the hearings, outlining the case for retaining the clear channels and granting superpower. Dingell's letter noted that unless Congress took action against the FCC's proposal, "irreparable national harm will be done and the nation will remain anchored to the outmoded 50 kilowatt power ceiling." He also enclosed a list of reasons—including national defense and service to rural areas—that clear channels should not be duplicated as well as sample recordings demonstrating the potential difference in signal quality between 50,000 watts and 750,000 watts. "In short," he wrote, "we face a now or never situation." At the same time, Battles was telling CCBS members to start "thinking how you can secure a 'Yes' vote from as many Congressmen as possible."[50]

Just as Senators Wheeler and Johnson had done in earlier decades, Dingell applied pressure to the FCC through his personal correspondence with the chairman. The congressman said he was "terrible [*sic*] distressed by the Commission's ... reluctance in today's changed world to break away from the archaic 50 kw ceiling on Clear Channels" and again urged the FCC to delay action until Congress had ample time to consider the issue. Minow continued to resist further delay, noting that "a substantial portion of the public interest involved" was met by finally resolving the issue. Minow also referred to H.R. 8210 and noted that Commissioner Lee had introduced a similar plan to the commission that did not receive any support. "We must, in all honesty, add that there is not now a majority of Commissioners willing to vote immediately in favor of higher power," he said.[51]

Dingell's H.R. 8210 was passed by the Commerce Committee but did not come to a vote on the House floor. Fearing that the Senate would not act even if the House did pass the bill, Dingell and other clear channel proponents on the Commerce Committee replaced it with a House Resolution, H. Res. 714. The resolution, which, like the Senate's 1938 resolution would not carry the force of law, authorized the FCC to grant power in excess of 50,000 watts to stations that could improve rural coverage and asked the commission not to act on its Docket 6741 decision for one year after the resolution's passage. H. Res. 714 passed the House on July 7, 1962, and Battles bragged to Craig that the CCBS had essentially written the text of the resolution. "Language guidelines for the legislation," he wrote, "followed in principle and in part language approved at the April 1, 1962, CCBS annual meeting held in Chicago."[52]

The CCBS tried to get a similar resolution passed by the Senate but was unable to do so. Nonetheless, there was now a congressional resolution to cancel out the 1938 Senate resolution, and CCBS member stations began applying for higher power. The FCC affirmed its decision on Docket 6741 in November 1962 but agreed—albeit reluctantly—to postpone implementing the decision until the July 2, 1963, date requested by H. Res. 714. If Congress did not pass more forceful legislation by that time, the commission said, it would begin placing Class II-A stations on the designated clear channels. Two of the stations scheduled for duplication, WJR and WGN, challenged the FCC's action in the D.C. Circuit Court of Appeals; they contended that the Docket 6741 decision to add stations to their frequencies constituted a modification of their licenses and thus necessitated individual hearings, but the court ruled against them. At the same time, the FCC dismissed the nine pending superpower applications from clear channel stations. H. Res. 714 turned out ultimately to be merely a one-year moratorium on implementing the Docket 6741 decision, as Congress never passed further legislation. Duplications under the FCC decision began in 1963.[53]

CLEAR CHANNELS IN THE POST-DOCKET 6741 YEARS

The CCBS continued to pressure the FCC to approve super-power for its members, and there were rumors in the mid-1960s that the commission was drawing up plans to allow some experimentation with power in excess of 50,000 watts, but by this time, the differences of opinion on superpower simmering within the CCBS during the 1950s had come into the open. These disagreements were aggravated by the Docket 6741 decision, which, by setting four CCBS frequencies for duplication, made superpower operation on those frequencies far more difficult, if not impossible. Critics had long intimated that many CCBS members were not sincere about their stated desire for higher power but merely wanted to preserve the clear channels. The CCBS continued to deny these charges, but only eight CCBS members—KFI, WSM, WLW, WGN, WJR, WCCO, WHO and KSL—applied for increased power during the mid-1960s. Two of those—WJR and WGN—were scheduled for duplication but had not yet had stations assigned on their frequencies. Still, the clear channels' continuing, if no longer unanimous, efforts for higher power sparked intense opposition from other stations, with at least 20 state broadcasting associations passing resolutions against superpower. In Congress, several bills prohibiting the FCC from granting higher power were introduced.[54]

The CCBS, meanwhile, continued its efforts to promote clear channels as beneficial to radio listeners. In May 1963, it published a 16-page booklet, *Radio for ALL America: The Case for the Clears.* In it, the CCBS likened radio channels to highways, with clear channels comparable to "long distance express highways." It was crucial, the booklet noted, to keep these highways clear of congestion in order to provide long-distance service to rural listeners. Although the booklet stated that higher power was necessary in order to improve rural service and "better hemispheric understanding and neighborliness," there was no mention of the highly touted Twenty-Station Plan. Much like the Clear Channel Group position in the 1930s, it now seemed that the CCBS wanted to leave the door to superpower open yet not directly commit any or all of its member stations to it. Clear channel stations also were touted as vital to national defense and lauded for "distinguished program contributions" such as news, cultural information, emergency notices and farm programming. The CCBS ordered 10,000 copies of the booklet, while individual station orders totaled 40,000 additional copies. The group immediately distributed the booklet to state, regional and local farm representatives, and it is likely copies were shared with members of Congress as well.[55]

The CCBS-friendly house hearings, the ensuing resolution favoring increased power and the subsequent renewal of the push for superpower brought regional stations back together to oppose the clear channels. The long-dormant Regional Broadcasters Committee, now renamed Association for Broadcast Standards (ABS), incorporated and established a full-time presence in Washington, D.C. John Cross, the former FCC commissioner whose dissenting opinion in the Docket 6741 decision had called for the duplication of all 25 clear channels, was retained as a communications consultant. The ABS said its goals were working for optimum radio service and opposing proposals that would "decrease, impair or destroy radio service which is now available to the American people." Since it was made up primarily of regional stations, that meant that the group opposed both the CCBS efforts for higher power and the DBA efforts to increase the operating hours of daytime stations. Thus, ABS stood, in essence, for maintenance of the status quo in the AM band, or as the group's legal counsel later remarked half-jokingly, "we weren't for anything."[56]

ABS worked in Congress to thwart the efforts of both the CCBS and DBA and also made limited attempts to influence farm groups. In 1966, the group published an informational pamphlet, "4000 Local Community Radio Stations or 12 Distant Superpower Giants: The Growing Outcry Against 'Superpower,'" outlining arguments against increasing the power of clear channel stations. The ABS pamphlet warned of "concentration of control, destruction of local and regional service" and "widespread economic hardship" if the FCC granted power increases to clear channel stations. It also contended that granting such "extraordinary 'developmental' licenses" would "embarrass and frustrate" American efforts to negotiate international treaties. The networks, much to the dismay of the CCBS, also supported ABS, as they had long shared the new group's interest in preserving the existing configuration of the broadcast band.[57]

Beginning in the late 1950s, as it became clear that the FCC was unlikely to approve higher power for clear channel stations, a number of CCBS members became complacent about continuing to pursue the issue. In some cases, new ownership did not share a former owner's passion for clear channel issues, while in others it was purely an economic decision based on the loss of network advertising revenue. A number of stations doubted they could support 500,000- or 750,000-watt operation and thus were not enthusiastic about maintaining membership in the CCBS. A case in point was William F. Rust, who purchased WHAM from Riggs and Greene Broadcasting Company in 1962. After attending the CCBS meeting held in conjunction with the National Association of Broadcasters convention in 1962, Rust seemed both intrigued and concerned by CCBS efforts for superpower. He wrote a letter to Battles noting that FCC approval of superpower would put his station "on the spot," estimating that WHAM would have to increase national revenue by at least 50 percent to justify 500,000-watt operation.[58]

Battles encouraged Rust to "have a long rump session" with DeWitt and Quaal to discuss the clear channel issue and noted that no legislation CCBS was pursuing would force any station to go to higher power. At the same time, Battles sent a letter to Quaal noting that "it might save a membership" if some CCBS executives had a personal session with Rust. While there is no record of such a meeting or any further correspondence between Rust and the CCBS, WHAM eventually resigned from the group.[59]

The WHAM episode was indicative of what "old timers" such as Quaal, DeWitt and Battles viewed as a lack of historical understanding among contemporary station owners and executives of what clear channels were intended to do. Increasingly, clear channel licensees neither knew nor cared about the disputes that had begun as early as the 1920s. While Quaal urged Battles to visit

CCBS member stations as often as possible to drum up support for CCBS objectives, he discouraged him from putting things in writing, noting that many stations objected to coaching from Washington, D.C. Preoccupied with pressures of day-to-day operation of AM stations in an increasingly competitive and changing marketplace, the management of some stations viewed the activities of the CCBS as an unnecessary diversion. "As much as I like all of these people," Quaal wrote to Battles in the fall of 1962, "you will find no more Jack DeWitts and Ward Quaals in the line up anywhere."[60]

Stations also began to object to the cost of membership in the CCBS, a concern that grew more pronounced as individual stations dropped out of the group. From a high of 16 members during the 1940s, the group sporadically lost members during the late 1940s and 1950s, beginning with the departure of Westinghouse stations KDKA and WBZ in a disagreement over the Twenty-Station Plan in 1948. By 1960, WWL had resigned from the group and both WCAU and WLS had become ineligible for membership after being purchased by CBS and ABC respectively. Although longtime holdout KSL entered the group in 1962, efforts to encourage other stations to join failed. Thus, the expenses for paying Battles and a full-time secretary, maintaining the Washington, D.C., office and paying legal fees had to be spread among a smaller number of stations.[61]

Throughout most of the 1950s and 1960s, the CCBS worked on an average annual budget of about $60,000, with stations paying dues based on their hourly advertising rates with a maximum yearly assessment of $7,000. Until 1967, assessments ranged from $2,671 for WBAP and WFAA to $7,000 for KFI, WJR and WGN. However, by the end of 1967, the group's legal fees and other outstanding expenses had far outstripped its budget. The group voted to raise the annual budget to $80,000 and to eliminate the single-station cap of $7,000. As a result, the dues of a few stations decreased slightly, while the assessments of WGN and WJR more than doubled. Assessments on KFI, WLW and WSB also increased significantly.[62]

Less than a year later, AVCO Corporation, parent company of WLW, withdrew the Cincinnati station from the CCBS. The departure was both symbolically significant because of the station's long history of being at the forefront of battles for increased power and financially significant because the station made the fourth largest contribution to the CCBS budget. Facing a substantial decrease in revenue, the group had to either trim expenses or substantially increase individual stations' dues again. As the latter choice was likely to cause further defections, the group's executive committee voted in July 1968 to close the Washington, D.C., office and release Battles and the secretary. However, Quaal assured members that the group's executive committee "is dedicated to the principles for which we have stood since our formation … in 1934."[63]

CONCLUSION

The landscape of American broadcasting had changed dramatically in the years between the initial closing of the record in Docket 6741 and the FCC's final decision. The opportunity to make Docket 6741 the keystone in a more logically planned system of broadcasting including FM and perhaps television had passed. By the time the FCC resolved the issue, in fact, many said AM radio had become irrelevant. Certainly, it was clear that many—if not most—clear channel stations no longer sought higher power.

But the industry interest groups had continued to pursue their policy goals, working at the FCC, in Congress and in the public arena. By the mid-1950s, the organized clear channel interests and regional interests were joined by a newly organized daytime station presence. The additional point of view no doubt further thwarted the FCC's efforts to resolve the issue, as did the continuing congressional attention, itself instigated by industry factions. As a result, the much delayed final Docket 6741 decision was largely an affirmation of the status quo: new stations would be added on some clear channels, but the overall structure and practical service area of the clear channels remained intact.

In 1980, the FCC finally resolved the clear channel debate by duplicating the remaining "clear" frequencies. Throughout the late 1960s and 1970s, the CCBS had continued its call for higher power, but with neither the enthusiasm nor continuity it had had in the 1940s and 1950s. In 1981, the group's executive committee passed a resolution stating the organization's objectives as providing government entities and the general public "information ... on wide-area clear channel service and the vital role it plays in the nation's communications and Defense needs." It was a rather timid set of ambitions for a group that had once fought for a network of 20 750,000-watt stations, but times had changed. The clear channels were clear no more.[64]

NOTES

1. Sid Hix, Cartoon, *Broadcasting*, September 5, 1949, 28.

2. Christopher H. Sterling and John M. Kittross, *Stay Tuned: A Concise History of American Broadcasting* (Belmont, Calif.: Wadsworth Publishing Company, 1990), 83.

3. See "Clear Breakdown," *Broadcasting*, January 17, 1949, 23; April 20, 1949, *Congressional Record*, 81st Cong., 1st Sess., 4782, 4788; and Ed Keys, "Johnson Prods Anti-Clears," *Broadcasting*, January 31, 1949, 22.

4. See Edwin Johnson to Wayne Coy, May 4, 1949, Volume 3, Docket 6741, Docketed Case Files, RG 173, National Archives, College Park, Md. (hereafter referred to as NACP); Rosel Hyde to Edwin Johnson, May 15, 1949, Volume 3, Docket 6741, Docketed Case Files, RG 173, NACP; and Edwin Johnson to Rosel Hyde, May 18, 1949, Volume 3, Docket 6741, Docketed Case Files, RG 173, NACP.

5. See William H. Sylk to Edward Martin, April 21, 1950, Volume 3, Docket 6741, Docketed Case Files, RG 173, NACP; Edward Martin to Wayne Coy, April 27, 1950, Volume 3, Docket 6741, Docketed Case Files, RG 173, NACP; Wayne Coy to Richard B. Wigglesworth, January 5, 1950, Volume 3, Docket 6741, Docketed Case Files, RG 173, NACP.

6. See "Anti-Clear Group," *Broadcasting*, January 24, 1949, 32; Louis Caldwell and R. Russell Eagan to CCBS Members, November 22, 1948, Box P-1142, Clear Channel Group Records, Wiley, Rein and Fielding, Washington, D.C. (hereafter referred to as WRF); Louis Caldwell and R. Russell Eagan to CCBS, December 12, 1948, Box P-1142, WRF; "Craney Elected Head of Anti-Clear Group," *Broadcasting*, January 31, 1949, 4; and Keys, "Johnson Prods Anti-Clears," 22.

7. January 31, 1949, *Congressional Record*, 81st Cong., 1st Sess., A410, A411.

8. See CCBS to Members, June 26, 1947, Box P-1130, WRF; and

Senate Interstate and Foreign Commerce Committee, *Hearings on S. 1973*, 81st. Cong., 1st Sess. (1949), 60, 170.

9. Senate, *Hearings on S. 1973*, 108–11, 117, 132.

10. "NARBA Action," *Broadcasting*, November 14, 1949, 19.

11. "Sholis Hits NAB Channels Stand," *Broadcasting*, June 13, 1949, 60.

12. See "NARBA Signed," *Broadcasting*, November 20, 1950, 19; and Ward Quaal, Memorandum, n.d., Box P-1148, WRF.

13. See Quaal, Memorandum; and May 21, 1951, *Congressional Record*, 82nd Cong. 1st Sess., A2886; FCC, *Annual Report* (Washington, D.C., 1955), 94–95; and FCC, *Annual Report* (Washington, D.C., 1959), 67–68.

14. See Memorandum, December 9, 1954, Box P-1135, WRF; "U.S.-Mexico AM Talks Collapse," *Broadcasting*, December 20, 1954, 68; and Memorandum, December 2, 1954, Box P-1135, WRF.

15. See FCC, *Daytime Skywave Transmissions*, 24 FR 7756 (1959); and "Clears Ask FCC to Reconsider Day Grants on Their Channels," *Broadcasting*, October 14, 1946, 18.

16. See "Clears Ask FCC"; FCC, *In the Matter of Petition of Clear Channel Group*, 11 FCC 842 (1947); "WCKY Decision," *Broadcasting*, May 3, 1948, 36; and FCC, *Daytime Skywave Transmissions*, 24 FR 7756 (1959).

17. See DBA, Petition, February 26, 1954, Docket 8333, Docketed Case Files, RG 173, NACP; and CCBS, Brief, March 12, 1954, Docket 8333, Docketed Case Files, RG 173, NACP.

18. FCC, Report and Order, March 12, 1954, Docket 8333, Docketed Case Files, RG 173, NACP.

19. Roy Battles, telephone conversation with author, January 5, 1994; and William Jennings Bryan Dorn to Robert E. Lee, March 17, 1954, Docket 8333, Docketed Case Files, RG 173, NACP.

20. See DBA, Brief, July 8, 1954, Docket 8333, Docketed Case Files, RG 173, NACP; Various Stations, Brief, July 8, 1954, Docket 8333, Docketed Case Files, RG 173, NACP.

21. See FCC, *Daytime Skywave Transmissions*, 24 FR 7757 (1959); George Harry Rogers, "The History of the Clear Channel and Super Power Controversy in the Management of the Standard Broadcast Allocation Plan" (Ph.D. Diss., University of Utah, 1972), 57; "Daytimers Oppose Treaty in Chicago Resolution," *Broadcasting*,

April 15, 1957; "Daytimers Block Okay of NARBA," *Broadcasting*, July 15, 1957, 76; and "Senate Group Considers NARBA," *Broadcasting*, July 13, 1959, 72, 74.

22. See "Senate Unit Schedules Hearings on Daytimers," *Broadcasting*, April 1, 1957, 51; and "Morse Warns Daytimers of FCC Status Quo," *Broadcasting*, April 8, 1957, 39.

23. Senate Committee on Small Business, *Daytime Radio Broadcasting—1957*, 85th Cong., 1st Sess., Washington, D.C., 1957, 43, 54, 58–59.

24. Senate Committee on Small Business, *Daytime Radio Broadcasting*, 30, 40.

25. Senate Committee on Small Business, *Daytime Radio Broadcasting*, 79, 136, 139, 144, 177, 302–5, 316–17.

26. Senate Select Committee on Small Business, *Daytime Radio Stations*, Senate Report No. 1168, 85th Cong., 1st Sess, 1957, 1, 12, 19, 24–25, 30.

27. See FCC, *Daytime Skywave Transmissions*, 22 FR 10497 (1957); and FCC, *Daytime Skywave Transmissions*, 24 FR 7757, 7759 (1959).

28. Eric F. Brown, "Nighttime Radio for the Nation" (Ph.D. Diss., Ohio University, 1975), 62–63.

29. FCC, Further Notice of Proposed Rule Making, 23 FR 2612, 26, 18–19 (1958).

30. Brown, "Nighttime Radio for the Nation," 71–72; and FCC, Further Notice of Proposed Rule Making, 23 FR 2617 (1958).

31. FCC, *Clear Channel Broadcasting in the Standard Broadcast Band*, 24 FR 7737 (1959); and FCC, Further Notice, 23 FR 2612, 2617.

32. FCC, *Clear Channel Broadcasting in the Standard Broadcast Band*, 24 FR 7737, 7738, 7740 (1959).

33. See Briefs, Volume 7, Volume 9, Volume 86, Docket 6741, Docketed Case Files, RG 173, NACP.

34. See CCBS, Brief, April 1, 1960, Volume 85, Docket 6741, Docketed Case Files, RG 173, NACP; and CCBS, Reply Comments, June 1, 1960, Volume 86, Docket 6741, Docketed Case Files, RG 173, NACP.

35. "Closed Circuit," *Broadcasting*, May 8, 1961, 5.

36. See Hollis Seavey, telephone conversation with author, May 12,

1994; and Brown, "Nighttime Radio for the Nation," 102.

37. Oren Harris to Newton H. Minow, September 7, 1961, Box P-1145, WRF; Newton H. Minow to Oren Harris, September 13, 1961, Volume 87, Docket 6741, Docketed Case Files, RG 173, NACP.

38. William Potts, telephone conversation with author, June 1, 1994.

39. See Sangamon Valley Television Corporation v. FCC, 269 F. 2d 223–24 (1959); and CCBS, Minutes of Special Meeting, September 14, 1961, Box P-1145, WRF.

40. FCC, *In the Matter of Clear Channel Broadcasting in the Standard Broadcast Band*, 31 FCC 565 (1961).

41. FCC, *In the Matter of Clear Channel Broadcasting in the Standard Broadcast Band*, 609–12.

42. See "Name Battles to Head Clear Channel Fight," Chicago *Tribune*, October 24, 1961; Roy Battles to Ward Quaal, October 8, 1961, Box P-1145, WRF; Roy Battles to Ward Quaal, October 13, 1961, Box P-1145, WRF; and Ward Quaal, telephone conversation with author, November 12, 1998.

43. Roy Battles to Edwin W. Craig, January 3, 1962, Box P-1145, WRF.

44. John H. DeWitt to Members, August 28, 1961, Box P-1127, WRF.

45. See John H. DeWitt, telephone conversation with author, May 27, 1994; Memorandum, July 17, 1963, Box P-1127, WRF; and October 11, 1962, *Congressional Record*, 87th Cong., 2d Sess., 23144.

46. See Roy Battles to John H. DeWitt, September 14, 1964, Box P-1127, WRF; John H. DeWitt to R. Russell Eagan, October 17, 1963, Box P-1127, WRF; John H. DeWitt, telephone conversation with author, May 27, 1994; Roy Battles to Edwin W. Craig, January 4, 1963, Box P-1145, WRF; and CCBS, Bulletin No. 37, October 25, 1962, Box P-1145, WRF.

47. House Committee on Interstate and Foreign Commerce, *Clear Channel Broadcasting Stations*, 87th Cong., 2d Sess. (Washington, D.C., 1962), 1–2.

48. House Committee on Interstate and Foreign Commerce, *Clear Channel Broadcasting Stations*, 2, 51, 55, 65, 85–86.

49. See "House Unit Hears FCC Ideas on Clears," *Broadcasting*, February 19, 1962, 68; House Committee on Interstate and Foreign

Commerce, *Clear Channel Broadcasting Stations*, 262, 283.

50. See Roy Battles to James Quello, November 15, 1961, Box P-1145, WRF; and CCBS, Bulletin No. 9, May 9, 1962, Box P-1145, WRF.

51. See John Dingell to Newton H. Minow, March 20, 1962, Volume 88, Docket 6741, Docketed Case Files, RG 173, NACP; Newton H. Minow to John Dingell, March 30, 1962, Volume 88, Docket 6741, Docketed Case Files, RG 173, NACP.

52. See Brown, "Nighttime Radio for the Nation," 120; and Roy Battles to Edwin W. Craig, July 24, 1962, Box P-1145, WRF.

53. See Roy Battles, interview by Eric F. Brown, June 1972, Broadcast Pioneers Library, Washington, D.C.; Roy Battles to Edwin W. Craig, January 4, 1963, Box P-1145, WRF; and Goodwill Stations v. FCC, 325 F. 2d 637 (1963).

54. See "Un-Clear Channel Case," *Broadcasting*, July 11, 1949, 46; Hollis Seavey to John Doerfer, December 24, 1957, Volume 3, Docket 6741, RG 173, NACP; "FCC Makes Move on Duplication of Clears," *Broadcasting*, June 29, 1964, 48–49; "FCC Asked to Deny High-Power Applications," *Broadcasting*, June 29, 1964, 48; "Clears to Ask for Higher Power," *Broadcasting*, October 15, 1962, 27–29; and "Resolution Opposes Superpower," *Broadcasting*, March 22, 1965, 130, 134.

55. CCBS, *Radio for ALL America: The Case for the Clears* (Washington, D.C.: CCBS, 1963).

56. See William Potts, telephone conversation with author, May 24, 1994; Brown, "Nighttime Radio for the Nation," 132; ABS, Press Release, n.d., Box 3403, WRF; William Potts, telephone conversation with author, August 17, 1998.

57. See ABS, "4000 Local Community Stations or 12 Distant Superpower Giants: The Growing Outcry Against Superpower," April 1966, Clear Channels 194-1, General Correspondence, 1957–1966, RG 173, NACP; and Clark B. George to Joe Kjar, November 10, 1967, Box P-1145, WRF.

58. William F. Rust to Roy Battles, April 9, 1962, Box P-1145, WRF.

59. See Roy Battles to William F. Rust, April 17, 1962, Box P-1145, WRF; and Roy Battles to Ward Quaal, April 17, 1962, Box P-1145, WRF.

60. Ward Quaal to Roy Battles, September 18, 1962, Box P-1145, WRF.

61. Roy Battles to Edwin W. Craig, January 4, 1963, Box P-1145, WRF.

62. See CCBS, Lobbying Reports, 1949–1966, Box P-1148, WRF; CCBS Proposed Dues Structure, October 10, 1967, Box P-1145, WRF; and CCBS, Meeting Minutes, October 5, 1967, Box P-1145, WRF.

63. Ward Quaal to CCBS Members, July 8, 1968, Box A401, WRF.

64. See FCC, Report and Order, 78 FCC 2d 1345 (1980); CCBS, Minutes, April 7, 1975, Box P-1143, WRF; David Hilliard to R. Russell Eagan, March 26, 1981, Box P-1143, WRF; and CCBS, Resolution, April 14, 1981, Box P-1143, WRF.

CHAPTER SEVEN

A Romance Needs Cultivation

Among the most important aspects of the clear channels' political strategy during the 1940s, 1950s and 1960s was the so-called farm alliance. Hoping to tap into one of the most powerful networks of political influence and grassroots strength in the United States, clear channel stations worked through the Clear Channel Broadcasting Service to engage national farm organizations in the clear channel debate. Naturally, the CCBS sought such involvement on terms favorable to the preservation and enhancement of clear channels and thus attempted to convince individual farmers and the groups that represented them that clear channels with high power were the most practical way to provide radio service to rural areas where most farmers lived.

Clear channel stations pursued such efforts at several levels, involving both individual farmers and the leaders of farm organizations at the local, state and national levels. The CCBS shepherded resolutions favoring the preservation and enhancement of clear channels through farm organizations at annual conferences, then pointed to such resolutions as evidence that clear channels were providing the best service to farmers. Whenever possible, leaders of farm organizations were urged to present testimony—often substantially influenced, if not directly written, by the CCBS—before the Federal Communications Commission and congressional committees. At various times, the CCBS asked farm organization leaders to write letters to the FCC and individual members of Congress and urged them to have their members do the same. Representatives of individual clear channel stations pushed farmers to write letters in support of their "local" clear channel stations, citing specific programs they found particularly valuable.

To the Clear Channel Broadcasting Service, then, farm organizations represented something of a fourth branch of government. The CCBS lobbied representatives of farm groups just as they would FCC commissioners or members of Congress. Although opposition groups such as the Regional Broadcasters Committee (RBC) and Daytime Broadcasters Association (DBA) did not initially emphasize farm groups in their own political strategies, the natural inclination of many farm organization leaders was to oppose clear channels. In some cases, this opposition was rooted in a philosophical aversion to the perceived monopoly status of high-power, clear channel stations; but more commonly it was because other stations supported by farm organizations found their broadcast rights restricted by the FCC's clear channel policy. In these cases, the CCBS had to downplay the effect on particular stations and instead couch the issue in terms of improving service to the nation as a whole. More broadly, the CCBS also was forced to accept the fact that the clear channel debate meant much more to clear channel stations than it did to most farm groups and individual farmers. While farmers and their representative groups were concerned with rural access to media—and thus the clear channel debate—the controversy did not possess the same salience or urgency that issues such as crop subsidies or farm loan policies did. The fate of clear channels, to be sure, made little difference to the average farmer's bank account. Thus, the CCBS usually found itself having to prod the farm groups to maintain the depth and continuity of involvement in the clear channel debate that it desired.

The keystone of the farm alliance, of course, was programming, and the CCBS continually encouraged member stations to maintain and improve farm service. As time passed, however, such efforts were increasingly futile as clear channel stations adapted to the economic realities of the changing population. By the 1960s, many clear channel stations with long traditions of farm service were replacing rural shows with programming directed at the metropolitan and growing suburban audience. "There are some officials here who feel it [farm programming] 'hurts' the rest of their audience and particularly the metropolitan people and the youth," one clear channel farm director complained in the 1960s. While some clear channel stations, such as WGN, KFI and KSL, maintained an emphasis on farm programming, by the 1960s many other clears were scaling it back.[1]

This chapter examines the Clear Channel Broadcasting Service's efforts to engage farm groups in the clear channel debate from the early 1940s to the mid-1960s. It concentrates on the CCBS's relationship with the American Farm Bureau Federation (AFBF) and National Farmers Union (NFU), two of the largest and most influential farm groups during the time of the study. While the CCBS also sought to enlist the support of other large farm organizations such as the National Grange and National Council of Farmer Cooperatives, concentrating on the CCBS's relationship with the Farm Bureau and NFU is especially instructive because of the radical differences between the two farm organizations' views and membership. Establishing and maintaining these relationships was a complex process, as indicated by this chapter's opening discussion. Nonetheless, the support of farm groups was a key element in the CCBS's strategy to maintain and enhance the position of clear channel stations.

RADIO AND THE FARMER

Farmers and broadcasters alike could see radio's potential benefit to the rural constituency almost from the moment broadcasting began. "When you come right down to it, is there any one group of people whom radio can serve more efficiently than farm folks?" George C. Biggar of Chicago's WLS asked in 1938. At a 1922 Department of Commerce radio conference, General Electric's radio department manager E.P. Edwards predicted that broadcasting would be a great boon to farmers:

> I do not believe, for instance, that there is any other one thing which will have the same influence on agrarian interests as will radio. ... [The farmer] would like a little something beyond his fourteen-hour day drudgery in the way of entertainment. He also wants to know what the market is and the weather reports.

Historian Reynold Wik affirmed that radio ultimately played both an informational and socializing function for rural people. "Following rural free delivery, the telephone, automobile and hard roads," he wrote, "radio has probably done more than anything else to lessen rural isolation." Indeed, the farmer certainly benefited from having the latest market prices nearly instantaneously rather than waiting for the newspaper, and up-to-date weather reports were valuable as well. Radio could provide both.[2]

But despite radio's potential value to the farmer, rural areas lagged well behind urban centers in purchasing home receivers during the pre–World War II era. As late as 1930, well less than half of American farmers owned a radio, and in certain areas—such as the South—the figure was less than 10 percent. One reason for this slow adoption rate was the lack of electricity in many rural areas; while battery-powered radios were available, they were cumbersome and expensive. The creation of the Rural Electrification Administration in 1935, however, did much to bring electric power to the farm, hooking up three rural households for every one served by private utilities during the late 1930s; although only 10 percent of farms had electricity in 1930, by 1945 that number had risen to 40 percent. A survey conducted in 1938 by the Joint Committee on Radio Research showed that 69 percent of rural homes had radios, a total of nearly 9.5 million families. Although the urban penetration level was more than 90 percent, that gap continued to close in ensuing decades.[3]

While providing service to farmers was a cornerstone of the efforts of many nonprofit educational stations, commercial interests discovered that farmers also were a potentially profitable audience. In the mid-1920s, radio manufacturers began marketing radios as a farm necessity rather than a luxury, and once a farm had a radio, advertisers discovered, a multitude of other items could be marketed to farm families. "He was told and sold on the convenience of running water and outside plumbing," noted a WLW promotional brochure. "His wife learned that she could save hours of back-breaking labor by doing the family laundry in a washing machine." Thus, stations such as WLW that reached a large farm population found advertisers ready and willing to pay to sponsor farm programs. These clients included not only national manufacturers of farm implements, appliances and household products, but the local dealers who sold them. "Everytime [*sic*] the farmer or his family decided on a new item of convenience and comfort," WLW pointed out to local merchants, "there was a dealer in the picture to deliver the product radio advertising had pre-sold."[4]

Thus, the farm programming on clear channel stations, which in many cases had started out as a purely noncommercial, informational service, had by World War II become decidedly commercial. The change was, of course, symptomatic of radio's broader shift in emphasis from providing informational and educational programming to becoming first and foremost a vehicle for commercial advertising. While market and weather information remained a part of farm programming fare, stations began to expand into entertainment, personality and farming technique segments as well. Several clear channel stations developed elaborate farm-related events designed not only to spotlight farm and rural interests but to promote the stations and their programs to advertisers.

In 1939, WHO (Des Moines) began holding an annual regional plowing contest, which soon expanded into a national competition. The event attracted crowds of up to 200,000 people and became a regular stop for presidential candidates and other office seekers. Perhaps most elaborate was WLW's so-called Everybody's Farm, a working farm that began operating in 1941 on 137 acres of land near the station's transmitter. It was the focal point of WLW's rural programming, including the daily *Everybody's Farm Hour,* which featured segments on farming technique and interviews with representatives of farm organizations, politicians and farm equipment vendors. Roy Battles, who was director of the CCBS during the 1960s, became WLW's farm director in 1944, and although he later claimed that he almost did not take the WLW position because he believed the station was too commercial, he proposed expanding Everybody's Farm in the late 1940s so that it could be used to promote New Idea brand farm equipment. "The addition of dairy or beef cattle would allow us a far better chance to support a soil building program that makes a manure spreader one of our most vital tools," he told station manager James Shouse. "This better falls in line with the New Idea theme." These and additional expansions, Battles noted, would "broaden our appeal for commercial accounts without destroying any present accounts."[5]

Similarly, the long-running *National Farm and Home Hour* eventually succumbed to the pressures of commercialism. Produced as a joint effort between NBC and the Department of Agriculture beginning in 1928, the program went to the Blue network when NBC was split in 1943. By 1944, the network was pressuring the Department of Agriculture to eliminate the market reports, despite the fact that many farmers valued them. The Department of Agriculture resisted these efforts, and the network moved the program to Saturdays in June 1944, canceling it completely at the beginning of 1945. By September, *National Farm and Home Hour* was back on NBC, after the Department of Agriculture agreed to allow the sponsorship of Allis-Chalmers and to pare market reports back to a mere two minutes.[6]

THE FARM LOBBY

Since a number of the independently owned clear channel stations had embraced farm programming—albeit commercially oriented farm programming—it was natural for the CCBS to seek to enlist farm groups as allies in its fight for clear channels. Such an alliance, if successful, could have substantial political benefits for the clear channel stations, as the farm lobby was among the most influential in Washington, D.C. This power traced its roots to the Populist political movements of the late 1800s. At that time, as the Industrial Revolution was just getting under way, farmers made up more than 40 percent of the country's population, and more than 60 percent of Americans lived in rural areas. Populism embraced the so-called agrarian myth, which painted the yeoman farmer as the country's ideal citizen. Historian Richard Hofstadter noted that such high regard carried with it the notion that farmers were thus entitled to "a special right to the concern and protection of government." During the 1920s, farm organizations, led by the American Farm Bureau Federation, assembled the so-called Farm Bloc alliance of Republicans and Democrats in the Senate and then proceeded to push through a series of bills expanding farm credits and subsidies. The power of farm groups reached its pinnacle during World War II, as farmers were able to win and preserve price supports and production controls. "In sheer reputation for power, the agricultural organizations reigned alongside the business lobbies and the labor unions as the 'big three' of American politics," John Mark Hansen noted. Although the farm population had been declining as a percentage of the total population since the turn of the century and in real numbers since the 1920s, farmers became a more powerful political force as their numbers grew smaller.[7]

Yet the farm lobby was by no means homogenous. Edward A. O'Neal, longtime president of the American Farm Bureau Federation, once described the complex structure of agricultural politics as "wheels within wheels." The Farm Bureau and National Farmers Union maintained a particularly adversarial relationship; their differences usually arose as a result of the fact that each group had a unique constituency as well as a distinct philosophy. The American Farm Bureau Federation, formed as the conglomeration of the Department of Agriculture's county agent system in 1919 and 1920, became a potent political force in its own right early in the New Deal era. Made up largely of wealthy family farmers in the Midwest, the Farm Bureau's membership grew from less than 400,000 members in 1939 to more than 1.3 million by 1949. Opposing the unionization of farm workers and measures designed to help poor farmers, the Farm Bureau pursued a conservative, anti-labor agenda. The National Farmers Union, in contrast, continually attempted to bring together the interests of farmers and laborers but ultimately with little success. The smallest and most liberal of the so-called big three farm organizations

(National Grange, AFBF and NFU), it also was the only farm group to fight consistently for dispossessed farmers. The philosophical differences between the two groups led not only to political disagreements but to pointed rhetorical exchanges as well. The Farm Bureau continually intimated that the NFU was a communist organization, while the NFU criticized the Farm Bureau as a shill of big business. The Farm Bureau was "born a bastard of the Railroads and Chamber of Commerce," Milo Reno, president of the Iowa Farmers Union, once said. "No farmer had anything to do with organizing [it]."[8]

CCBS AND FARM GROUPS

When the Clear Channel Broadcasting Service was formed in 1941, one of its first priorities was to engage as many farm groups as possible in the clear channel debate. Although its predecessor, the Clear Channel Group, had made no organized effort to influence farm organizations, both the National Grange and American Farm Bureau Federation had expressed support—albeit in vague terms—for the concept of clear channels to provide rural service. The Farm Bureau's most recent resolution on the topic, passed in 1930 at the height of debate over the commercial broadcasting system, called for the Federal Radio Commission to allocate to agriculture "such wave length or lengths, cleared channels, and power as are necessary permanently to preserve its rightful interests of the air." In a 1940 letter to FCC Chairman James Lawrence Fly, O'Neal asked the FCC to preserve rural radio service but made no reference to any specific issue. "If farmers and their organizations have not been active in recent years in making representations relative to their reception of radio programs," O'Neal reported, "it is no doubt due to their general satisfaction with the present quality of service."[9]

Ignoring the 1930 resolution's call for specific allocations to noncommercial entities, the CCBS would have argued that both the resolution and O'Neal's stand on the present allocation system represented an affirmation of clear channels. Whenever farm groups intimated for anything but the existing free market, advertiser-supported broadcasting system, the CCBS dismissed the requests as impossible and thus irrelevant. A significant part of the CCBS's challenge in enlisting farm group support was convincing farmers that commercial clear channel stations could meet the needs of farmers better than the limited number of existing noncommercial stations and better than any proposed re-allocation that would upset the existing commercial structure.

To that end, CCBS Director Victor A. Sholis convened a meeting of clear channel farm directors in the group's Washington, D.C., office soon after he was hired in 1941. He urged farm directors to contact local farm representatives and describe the clear channel situation in "simple, non-technical terms" while explaining why rural listeners had a stake in the preservation of clear channels. Sholis prepared sample discussion guides and a series of articles on clear channels and rural service, noting his desire to establish "groundwork for constructive future action." Farm directors also were instructed to make periodic reports to the CCBS central office so that information could be shared among all member stations. The CCBS also urged stations to work to improve their farm programming and offered to help stations struggling to fit such programming into their schedules.[10]

The ongoing discussion of the FCC's announced decision to duplicate KOA's 850 kHz clear channel provided additional talking points for clear channel stations' discussions with farm leaders. Here was a situation that played directly into CCBS arguments that duplication would sacrifice rural service for the benefit of urban listeners. The commission's proposal to allow Boston's WHDH to broadcast full-time on KOA's clear channel would significantly impact the Denver station's ability to reach rural listeners east of the station, and listeners in metropolitan Boston, the CCBS pointed out, were hardly in need of more radio service. In the late fall of 1941, having established lines of communication with leaders of farm groups through individual stations' farm directors, the CCBS then orchestrated a letter-writing campaign from farm group leaders and members. The CCBS hoped that a strong showing of support from farm groups would not only curb the trend toward piecemeal duplication presaged by the KOA case but encourage the FCC to examine the overall clear channel structure. The group's timing, however, could not have been worse, as letters began rolling into the Federal Communications Commission just days after the Japanese attack on Pearl Harbor drew the United States into World War II. Nonetheless, CCBS efforts toward the Farm Bureau paid off in the form of a new resolution at the end of 1941, in which the group acknowledged clear channel broadcasting services as "an invaluable source of news, education, information and entertainment for American farm families" and opposed "any action tending to reduce the number of clear channel stations."[11]

The CCBS made little progress in swaying the National Farmers Union, despite the fact that KOA had a good reputation for farm programming and provided service to the heart of the NFU's geographic membership base. The WHDH duplication, in fact, was likely to keep many NFU members from receiving KOA's signal. But the concurrent dispute between KFI of Los Angeles and WOI of Ames, Iowa, strengthened the NFU's opposition to clear channels. WOI, as discussed in Chapter 5, wanted to increase its hours of operation in the morning to provide service to farmers in rural Iowa, but KFI protested, and the FCC denied WOI's request. This particularly angered NFU President James Patton, who in 1944 urged interim FCC chairman Ewell K. Jett to reverse the decision. The Los Angeles station, Patton noted, used the time in which WOI was forced off the air to play phonograph records, thus depriving farmers in Iowa of early morning agricultural reports:

> We believe that the principle here goes far beyond the interests of agriculture. It is the issue of the public good, the issue whether commercial stations shall be given preferential treatment over noncommercial, whether educational, governmental and similar radio stations dedicated to the good of all the people, are to be ignored in order that the greed of private radio interests may be subserved.

The KFI/WOI dispute also would lead other farm groups to reassess their support for clear channels, although none would oppose the existing clear channel structure with the stridence of the NFU. While the National Grange, for example, had expressed its support for clear channel broadcasting in 1941, in 1945 the group passed a resolution saying that the clear channel structure discriminated against farmers.[12]

But while Sholis had developed a strategy for wooing farm support upon taking the CCBS reins, the United States' entry into World War II diverted the group's focus. Both Sholis and Jack DeWitt, in fact, left their CCBS positions to enter the service in 1942. Despite the relative lack of organized lobbying activity from the CCBS, however, the Farm Bureau continued to express its support for clear channels throughout the war years. In 1944, it strengthened its 1941 stand by calling clear channels invaluable to rural America and urging no limitation of clear channel broadcasting. The following year, it affirmed the value of clear channels again, echoing the CCBS contention that FM's growth in urban areas would eventually leave rural people even more dependent on clear channel stations. "[W]e insist that clear channel radio service be maintained and improved to the end that rural people may enjoy the best in radio programs," the resolution concluded.[13]

FARM GROUPS IN DOCKET 6741

The fact that the war and the postwar NARBA negotiations had hindered the CCBS's efforts in rallying farm groups to its side became apparent at the start of Docket 6741 hearings. The sessions were disastrous from the CCBS point of view as farm interests soundly criticized clear channel farm programming. Representatives from the U.S. Department of Agriculture, National Council of Farmer Cooperatives and National Grange all called farm programming on clear channels inadequate, most often criticizing the fact that programs of interest to farmers were broadcast only at times during the day when commercial programming could not be sold. And, witnesses pointed out, the limited amount of farm programming that was offered by clear channels was becoming more commercialized. In general, clear channels were portrayed as more interested in providing programs of interest to city dwellers. "In its overall program structure," John Baker of the Department of Agriculture noted, "the average clear channel station is governed by urban tastes, whether the programs are produced locally or taken off a network." Baker, however, did note that clear channel stations were making an effort to improve farm programming by hiring full-time farm directors, but he contended that the best farm service still came from daytime-only stations such as WOI and Michigan State University's WKAR.[14]

The most pointed criticism, however, was offered by Russell Smith, legislative secretary of the National Farmers Union. Citing the inadequacy of farm programming on clear channels, Smith told the commission that the situation was indicative of the larger problem of commercial control of radio. "[R]adio as it is now conducted does not bring to farmers the information that they need as functioning citizens of a democracy," he said. "The effort put into public programs rarely equals that put into commercial programs." Farmers, Smith said, were made to feel like "aliens in their own land" by radio:

> [T]here is a widespread belief among farmers and rural people that radio belongs to the advertising business, and that their appropriate attitude toward sponsored programs is to be grateful for what they get and uncritical of defects. Such programs as they enjoy are regarded as manna providentially and accidentally dropped from a far-off heaven of honey-tongued announcers and business concerns.

Citing such "control of broadcasting stations by giant aggregations of wealth," Smith called for the commission to eliminate large corporations' "dominance over the minds of the people."[15]

Clear channel stations, Smith contended, demonstrated the worst result of such corporate control of the airwaves. He told the commission that NFU members were increasingly dissatisfied with programming offered by clear channel stations. "[W]e have grave doubts as to the wisdom of permitting the operation of any cleared channel stations," he said, noting that adding more local stations to clear channel frequencies would serve rural listeners more effectively. If clear channels should be preserved at all, Smith said, the stations on them should be operated by the government for broadcasting the proceedings of Congress, and if the commission insisted on allowing them to operate as commercial enterprises, they should be relocated to better cover rural areas.[16]

CCBS counsel Louis Caldwell, of course, objected to such programming considerations in what he viewed as a strictly "techni-cal" proceeding. But, overruled by the FCC, he was forced con-tinually to resort to playing up technical issues at the expense of programming concerns. In cross-examining witnesses critical of clear channel farm programming, Caldwell attempted to establish that before rural listeners could enjoy good programming they had to have good reception. He also tried to deflect criticism by playing the CCBS line that farmers essentially enjoyed—and were entitled to—the same entertainment programming city residents received. More than once, Caldwell attempted to illustrate this point by asking witnesses whether they would choose to listen to a talk on how to raise livestock or *Fibber McGee*. Baker, for one, noted that it was unfortunate that farmers could not have both.[17]

When Docket 6741 hearings resumed three months later, one of the CCBS's first orders of business was to minimize the damage done by its poor showing at the first set of hearings. The corner-stone of this effort was the Farm Bureau's O'Neal, who urged the FCC to do whatever was necessary to improve clear channel ser-vice. He noted that farmers were dependent on clear channel sta-tions but often had trouble hearing them because of interference. He particularly objected to the breakdown of KOA's clear chan-nel because he saw very little need to add another nighttime sta-tion in Boston. O'Neal's obvious toeing of the CCBS line angered Paul D.P. Spearman, counsel for the Regional Broadcasters Com-mittee, who attacked O'Neal's "prepared statement," which was prepared, as he suspected, with the help of the CCBS.[18]

But despite O'Neal's strong stand in favor of clear channels at the 1946 hearings, sentiment against clear channels was building within his organization. The strongest opposition originated in the Iowa and Ohio state Farm Bureaus: Iowa was angered over WOI's inability to increase its operating hours on KFI's clear channel, and Ohio was itself planning a broadcasting station. In the sum-mer of 1947, WRFD, operated by the Peoples Broadcasting Cor-poration, went on the air in Worthington, Ohio, just north of Co-lumbus, promising to provide news, market reports, group dis-cussions and "wholesome entertainment" for the benefit of Ohio farmers. Supported by the Ohio Farm Bureau, the organization made up of 26 "farmer-directors" received a license to broadcast during the day on 800 kHz, a Mexican I-A frequency. A change in the clear channel policy allowing duplication of U.S. I-A frequencies would likely be the only way WRFD could ever increase its operating hours.[19]

Still, the national Farm Bureau once again affirmed its stand in favor of preserving clear channels at its 1946 convention. The new resolution, in fact, went even further, urging that clear channel frequencies "be held inviolate by international agreement" and that clear channel stations' power "be increased to allow for complete coverage to all areas." At the Farm Bureau's board of directors meeting in June 1947, however, James Moore, information director of the Ohio Farm Bureau, and Richard Hull of WOI made a presentation on the clear channel issue. They brought with them an anti-clear channel resolution passed by the Ohio Farm Bureau and asked the AFBF to reconsider its support of clear channels. As a compromise, the board subsequently approved a resolution designed to set down certain principles to guide the FCC in its clear channel deliberations. Those principles were (1) that a person with a background of experience in agriculture and rural radio be appointed to the FCC, (2) that clear channel wavelengths be more equitably distributed to provide rural radio service, (3) that any new frequencies created by an expansion of the broadcast band be made available to applicants that would provide rural programming and (4) that every station providing rural service devote a fair portion of airtime throughout the day to programs of distinctly rural nature. The final point, the resolution noted, should be particularly enforced on stations granted power in excess of 50,000 watts.[20]

The resolution was presented in a letter to the FCC on October 30, 1947, just days after the CCBS had unveiled its Twenty-Station Plan. It was significant because it showed that internal forces in the AFBF were gaining control of the group's policy position. The resolution, in fact, did not contradict the one passed by the AFBF convention in 1946, yet it did put the group on record as seeking improvements in rural programming outside of the commercial clear channel structure. More importantly, the CCBS was no longer in a position to unilaterally control the Farm Bureau's position. A backlash against the AFBF's strong stand at the 1946 hearings had quickly developed, and that difference of opinion within the group would temper its support for clear channels in the coming years.

But in keeping with the AFBF's 1946 resolution, Willis Tobler of the group's Washington, D.C., office testified against the Johnson Bill in 1948, while within the organization debate on the clear channels continued. The AFBF's director of information, John Lacey, had been put in charge of gathering data on the clear channel issue, and he made his final presentation at a board meeting in September 1948. "I can see no valid reason why the American Farm Bureau Federation should alter its policy on this issue," his report noted. "On the contrary, it is my opinion that the organization should reiterate its stand against any general breakup of the present clear channel system." He characterized the situation as "the 'have-nots' trying to take from the 'haves'":

> It is quite similar to the agitation by some groups for a breakup of existing farms in this country into much smaller units so that more people could have the advantage of living on the land. The result of such a development would be to spoil the farming business for everybody engaged in it. The breakup of the clear channel system would have comparable results in the radio business.

The report acknowledged criticisms that some clear channel stations did not provide adequate informational programming but noted that farmers enjoyed other types of programs as well. "[W]e must remember that farm people demand and are entitled to music and drama and world news on a par with that supplied to city people," it said, echoing the CCBS position.[21]

Lacey also pointed out that any new stations licensed under a breakup of the clear channels were likely to go to metropolitan areas and that "farm people are the ones most likely to lose." He contended that "a realistic appraisal of the situation indicates that the reason covetous eyes are being cast on the clear channels is that they are very valuable properties. Most of those who seek a slice of them want them for their money-making possibilities." Thus, in his view, new stations would be no more likely to program to farmers than existing clear channel stations.[22]

Despite the fact that Lacey's report read as if it had come directly from the Clear Channel Broadcasting Service, the CCBS was apparently unaware of its existence. A memo written to stations in October 1948 by Caldwell and R. Russell Eagan chronicled developments at the Farm Bureau but made no mention of the strong support supplied by Lacey. However, while no documentation could be found connecting the CCBS to Lacey's report, it is obvious that he relied substantially on information supplied to him by CCBS interests. Nonetheless, as the Farm Bureau's 1948 convention approached, the CCBS feared that the Iowa and Ohio Farm Bureaus would hold sway over the national organization's clear channel position. Caldwell and Eagan noted that it was extremely important for individual stations to contact representatives of national and state farm bureaus in their area "to ensure that the present favorable position ... is not modified." Despite the consternation within the CCBS, however, the 1948 Farm Bureau convention took no action on the clear channel issue. One resolution, noting that rural residents still depended on clear channel stations in spite of the fact that more than 1,000 new stations had been added to the broadcast band since World War II, was referred to the board of directors by the resolutions committee. Following discussion, however, the board concluded that its position was well established and saw no need to further consider the issue.[23]

CCBS EFFORTS TO ENGAGE FARM GROUPS

During this period, the CCBS also emphasized gaining the support of state and local farm organizations. Member stations' farm directors attended conventions in surrounding states, urging them to pass pro-clear channel resolutions, and the CCBS's lawyers in Washington, D.C., developed a "template" to guide local farm directors in drawing up state and local resolutions. The template noted that the resolution should first spell out that farmers depend primarily on clear channel stations for their radio reception, that radio is an invaluable source for news, information and entertainment and that existing service was not adequate because of interference and static. Then, the resolution should conclude that there should be no reduction in the number of clear channels either by domestic action or through international agreements and that clear channel stations should have higher power. Using these guidelines, local clear channel representatives were able to push numerous resolutions through state contingents of national groups as well as independent state, regional and local organizations. After passage, these resolutions were then forwarded to the FCC and congressional committees, either by the organization itself or by the CCBS.[24]

Ward Quaal, who took over as director of the CCBS in 1949, placed greater emphasis on "educating" farmers and rural people about the clear channel issue. To this end, he instituted the *CCBS Farm Paper Service*, which distributed informational material to farmers and farm group leaders through individual clear channel stations. The purpose of the material, as noted on each dispatch, was "to let radio listeners know of a movement afoot to deprive them of their radio service." Quaal increased member stations' coverage of farm organization conventions by using pooling systems to provide individual stations with audio of important speeches and interviews with farm leaders. He also facilitated *Agriculture U.S.A.*, a cooperative effort with the U.S. Department of Agriculture to distribute in-depth farm stories to CCBS members. The series continued cooperatively until 1959, when the USDA took sole control of production to make it available to more stations. By this time, too, it should be pointed out, the number of clear channel stations actually airing *Agriculture U.S.A.* had dramatically decreased. Although possessing little in the way of a farm background himself, Quaal also made an effort to educate himself on farm issues and to attend as many farm conventions as possible. "We told them that they needed us," he later said.[25]

The ongoing disputes involving NARBA during the early 1950s provided an additional line of attack for the CCBS. The group had worked with KFI during the 1946 discussions of the NARBA Interim Agreement and protested the authorization of Cuban stations on the Los Angeles station's frequency. Similarly, the CCBS opposed the pending agreement reached in Washington, D.C., in 1950 because it did not include Mexico. In communications with farmers during the early 1950s, the CCBS played up the specter of foreign intrusion on U.S. airwaves. "We've given other nations nearly everything else," one *Farm Paper Service* noted. "Shall we now give them our 'radio air' also?" The CCBS warned that rural listeners stood to lose the most in this giveaway of American natural resources and noted that if the clear channels were broken down, either by international treaty or congressional action, farmers might receive stronger signals from foreign stations than from U.S. stations. "Won't that be a fine kettle of fish?" one paper asked. "American farmers unable to get U.S. radio stations on their receivers, so they have to listen to Mexico, Cuba and Canada!" Clear channel stations also were described as a crucial link in national defense: "It looks like this effort to deprive us of clear channel service plays right into the hands of some subversive elements at home and abroad, who would like to keep us from having good communication with one another."[26]

Hollis Seavey, who took over as director of the CCBS after the departure of Quaal in 1953, tried to continue the close cultivation of farm groups but was not as successful as his predecessor. "[A]s someone who grew up in Cambridge, Massachusetts, I really wasn't very close to the soil," he later lamented. During Seavey's tenure, much of the responsibility for courting farm support and covering farm issues shifted back to individual stations' farm directors. Still, he continued to attend the meetings of national, regional and local farm groups and made tape recordings of addresses and news of the meetings available to CCBS members. Until the early 1950s, only the CCBS had made organized efforts to influence the policy of farm groups on the clear channel issue. However, in 1951 Edward B. Craney began to make overtures to AFBF representatives; his letter to Farm Bureau president Charles Shuman led to a discussion of the group's stand on clear channels at a 1951 board of directors meeting. The board came to no consensus to change the AFBF's existing stand but resolved only to "remain active ... and keep informed on current developments." Craney's efforts, however, would eventually show results.[27]

Resolutions passed by the AFBF in 1950, 1951 and 1953 reiterated support for clear channels and urged the FCC to allow them to increase their power. Internally, Farm Bureau leaders resolved to oppose ratification of the NARBA treaty, and a 1954 resolution urged the U.S. government to protect its radio frequencies from foreign interference. However, the Farm Bureau's 1955 resolution was decidedly nebulous:

> Reduction of broadcast interference, particularly as it applies to clear channel stations, is a constant challenge to governmental agencies. We are firmly opposed to any government regulations which might reduce, or threaten to reduce, service to rural listeners.

The following year, the group's resolution was even more vague, noting Farm Bureau support for "the efforts made by the industry to expand and improve its coverage of news and farm affairs." The 1957 resolution, reaffirmed in 1958, added support for the 1950 NARBA agreement but presented no strengthening of its clear channel stand. The CCBS, of course, had also done an about-face on NARBA after Mexico was brought into the agreement and now supported the treaty as well.[28]

But by this time, organized opposition to the clear channels by the Daytime Broadcasters Association and Craney was starting to show results with the Farm Bureau. While there had been disagreement within the Farm Bureau since the mid-1940s on the clear channel issue, the CCBS had been able to thwart insurgencies through its organized lobbying efforts. Now, however, the opposition was equally organized, and just as the DBA boasted the advantage of having a member station in nearly every congressional district, it also had member stations near many farm areas. Seavey and the CCBS redoubled efforts toward the Farm Bureau, and prior to the group's 1958 convention, Seavey gave a presentation at the Rural Living Resolutions Subcommittee's meeting, in which he outlined "the facts" of the clear channel situation. The CCBS director believed he had been well received by the committee and was surprised by the resulting resolution. "While there is nothing detrimental in this resolution," he complained, "I must say that it does not represent a strong affirmative stand." Nonetheless, the Farm Bureau did go on record against the FCC's 1958 proposal to duplicate 12 clear channels.[29]

As opposition groups increased their contact with farm groups, the CCBS attempted to portray them as naïve newcomers concerned only with their own interests. Since the CCBS had had a long—if at times rocky—affiliation with each of the major farm groups, it termed its relationship with them a "friendship" as opposed to the "pressure" exerted by the other groups. Continually, the CCBS reminded farm leaders that the clear channel problem was at its heart an engineering issue and that powerful clear channels provided the best engineering solution to rural area service. This approach, of course, not only allowed the CCBS to rely on its voluminous technical exhibits but to sidestep the fact that many— if not most—clear channels did not have impressive farm programming records. In a 1960 letter to Shuman, Quaal characterized the CCBS's efforts toward farm groups as mutually beneficial. "I have always wanted to have it [our relationship] understood as informational and educational in nature," Quaal wrote, "for as expert as you people are in a good many things, you are lacking the technical knowledge engineering-wise and this is strictly an engineering matter."[30]

Beginning in the summer of 1960, Quaal and John McDonald, WSM's farm director, began further efforts to strengthen Farm Bureau support for clear channels. Quaal lobbied Shuman, while McDonald worked on Tom Hitch, an officer of the Tennessee Farm Bureau. By this time, the CCBS had traced the nexus of opposition within the Farm Bureau to Jack Angell, a former NBC newscaster who was now the bureau's director of radio-television services. By lobbying other Farm Bureau representatives, the CCBS hoped to neutralize Angell, and the strategy showed quick results. The bureau's 1960 resolution called on the FCC to "determine the number of clear channel stations needed to provide adequate service" and to "prescribe standards of service and performance for them." While certainly not as vigorous or unconditional as previous resolutions on the clear channel issue, the CCBS could reasonably assert it was an acknowledgment that adequate service could only be provided through the use of clear channels.[31]

THE NFU AND CLEAR CHANNELS

In contrast to the varying support offered by the American Farm Bureau Federation throughout the 1940s and 1950s, the National Farmers Union consistently opposed the clear channels. Farmers and other noncommercial interests, according to the NFU, were getting short shrift in the commercial radio structure, and conservative, pro-business interests dominated the airwaves. "Too many of our radio stations are owned by the Hearsts, the Colonel McCormick's and the Pew's," Smith noted. "Too few of them are owned by labor unions, cooperatives or farm organizations." Such beliefs naturally caused the NFU to oppose clear channels, which included many of the wealthiest broadcasting interests, all with network affiliations. In addition, since its membership was concentrated in the West, the group particularly opposed granting higher power to stations located mostly in the East. Thus, the NFU testified against superpower at the Docket 6741 hearings in 1946 and strongly urged passage of the Johnson Bill in 1948.[32]

Patton's testimony at the Johnson Bill hearings emphasized the fact that the group's opposition to clear channels was rooted in a larger antipathy for monopoly power and commercial control of broadcasting. "[W]e are against monopoly power in any form," Patton said, "and believe that the operation of stations in excess of 50,000 watts would contribute to a monopoly of a natural resource of all the people, the air." Granting superpower, Patton contended, would "squeeze small stations off the air" and concentrate radio power in the hands of a few powerful corporations. "You can draw your own conclusions as to what would happen if 750,000 watts of power were granted to Colonel McCormick [the conservative owner of the *Chicago Tribune* and WGN]," Patton said. "The result probably would be a *Chicago Tribune* of the air."[33]

Patton then decried the dearth of farm programming on radio, especially on powerful stations. "Private monopolists" engaged in radio broadcasting, he asserted, believed that "great organizations of people, or for that matter, average citizen[s], in general, have no claim upon them." The commercialization of the Department of Agriculture's *National Farm and Home Hour* was but one example of the way business interests were squelching farm programming. "[A] farm program in the evening is almost unheard of, yet that is the time when many farmers would prefer them," he said. Some clear channel stations, he noted, had marginally improved their farm programming, but he doubted that the changes would last:

It must be said that since the FCC has begun its investigations of the rural service of clear channel stations there has been a decided improvement in their farm broadcasts. Most of them have hired radio farm directors. I am not sure that this improved service will continue once the FCC has rendered a final decision on clear facilities.

Meanwhile, Patton contended, the existing clear channel policy was thwarting the efforts of many farm-oriented stations to improve their service. Passing the Johnson Bill, Patton noted, would provide increased opportunities for stations like WRFD, WOI and WKAR. "One of the great scandals of our day is the fact that our great agricultural colleges cannot broadcast the information which they have to the farmer at times when the farmers wish to listen," he said.[34]

Patton acknowledged that there were many areas of the country, especially west of the Mississippi River, that lacked adequate radio coverage, but he doubted that granting superpower to clear channel stations would alleviate the problem. Instead, he called on the FCC to "make a thorough overhauling of its whole allocation system" and devise a plan that would give all farmers day and night radio service. Noting that he was not an expert in radio matters, he offered no specifics on how such a plan could be carried out, except to urge that clear channel stations be relocated, that room in the AM band be opened up by serving urban areas with FM stations and that frequencies be allocated to noncommercial interests.[35]

The NFU continued to oppose the clear channels throughout the 1950s, and this fact, coupled with the mercurial support offered by the American Farm Bureau Federation, prompted the CCBS to place even greater emphasis on wooing farm groups. Quaal, who was the group's spiritual if not official leader throughout the 1950s, was convinced that maintaining farm support was the only way to keep the FCC from breaking down the clear channels. The 1961 hiring of Battles, a former clear channel farm director and high-ranking official with the National Grange, was a last-ditch effort to cement the farm groups behind the CCBS. Never before had a CCBS director boasted such a close relationship with farm groups and possessed such an intimate knowledge of farm issues apart from the provincial interests of the clear channel group. Battles prided himself in knowing about farm issues. "It's my life," he later said. "I had a lot of contacts." Quaal, too, noted that Battles' knowledge of farming was invaluable to the CCBS's agenda.[36]

When Battles began his CCBS work in October 1961, he had little opportunity to take time to settle into his new position. Only weeks before, the FCC had issued its decision in Docket 6741 to duplicate half of the remaining clear channels. Battles, of course, knew he had been hired because of his farm contacts, and he quickly put them to work in aligning farm organizations against the FCC's Docket 6741 decision. The most significant early result of Battles' work was a pro-clear channel resolution passed by the NFU in 1962. "[This is] a major breakthrough," he noted in a memo to member stations. "You will recall that the Union fought us tooth and toenail back during the Johnson Bill hearings." While this particular show of support would be short-lived, the reasons behind it foreshadowed a change in philosophy of the NFU.[37]

By this time, Battles and the CCBS had convinced Patton, at least, to soften his stance against clear channels. While it is not clear what specific events led to this change, it is likely that the CCBS finally persuaded Patton that at least some of the clear channel stations were making an effort to provide service to farmers. It is also likely that the FCC's Docket 6741 decision showed Patton that support for educational, noncommercial and farm-specific AM radio was not forthcoming from the FCC. Even though the commission had in a sense given the NFU what it had asked for since the 1940s—a breakdown of the clear channels and the addition of more stations—in a larger sense it had not. The Docket 6741 decision made no provision for anything but more commercial, advertiser-supported radio stations. Patton probably believed that the best practical way to improve farm programming was no longer to rail against the business of radio but to work within the system with those who seemed most apt to provide farm service. And for the time being, that meant the CCBS.

But not everyone in the NFU shared in Patton's gradual conversion. Once again, the preservation of clear channels conflicted with a smaller station's excellent reputation for farm coverage. This time, it was Max Brown's KRVN in Lexington, Nebraska, a station started in 1951 by a corporation made up of 5,000 farmers and dedicated to farm service. The NFU had supported Brown in his efforts to obtain the license, which authorized the station to broadcast daytime only on 1010 kHz, a Canadian clear channel frequency. The FCC's Docket 6741 decision, however, would give KRVN a chance to improve its coverage significantly because on 880 kHz, currently WCBS's clear channel frequency, the FCC proposed a new full-time station in North Dakota, South Dakota or Nebraska. Since the new assignment would allow full-time operation, Brown decided to pursue the frequency for KRVN. "It is likely there will never be another opportunity to obtain an AM broadcast license that would have enough power to cover all Nebraska and be able to operate both day and night," Brown told the NFU.[38]

The NFU's efforts for Brown precluded support for clear channels, at least for the time being. The NFU did not testify at the 1962 congressional hearings orchestrated by the CCBS, but Battles still pointed to the group's earlier resolution opposing the breakdown of the clear channels. Other farm groups, however, supported the CCBS at the House hearings, although all expressed a belief that clear channel stations varied greatly in their level of support for rural programming. Hershel D. Newsom, national master of the National Grange and Battles' old boss, testified in favor of the pending legislation but, when asked about complaints lodged by rural residents, noted that a few clear channel stations "are not doing the job I think they ought to do." Kit H. Haynes of the National Council of Farmer Cooperatives also testified in favor of clear channels, and John C. Lynn of the American Farm Bureau Federation supported clear channel stations such as WGN and KMOX that carried significant farm programming. Lynn, however, criticized stations such as WLS that aimed much of their programming at urban areas and suggested that these stations were not serving the rural population and thus should have their channels duplicated. WLS, formerly owned by *Prairie Farmer* magazine, had an excellent reputation for farm programming until coming under ABC ownership in 1954. ABC quickly shifted the station's emphasis to the Chicago metropolitan area, sharply curtailing farm programs.[39]

CCBS AND RIVALS COMPETE
FOR FARM GROUP SUPPORT

Under Battles' tenure, the Clear Channel Broadcasting Service finally was able to implement the farm initiatives it had attempted since its inception. The CCBS director became the point person in a well-organized system that allowed the group to maintain alliances with farm organizations and their members. Battles toured the farm circuit regularly, attending meetings, giving speeches and making sure groups received coverage on appropriate clear channel stations. Battles found himself very much at home with farmers and proved skillful at adapting the clear channel issue to different farm organizations by exploring various angles of the debate in terms that would most interest the group to which he was speaking. At a meeting of the National Apple Institute in 1962, for example, Battles gave a presentation called, "The Case For Clear Channel Broadcasting in Weather Reports to Growers." Afterward, the NAI's executive vice president praised the CCBS director, noting that his talk "aroused much interest and evoked many enthusiastic comments."[40]

Most importantly, however, Battles brought an extensive knowledge of and interest in farm issues apart from the clear channel debate. He had to decline an invitation to return to the National Apple Institute in 1963, for instance, so that he could attend a meeting of the National Hog Cholera Eradication Committee that had no relation to the clear channel issue. At other times, Battles offered to exchange coverage on CCBS member stations for the opportunity to appear at a group's convention or for favorable testimony. After Ed Marsh of the National Wool Growers Association had supported the CCBS at the House hearings, Battles urged CCBS member stations to "do Ed a good turn" by covering his side of a dispute within the lamb and wool industry. Quaal encouraged Battles' "outside" interests because both men knew that cultivating such involvement in farm issues would make Battles all the more influential when it came to clear channel matters.[41]

But Battles' familiarity with farmers and their issues was often not enough, especially when equally influential and respected people opposed the CCBS position. Brown, especially, urged farm groups not to toe the CCBS line, citing opportunities that would be given to smaller stations if the clear channels were duplicated. "He is really a thorn in our side," Battles said in 1963. Where for so many years the CCBS was the only group presenting its point of view at national and state farm conventions, now Brown and representatives from the DBA and the Association on Broadcast Standards, Inc., were often in attendance as well. "Opposition to the Clear Channel position from other classes of Broadcasters is becoming more and more difficult to overcome in national agricultural circles," Battles complained in 1962.[42]

Brown especially concentrated on the NFU, whose support of clear channels the Nebraskan knew was tenuous at best. At the group's 1962 convention, he distributed a brochure outlining his case against clear channels. Most of them, Brown pointed out, were located in the East (far from the NFU's Western base), and as a group they devoted only 2 percent of their airtime to farm programming. "A Nebraska farmer tuned to a Clear Channel Station will receive little information on sudden storm warnings, but he can learn that traffic is heavy on Lakeshore Drive in Chicago, or that it's a wonderful evening in Dallas," Brown noted. In 1963, the NFU's resolution in support of retaining the clear channels was replaced by a much less definitive one:

> We urge the Congress and the Federal Communications Commission to reject proposals which would decrease, impair or destroy radio service and to support the adoption of legislation and FCC policies which will safeguard and improve radio service now available to farmers and residents of rural areas.

Battles, meanwhile, worked to make sure that the NFU's vague stance did not evolve back into opposition to the clear channels. In a letter to Patton in early June, he defended the clear channels' farm efforts. "These are the boys, Jim, who for the most part form the backbone of the farm broadcasting business," he wrote. "These are the men who have given you and the Farmers Union a square break for a long time." Clear channel stations,

Battles contended, were being "gored" by FCC policies that were "anything but compatible with rural interests."[43]

Battles then addressed the KRVN issue, calling it "simply another case of a local interest being at variance with the national interest." While he called Brown a "fine and ethical" farm broadcaster, he noted that other interests supporting the breakdown of clear channels were big business "license hucksters" who hoped to secure and then sell the stations created by the duplication of the clear channels. "They make most of our CCBS members look like peanuts," he claimed, "their interests are largely urban." Battles said that these wealthy companies hoped to dupe farmers into believing that their new stations would provide better rural coverage. "It compares with the big lie technique that Hitler perpetuated," Battles noted with no hint of sarcasm. Patton's reply acknowledged the difference of opinion within the NFU, but he said he would try to prevent anyone from coming out against the CCBS.[44]

Battles also attempted to neutralize Brown by writing him a 10-page letter he told Eagan would "either kill or cure" the KRVN owner. The focal point was Brown's brochure; Battles attempted to point out what he believed were inaccuracies and misleading information in it. "May I make some comments about it in an atmosphere of friendship which I hope will pave the way for us to agree on certain facts relating to the mutual problem we both wish to solve?" Battles asked. The CCBS director then critiqued the brochure literally line-by-line, offering with a cordial tone the CCBS position that Brown was no doubt already quite familiar with. Still, Battles' purpose, as he told Eagan, was to make "his attack on us ... less vicious," and so he attempted to present the CCBS arguments in a nonconfrontational way. "Confidentially, Max, what worries me most ... is that I seem to sense an undertone in the brochure of antagonism, hostility or suspicion toward CCBS and other clear channel operators," he wrote. He invited Brown to let him know what, if anything, Battles had done to create this atmosphere "so I can get myself straightened out." Finally, he warned Brown that if he did win the Class II assignment on 880 kHz, he would eventually find that his station provided little usable skywave service at night because the FCC would inevitably duplicate the frequency with more stations after it had duplicated it once. "[Y]ou will [then] be fighting duplication shoulder to shoulder with the clear channel group," he predicted. Battles closed the letter by offering to meet with Brown and an engineer to discuss the clear channel issue. "Once we get our facts clear," Battles wrote, "I believe our differences to some degree will evaporate." There is no record of a reply from Brown.[45]

Since the CCBS was unable to get Congress to pass a more forceful directive to the FCC during the one-year delay in implementing Docket 6741, the FCC began processing applications for new stations in 1963. The NFU continued to help Brown in his efforts to secure a new license on 880 kHz by writing letters of support to the FCC. In October 1967, the FCC awarded KRVN a license to broadcast with 50,000 watts full-time on 880 kHz. Brown thanked Patton and National Secretary Tony DeChant for their help. "This has been a long, expensive, difficult project," Brown wrote. "However, if we had not had help from you and your organization, as well as many others, we could not have won."[46]

Other farm organizations such as the American Farm Bureau Federation and National Grange continued to support the CCBS throughout the 1960s, but the decline of farm programming on clear channel stations became more noticeable. In a 1966 letter to the CCBS's law firm, Battles chronicled the recent changes: several clear channel stations had dropped farm programming completely, while others had curtailed it significantly or moved it to less desirable hours of the broadcast day. Some stations, such as Chicago's WGN, Salt Lake City's KSL and Minneapolis's WCCO maintained farm coverage, but they were in the minority. "Without getting into the merits or demerits of the above trends, the question comes up very clearly," Battles noted. "How long can we expect enthusiastic agricultural support for CCBS positions in this climate?"[47]

This point was not lost on CCBS opponents, who had always called clear channel farm programming marginal at best. The most scathing assessment of the relationship between the CCBS and farm organizations was offered in 1948 by Richard B. Hull, who, in addition to running WOI, was also president of the National Association of Educational Broadcasters. He testified at the Johnson

Bill hearings that the clear channels' emphasis on farm groups was "more a matter of interest than concern":

> This ardent courtship over a period of years, directed at the American Farm Bureau Federation, the National Grange, and scores of colleges and agriculture groups has resulted in many weddings. Too often, I think, the record will show the unions were barren and the spouse unfaithful. Obviously, the clear channel group's interest in the farmer as a farmer is secondary to their interest in him as part of an advertising market.

Similarly, a DBA representative wrote a letter to FCC Chairman Newton H. Minow in 1962 in which he discussed WGN's efforts to promote its new Trafficopter. "Who in Wisconsin, Indiana, or Michigan cares about a traffic jam on the Outer Drive?" he asked.[48]

Still, upon Battles departure from the group in 1968, he could boast that the major farm organizations had for the most part fallen in line behind the clear channel cause. However, their support was certainly not strident, and an increasing number of clear channel stations were at best indifferent to farm programming. Nonetheless, Battles still believed that farm groups were key to preserving those clear channels that remained, and that strong farm programming represented the best defense against duplication. He urged individual clear channel farm directors to keep farm groups up-to-date on the clear channel issue, especially since clear channel opponents were "forever planting 'electronic and economic lies' in the hands [*sic*] of our friends." Battles noted that the CCBS must "reassure them with facts. ... Even a romance, you see, needs cultivation."[49]

The CCBS continued to operate on a less formal basis following Battles' departure and the closing of the group's Washington, D.C., office in 1968. When the FCC revisited the clear channel issue in 1975, the CCBS urged preserving the remaining 12 clear channels, and DeChant, who by this time had taken over leadership of the NFU, obliged when the CCBS asked for a letter of support to the FCC. By now, the NFU readily agreed to support those clear channel stations providing farm coverage. "The Farmers Union strongly supports the concept of clear channel broadcasting,"

DeChant's letter began. "Although we see areas for improvement by the clear channel stations, we feel this kind of broadcasting provides an important service to rural America." DeChant cited the farm work of stations such as WGN:

> There are other fine examples we could cite, but we also want to point out that there are clear channel stations which provide only minimal farm news coverage, in spite of the fact that they reach millions of listeners at nighttime in the rural areas of the country. … Indeed, one can assume at times that the signals from these stations at nighttime are intended strictly for truckers and teenagers.

DeChant wrote similar letters of support for WHO in Des Moines and WCCO in Minneapolis.[50]

CCBS interest in farm groups waned, but it continued to pursue alliances with other groups it perceived as having a stake in the clear channel issue. During the 1970s, for instance, the CCBS attempted to rally trucking organizations in support of clear channels, noting long-distance truckers' need for reliable radio service while driving the interstate highway system. These efforts, however, never approached in scope or result the CCBS's relationship with farm groups during the 1940s, 1950s and early 1960s.

CONCLUSION

Through their relationships with various farm groups, the CCBS and other broadcasting groups sought to strengthen support for their positions in the policy-making process. Farm groups such as the AFBF and NFU, of course, were particularly influential in the political process. By rallying the support of these groups, commercial broadcasters sought to demonstrate grassroots support for their policy positions.

Examining the CCBS's attempts to engage farm groups in the process reveals that maintaining the support of these groups was a continuing—and ever-changing—process. Just as the CCBS continually faced shifting beliefs among FCC commissioners and members of Congress, it also had to react to changes among state and national farm group leaders. Initially, the CCBS faced little opposition in winning the favor of farm groups, and only the NFU—

whose disdain for clear channels was rooted in the group's radical anti-monopoly beliefs—remained recalcitrant. However, as smaller farm broadcasters such as WOI and WRFD came into conflict with the clear channels and as opposition groups such as the DBA began to turn their attention to farm groups, it was increasingly difficult for the CCBS to preserve support for its positions. Nonetheless, through its efforts to become involved in other issues facing farmers and to portray clear channels as crucial to providing rural service, the CCBS was able—at least until the mid-1960s—to maintain at least some measure of farm group support. Although it was a strained relationship at times, CCBS leaders believed that the support offered by farm groups during the heated debates on clear channels prevented further erosion of clear channel broadcasting. "We couldn't have gotten anywhere without the farmers," Quaal later said.[51]

More broadly, the involvement of farm groups in the clear channel debate illustrated the manner in which interests that did not have direct commercial interest in broadcasting were assimilated into the commercial structure. Commercial groups, such as the CCBS and the networks, controlled the terms of policy debate, and groups without commercial standing—such as farm groups—essentially had to choose one or more commercial positions to support. By not bowing to one of the commercially endorsed positions, groups such as the NFU in the 1940s found that their arguments were in vain. Noncommercial groups and groups without direct commercial interest in broadcasting could become materially involved in policy-making discussion only by adopting the positions of one or more commercial interest groups.

NOTES

1. Herb Plambeck to Victor Ray, December 16, 1969, News Media, Box 14, Series III, National Farmers Union Archives, University of Colorado at Boulder Library (hereafter referred to as NFU Archives).

2. See George C. Biggar, "Renewed Interest Shown by Radio in Rural Market," *Broadcasting*, August 1, 1938, 22; Department of Commerce, *Minutes of Open Meeting of Department of Commerce Conference on Radio Telephony*, February 27 and 28, 1922, FCC Library, Washington, D.C., 20; and Reynold M. Wik, "The Radio in

Rural America During the 1920s," *Agricultural History* 55 (October 1981): 340–42.

3. See Z.R. Pettet, "Marked Increase in Radios on Farms is Shown in Survey by Census Bureau," *Broadcasting*, August 1, 1938, 22; Anthony Badger, *The New Deal: The Depression Years, 1933–1940* (New York: Noonday Press, 1989), 147, 179–80; "Retail Radio Sales in the United States, 1922–1944," *Broadcasting Yearbook, 1945*, 50; "Caldwell Reports Record High in Radio Homes, Despite War," *Broadcasting*, January 3, 1944, 10; and "More Radio Homes Despite War—NAB," *Broadcasting*, January 1, 1945, 65.

4. See Katherine Jellison, *Entitled to Power: Farm Women and Technology, 1913–1963* (Chapel Hill: University of North Carolina Press, 1993), 55, 60; and WLW Radio News, "Buy-Way of the Nation," Spring 1947, Box 31, Howard E. Babcock Papers, Kroch Library, Cornell University, Ithaca, N.Y. (hereafter referred to as HEB Papers).

5. See John C. Baker, *Farm Broadcasting: The First Sixty Years* (Ames: Iowa State University Press, 1981), 128, 216; WLW, "Farming Is Serious Business," n.d., Box 31, HEB Papers; WLW, "A Partial List of Guests Who Have Appeared on WLW Farm Programs During the Past 18 Months," June 25, 1947, Box 31, HEB Papers; and Roy Battles and John Butler to James Shouse, n.d., Box 31, HEB Papers.

6. John Baker to Rosel Hyde, January 29, 1946, Volume 38, Docket 6741, Docketed Case Files, RG 173, National Archives, College Park, Md. (hereafter referred to as NACP).

7. See Calvin L. Beale, "Nonfarm Rural America," in Senate Committee on Agriculture, Nutrition and Forestry, *Farm Structure: A Historical Perspective on Changes in the Number and Size of Farms*, 96th Cong., 2d Sess., Washington, D.C., 1980, 37; Richard Hofstadter, *The Age of Reform* (New York: Vintage Books, 1955), 24; John Mark Hansen, *Gaining Access: Congress and the Farm Lobby, 1919–1981* (Chicago: University of Chicago Press, 1991), 31, 94, 108; and Grant McConnell, *The Decline of Agrarian Democracy* (Berkeley: University of California Press, 1953), 58.

8. See Christiana McFayden Campbell, *The Farm Bureau and the New Deal: A Study of the Making of National Farm Policy, 1933–40* (Urbana: University of Illinois Press, 1962), 3, 4, 12, 27, 169; Samuel R. Berger, *Dollar Harvest: The Story of the Farm Bureau* (Lexington,

Mass.: Heath Lexington Books, 1971), 102, 106, 133; Hofstadter, *The Age of Reform*, 123; and John A. Crampton, *The National Farmers Union: Ideology of a Pressure Group* (Lincoln: University of Nebraska Press, 1965), xi, 4, 13.

9. See Fred Brenckman to James Lawrence Fly, March 27, 1940, 194-2 Clear Channels, General Correspondence, 1927–1946, RG 173, NACP; AFBF, *1930 Resolutions*, American Farm Bureau Federation, Chicago, Illinois (hereafter referred to as AFBF Archives); Edward A. ONeal to James Lawrence Fly, March 22, 1940, 194-1 Clear Channels, General Correspondence, 1927–1946, RG 173, NACP.

10. Victor A. Sholis to CCBS Members, April 9, 1941, Box P-1130, Clear Channel Group Records, Wiley, Rein and Fielding, Washington, D.C. (hereafter referred to as WRF).

11. See Victor A. Sholis to CCBS Members, June 18, 1941, Box P-1130, WRF; Fred Brenckman to James Lawrence Fly; Earl C. Smith to James Lawrence Fly, March 27, 1941, 194-2 Clear Channels, General Correspondence, 1927–1946, RG 173, NACP; and AFBF, *1941 Resolutions*, AFBF Archives.

12. NFU, Press Release, December 2, 1944, September-December 1944, Box 1, Series VII, NFU Archives.

13. See AFBF, *1944 Resolutions*, AFBF Archives; and AFBF, *1945 Resolutions*, AFBF Archives.

14. See Victor A. Sholis to CCBS Members, February 23, 1946, Box P-1130, WRF; and Transcript, 198–312, Volume 16, Docket 6741, Docketed Case Files, RG 173, NACP.

15. Russell Smith, Statement on Docket 6741, January 14, 1946, Press Releases March–May 1948, Box 1, Series VII, NFU Archives.

16. Smith, Statement on Docket 6741.

17. Transcript, Docket 6741, 199, 257.

18. See Jack Levy, "Clear Channel Decision Seen by Fall," *Broadcasting*, April 22, 1946, 18; and Transcript, 911, Docket 6741.

19. "Ohio Farm Bureau Gets Green Light for Radio Station," *American Farm Bureau Federation Official News Letter*, June 25, 1947, 2.

20. See AFBF, *1946 Resolutions*, AFBF Archives; and AFBF, Minutes, Board of Directors Meeting, June 16–19, 1947, AFBF Archives.

21. See Senate Interstate and Foreign Commerce Committee, *To*

Limit the Power of Radio Broadcast Stations, 80th Cong., 2d Sess. (Washington, D.C., 1948), 303; AFBF, Minutes, September 28, 1948, AFBF Archives; and John Lacey to Board of Directors, September 27, 1948, AFBF Archives.

22. Lacey to Board.

23. See Louis Caldwell and R. Russell Eagan to CCBS Members, October 28, 1948, Box P-1130, WRF; and AFBF, Minutes, December 17, 1948, AFBF Archives.

24. R. Russell Eagan to CCBS, November 8, 1948, Box P-1130, WRF.

25. See CCBS *Farm Paper Service*, "Have Rural Radio Listeners Any Rights?" n.d., Box P-1146, WRF; Hollis Seavey to CCBS, January 7, 1959, Box 3403, WRF; Hollis Seavey to CCBS, March 31, 1959, Box 3403, WRF; Baker, *Farm Broadcasting*, 37; and Ward Quaal, telephone conversation with author, January 5, 1994.

26. See Various CCBS *Farm Paper Service* Reports, n.d., Box P-1146, WRF.

27. See Hollis Seavey, taped interview by Layne R. Beaty, October 28, 1986, Broadcast Pioneers Library, Washington, D.C.; Hollis Seavey, telephone conversation with author, May 12, 1994; Hollis Seavey to CCBS Members, December 12, 1956, Box P-1146, WRF; Roger W. Fleming to John Doerfer, August 12, 1958, Volume 4, Docket 6741, Docketed Case Files, RG 173, NACP; and AFBF, Minutes, Board of Directors Meeting, June 27–29, 1951, AFBF Archives.

28. See AFBF, *Resolutions*, 1950, 1951, 1953, 1955–1958, AFBF Archives.

29. Hollis Seavey to Jay W. Wright, December 16, 1958, Box P-1146, WRF.

30. Ward Quaal to Charles Shuman, September 15, 1960, Box P-1146, WRF.

31. See Gayle Gupton to John McDonald, September 7, 1960, Box P-1146, WRF; Ward Quaal to Tom Hitch, September 16, 1960, Box P-1146, WRF; and AFBF, *1960 Resolutions*, AFBF Archives.

32. Smith, Statement on Docket 6741.

33. James G. Patton, Testimony on S. 2231, April 14, 1948, Press Releases March–May 1948, Box 1, Series VII, NFU Archives.

34. Patton, Testimony on S. 2231.

35. Patton, Testimony on S. 2231.

36. See Roy Battles, telephone conversation with author, January 5, 1994; and Ward Quaal, telephone conversation with author, January 5, 1994.

37. See NFU, 1962 Convention, Series V, Box 6, NFU Archives; and Roy Battles to R. Russell Eagan, April 5, 1962, Box P-1146, WRF.

38. See Max Brown to Tony DeChant, September 6, 1967, Series III, Box 4, NFU Archives; and FCC, *In the Matter of Clear Channel Broadcasting in the Standard Broadcast Band*, 31 FCC 565, 604 (1961).

39. See House Committee on Interstate and Foreign Commerce, *Clear Channel Broadcasting Stations*, 87th Cong., 2d Sess. (Washington, D.C., 1962), 138, 144, 152; and WLS Advertisement, Chicago *Sun-Times*, April 1, 1954, 49.

40. See Ward Quaal to Roy Battles, October 12, 1962, Box P-1146, WRF; National Apple Institute, *Press Release*, April 25, 1962, Box P-1146, WRF; and James Moore to Roy Battles, July 6, 1962, Box P-1146, WRF.

41. See Roy Battles to James Moore, May 21, 1963, Box P-1146, WRF; Roy Battles to Ed Marsh, January 3, 1962, Box P-1146, WRF; and Roy Battles to CCBS Farm Directors, August 27, 1962, Box P-1146, WRF.

42. See Roy Battles to R. Russell Eagan, March 26, 1963, Box P-1145, WRF; CCBS, Bulletin No. 83, October 4, 1964, Box 3403, WRF; Roy Battles to CCBS, May 16, 1963, Box 3403, WRF; CCBS, Bulletin No. 45, December 10, 1962, Box 3403, WRF.

43. See NFU, 1963 Convention, Series V, Box 6, NFU Archives; Roy Battles to Murray Cox, et al., October 15, 1964, Box P-1146, WRF; and Roy Battles to James Patton, June 12, 1964, Yearly Files 1965, Box I, Series III, NFU Archives.

44. See Roy Battles to James Patton, June 12, 1964; and Roy Battles to Murray Cox, Bob Etheredge and Bill McReynolds, June 15, 1964, Box P-1146, WRF.

45. Roy Battles to Max Brown, March 26, 1963, Box P-1145, WRF.

46. Max Brown to Tony DeChant, October 18, 1967, News Media, Box 6, Series III, NFU Archives.

47. Roy Battles to R. Russell Eagan, March 3, 1966, Box P-1127, WRF.

48. See Senate, *To Limit*, 918; and David Potter to Newton H.

Minow, September 27, 1962, Volume 88, Docket 6741, Docketed Case Files, RG 173, NACP.

49. Roy Battles to Robert H. Harter, July 30, 1968, Box P-1146, WRF.

50. Tony DeChant to Richard Wiley, August 17, 1976, News Media, Box 34, Series III, NFU Archives.

51. Ward Quaal, telephone conversation with author, January 5, 1994.

CHAPTER EIGHT

Conclusion

Jack DeWitt, the longtime CCBS engineer, often remarked that the history of the clear channel allocation was like the history of the universe. Both began in chaos, he said, and both would end in chaos. The debate over clear channels, which began in the late 1920s, ultimately dragged on for more than a half century. It was, as demonstrated by this book, a high-stakes conflict marked by contentious disputes, political maneuvering, competition for public and congressional opinion and, of course, numerous delays. The battle, at least for the first 25 years, also could have substantially altered the entire system of broadcast allocation in the United States.[1]

Ironically, for all its potential to radically redefine the broadcast band, the clear channel debate ultimately did not do so. Since the FCC essentially preserved the sanctity of each clear channel station's usable service area (roughly 700 to 750 miles) while maintaining the existing 50,000-watt power limit, both the 1961 and 1980 decisions effectively upheld the status quo. Of course, they did allow the commission to add a number of new stations to the broadcast band, but these outlets made little contribution to the White Area service inadequacy. The FCC, in fact, later admitted that the stations added by Docket 6741 did nothing more than "nibble at the fringes of the problem of inadequate nighttime standard broadcast service." After hundreds of hours of testimony, thousands of pages of exhibits and countless technical studies, the clear channels in 1980 looked pretty much as they did in 1928. Not surprisingly, unless one considers the coverage of FM, broadcast television and cable, the White Area still looks much the same today as it did in 1945.[2]

The importance of this book, however, does not lie in passing judgment on the decisions made by the FCC in the clear channel debate nor in arguing that more radical options (i.e., approving superpower) should have been implemented. Rather, this book demonstrates that the true significance of the clear channel debate is gleaned from examining *how* the debate was conducted. Specifically, the book shows that the formation and activities of commercial interest groups substantially limited the scope of the debate over clear channels and in so doing restricted the options available for resolving the dispute. In that regard, various factions of the commercial industry not only competitively pursued goals that would be financially favorable to them but in a larger sense served to affirm and further validate the commercial system of broadcasting.

Two developments were precursors to the emergence of the pluralist commercial broadcasting industry in the pre–World War II years. The first of these was the Federal Radio Commission's 1928 allocation, which was based not on a considered plan to provide efficient radio service but on a desire to accommodate existing commercial stations with a minimum of "disruption." Thus, the allocation plan was decidedly tenuous, and it caused conflict among stations from nearly the moment of its implementation. Incessant hearings, necessitated by claims of interference or by competing applications under the commission's 90-day license renewals, forced broadcast stations to retain legal help and made radio law a lucrative undertaking for Washington, D.C., attorneys. "The lawyer plays as important a role in making radio broadcasting possible as the engineer or the announcer," noted an NBC lawyer in 1930. The allocation's tripartite setup, which granted individual stations power, frequency and operating hours based upon class, inevitably placed groups of stations in conflict with one another as well, leading to the formation of specialized interest groups combining legal, technical and public relations functions.[3]

The second development was the rather complete victory of the commercial broadcasting industry over noncommercial entities. Commercial interests, through the networks and the National Association of Broadcasters, presented a unified front during the late 1920s and early 1930s, arguing that American broadcasting was best left to for-profit enterprises, indeed that doing so was the only possible democratic option. Robert McChesney noted that the commercial industry "concurrently sought to establish monopoly control over the ether, eliminate any organized opposition to their modus operandi, and consolidate the industry economically, legislatively, and ideologically." The affirmation of this belief by the government in the Communications Act of 1934 essentially placed the commercial status of U.S. radio beyond challenge. Comfortably in the driver's seat, then, the commercial industry began to splinter into individual interests. "Hence the First Amendment was appropriated as trade legislation and brandished to remove the last vestiges of public control of the airwaves," McChesney noted.[4]

Thus, by 1936 commercial broadcasting was firmly entrenched, yet the industry itself was no longer united toward a common cause. As it was now clear that those arguing against the commercial broadcasting structure would play at best a gadfly role, disputes could be decided amongst the various factions of the commercial industry. The clear channel debate was the first and longest-running of these disputes, and it was originated, argued and resolved in a forum that commercial interests firmly controlled. Thus, the commission's vow to consider "social, political and economic effects" beginning with the 1936 allocation hearings was largely a smokescreen. Certainly, social, political and economic effects were discussed in the clear channel debate, but only as far as they did not conflict with the commercial structure itself. Issues impinging upon "givens" of the commercial structure, such as relocation of stations, broad programming issues, listener perceptions of advertising and alternatives to the network system, were never seriously a part of the dialogue. To be sure, industry factions pursued such discussions as far as they could use them to denigrate their opposition but united against calls to make comprehensive changes. Thus, the industry opposed broad stroke considerations of programming and was against any moves that would generalize the clear channel inquiry into an examination of the commercial system.

The role of parties without direct commercial interest in the policy debate was marginal at best. Commissioner T.A.M. Craven's gruff dismissal of educational and noncommercial groups during the 1936 allocation hearings was indicative of the attitude the commission and the industry would take toward such groups for the remainder of the debate. Nonindustry representatives that wished to have their views seriously considered had to work within the confines of the debate as established by the commercial industry. Thus, the calls of National Farmers Union's representatives for banishing the commercial radio system during the 1940s softened by the 1960s to merely opposing the portions of the commercial system that seemed not to be working. Similarly, other farm groups were assimilated into the debate through the efforts of commercial groups—chiefly the CCBS—that steered them toward their particular viewpoint. The clear channel debate was a complex engineering matter, the CCBS told farm groups, and thus outsiders should defer to the expertise of the industry. However, when needed, farm groups were rallied to support the CCBS's contention that clear channels were necessary to serve the farm audience. Educational interests were even worse off, their views strictly marginalized because their lack of political power meant they had little value to any of the commercial interests.

The activities of the commercial interest groups—including testifying at hearings, performing technical studies, rallying public support and direct lobbying—all were designed to control the conduct of the policy-making process. Populated largely by engineers, lawyers and political appointees, the FCC lacks appropriate economic and social scientific expertise and is forced to rely on the industry to supply such data. "At its heart," Jeffrey Berry noted, "regulatory lobbying is a process of interest groups bringing their data to policy makers and trying to make these data the information base from which decisions flow." To this end, interest groups usually supply the commission not with raw data but with interpreted data. In this way, the range of the commission's solutions is conveniently circumscribed by the industry.[5]

Similarly, through coalition-building efforts and direct lobbying, interest groups assimilate the public, independent groups and political figures into the policy-making process. In so doing, the groups not only build support for their own policy positions but validate the policy-making process through the use of symbolic representations of public service. The CCBS, for example, was able to elicit the support of farm groups and selected members of Congress by touting its interest in providing service to rural areas. Similarly, opposition groups gained support by portraying the clear channel stations as big-city monopolists, and superpower as the death knell for lesser classes of stations. The options for improving rural service, then, were largely narrowed to two choices: higher power for clear channel stations or duplication of clear channel frequencies. No other choice could be pursued without challenging the commercial structure or its inherent control of the policy-making process.

Thus, by working to strengthen external pressure—from Congress, the public and other interest groups—commercial interests lessen the power of regulatory agencies. A number of scholars, in fact, characterize regulatory commissions such as the FCC as "captured" by the industries they are charged with regulating. "[C]onflict threatens the autonomy of an organization situated amidst a sea of pressures and challenges to its authority," Robert Britt Horwitz noted. "The regulatory agency is in an inherently weak position." Since the FCC has never been given a clear definition of "public interest," Harry M. Shooshan and Erwin G. Krasnow noted, it is particularly vulnerable to pressure from members of Congress who "have little fear of political reprisal." Congressional pressure, usually instigated by a faction of the industry, was continually brought to bear during the clear channel debate, from the 1939 Wheeler Resolution to the 1962 House resolution and the various hearings in between. This pressure undoubtedly played a substantial role in influencing the FCC. Newton H.

Minow noted that "it is easy—very easy—to confuse the voice of one Congressman, or one Congressional committee, with the voice of Congress." And more often than not, this congressional voice is being raised at the behest of one or more factions of the commercial industry. The use of symbols was particularly important to creating and maintaining such external pressures. Of course, clear channels continually stressed their alleged value for defense communications while more often than not smaller stations portrayed themselves as "little guys" in danger of being squashed by the more powerful stations.[6]

It is not surprising that many policy debates, such as the one over clear channels, ultimately end in either incremental changes or the maintenance of the status quo. It is practically impossible to pursue revolutionary solutions not offered by the industry without undermining the policy process itself. Thus, the clear channel debate was in essence a battle first between clear channel stations and regionals, then among clear channel stations, regionals and daytime stations. These groups established the terms of the debate on the issue, appropriating public interest arguments into their own point of view and thus limiting outcomes to either/or decisions. The intense competition among these groups gave the illusion that a wide range of policy alternatives was being considered, when in reality the scope of choices had been substantially narrowed.

The same broad outlines of conduct can be seen in contemporary communications policy debates, although today entire industries are likely to be allied against other industries or potential competitors. The rampant consolidation of the radio industry, made possible under the Telecommunications Act of 1996, has made specialized groups such as the CCBS largely superfluous since, as William Potts pointed out, "everybody owns everything." Today, entire industries are more likely to unite against a common threat, much as the commercial broadcasters did during the early 1930s. As this is being written, for instance, the NAB is uniting against the FCC's plan to authorize so-called "microradio" FM broadcasters of between 10 and 1,000 watts. The NAB says it would "cause devastating interference to existing broadcasters." Such a plan, incidentally, is likely to create the same sort of haves versus have-nots situation caused by the licensing of daytime-only stations in the early days of AM radio. Similarly, we see the broadcasters and the computer industry battling over digital television standards and broadcasters and satellite companies squaring off over signal importation. In all such debates, the public interest is defined by commercial industries, and it can only end up being served as far as it benefits one or more commercial interests. Just as opposing sides did in the clear channel debate, various industries couch their demands in service to the public while systematically assimilating or excluding substantive public participation.[7]

The inherent ineffectiveness of such a policy-making process, purported to be based on overarching principles yet in practice deferring to industry interpretation of those principles, is apparent when considering today's AM band, where an ever-shrinking group of conglomerates is gobbling up all classes of radio stations and making local ownership a dying commodity. In many markets, in fact, a single corporation controls the majority of the radio stations, and local programming is rapidly pushed aside by Dr. Laura, Rush Limbaugh or some other syndicated host. In such a setting, the notion of individual 50,000-watt radio stations as "big voices of the air" seems positively quaint by comparison. The clear channel debate, of course, was an inherent conflict among the goals of providing rural service, preserving local outlets for self-expression and maintaining the largest number of choices for radio listeners. Today, AM broadcasting is a medium that seemingly has achieved none of those goals.

NOTES

1. CCBS, Meeting Minutes, October 5, 1967, Box P-1143, Clear Channel Group Records, Wiley, Rein and Fielding, Washington, D.C. (hereafter referred to as WRF).

2. See FCC, *Clear Channel Broadcasting in the Standard Broadcast Band*, 40 FR 58468 (1975); and FCC, Report and Order, 78 FCC 2d 1345 (1980).

3. "Lawyer Plays Important Part in Radio Broadcasting," *American Bar Association Journal* 16 (June 1930): 347.

4. Robert W. McChesney, *Telecommunications, Mass Media and Democracy* (New York: Oxford University Press, 1994), 5; and Robert

W. McChesney, "Free Speech and Democracy! Louis G. Caldwell, the American Bar Association and the Debate over the Free Speech Implications of Broadcast Regulation, 1928–1938," *The American Journal of Legal History* 35 (October 1991): 385.

5. Jeffrey M. Berry, *The Interest Group Society* (Boston: Little, Brown and Company, 1984), 37.

6. See Robert Britt Horwitz, *The Irony of Regulatory Reform: The Deregulation of American Telecommunications* (New York: Oxford University Press, 1989), 85; and Harry M. Shooshan III and Erwin G. Krasnow, "Congress and the Federal Communications Commission: The Continuing Contest for Power," *Hastings Communication and Entertainment Law Journal* 9 (1987): 620, 631–32.

7. See William Potts, telephone conversation with author, August 17, 1998; and Bill McConnell, "FCC Proposes Microradio Plan," *Broadcasting and Cable*, February 1, 1999, 11.

Bibliography

Arnold, R. Douglas. "Overtilled and Undertilled Fields in American Politics." *Political Science Quarterly* 97 (1982): 91–103.

Babcock, Howard E., Papers. Kroch Library, Cornell University, Ithaca, N.Y.

Badger, Anthony. *The New Deal: The Depression Years, 1933–1940.* New York: Noonday Press, 1989.

Baker, John C. *Farm Broadcasting: The First Sixty Years.* Ames: Iowa State University Press, 1981.

Barnouw, Erik. *The Golden Web: A History of Broadcasting in the United States, Volume II—1933–1953.* New York: Oxford University Press, 1968.

———. *A Tower in Babel: A History of Broadcasting in the United States, Volume I—to 1933.* New York: Oxford University Press, 1968.

———. *The Image Empire: A History of Broadcasting in the United States, Volume III—from 1953.* New York: Oxford University Press, 1970.

Battles, Roy. Interview by Eric F. Brown, June 1972. Broadcast
    Pioneers Library, Washington, D.C.
————. Telephone conversation with author, January 5, 1994.
Benjamin, Louise. "Working It out Together: Radio Policy from
    Hoover to the Radio Act of 1927." *Journal of Broadcasting
    and Electronic Media* 42 (Spring 1998): 221–36.
Berger, Samuel R. *Dollar Harvest: The Story of the Farm Bureau.*
    Lexington, Mass.: Heath Lexington Books, 1971.
Berry, Jeffrey M. *The Interest Group Society.* Boston: Little, Brown
    and Company, 1984.
Braun, Mark J. *AM Stereo and the FCC: Case Study of a Marketplace
    Shibboleth.* Norwood, N.J.: Ablex Publishing Company, 1994.
Brinkley, Alan. *Defining Vision: The Battle for the Future of Televi-
    sion.* New York: Harcourt Brace, 1997.
Brown, Eric F. "Nighttime Radio for the Nation: A History of the
    Clear Channel Proceeding, 1945–1972." Ph.D. Diss., Ohio
    University, 1975.
Caldwell, Louis G. "The Rules and Regulations of the FRC," *The
    Journal of Radio Law* 2 (January 1932): 66–99.
Campbell, Christiana McFayden. *The Farm Bureau and the New
    Deal: A Study of the Making of National Farm Policy, 1933–
    40.* Urbana: University of Illinois Press, 1962.
Cigler, Allan J. and Burdett A. Loomis, eds. *Interest Group Politics.*
    Washington, D.C.: Congressional Quarterly, Inc., 1998.
"Cincinnati Giant on the Air: WLW 20 Years Old This Week."
    Newsweek, April 14, 1941, 66.
Clear Channel Broadcasting Service. *Summary History of Allocation
    in the Standard Broadcast Band.* Washington, D.C.: Press of
    Byron S. Adams, 1948.
————. *Radio for ALL America: The Case for the Clears.* Washing-
    ton, D.C.: Clear Channel Broadcasting Service, 1963.
Clear Channel Broadcasting Service Legal Records. Wiley, Rein and
    Fielding, Washington, D.C.
Clear Channel Group Records. Wiley, Rein and Fielding, Washington,
    D.C.
Cohen, Jeffrey E. *The Politics of Telecommunications Regulation: The
    States and the Divestiture of AT&T.* Armonk, N.Y.: M.E.
    Sharp, 1992.

Coll, Steve. *The Deal of the Century: The Breakup of AT&T.* New
    York: Atheneum, 1986.
Congressional Record. Washington, D.C., 1926–65.
Courier-Journal Company v. Federal Radio Commission, 46 F. 2d. 614
    (1931).
Crampton, John A. *The National Farmers Union: Ideology of a
    Pressure Group.* Lincoln: University of Nebraska Press,
    1965.
"Death of Louis G. Caldwell." *Journal of the Federal Communications
    Bar Association* 12 (Spring 1952): 60–61.
Department of Commerce. *Minutes of Open Meeting of Department of
    Commerce Conference on Radio Telephony,* February 27 and
    28, 1922. FCC Library, Washington, D.C.
———. *Radio Service Bulletin,* 1922–26.
———. *Recommendations for Regulation of Radio.* Washington,
    D.C., 1924.
———. *Proceedings and Recommendations for Regulation of Radio.*
    Washington, D.C., 1925.
DeWitt, John H. Telephone conversation with author, August 8, 1993.
———. Telephone conversation with author, May 27, 1994.
Diehl, William Jr. "Crosley's Clear Channel Colossus." *Cincinnati,*
    March 1968, 26–33, 63.
Ditingo, Vincent M. *The Remaking of Radio.* Boston: Focal Press,
    1995.
Douglas, Susan J. *Inventing American Broadcasting, 1899–1922.*
    Baltimore: Johns Hopkins University Press, 1987.
Edelman, Murray. *The Licensing of Radio Services in the United
    States, 1927 to 1947.* Urbana: University of Illinois Press,
    1950.
Emery, Walter. *Broadcasting and Government.* East Lansing: Michi-
    gan State University Press, 1969.
Federal Communications Commission v. National Broadcasting
    Company, 319 U.S. 239 (1943).
Federal Communications Commission. *Annual Report,* Washington,
    D.C., 1935–65.
———. *Decision and Order on Petition for Rehearing,* 6 FCC 805
    (1939).

————. *In the Matter of the Application of the Crosley Corporation*, 6 FCC 798 (1939).

————. *In the Matter of Matheson Radio Company*, 8 FCC 397 (1940).

————. *Report on Chain Broadcasting*. Washington, D.C., 1941.

————. *In the Matter of Crosley Corporation*, 9 FCC 202 (1942).

————. *In Re Applications of Matheson Radio Company, Inc. and WJW, Inc.*, 10 FCC 128 (1943).

————. *In the Matter of Clear Channel Broadcasting in the Standard Broadcast Band*, 12 FCC 587 (1947).

————. *In the Matter of Petition of Clear Channel Group*, 11 FCC 842 (1947).

————. *Daytime Skywave Transmissions*, 22 FR 10497 (1957).

————. Further Notice of Proposed Rule Making, 23 FR 2612 (1958).

————. *Clear Channel Broadcasting in the Standard Broadcast Band*, 24 FR 7737 (1959).

————. *Daytime Skywave Transmissions*, 24 FR 7755 (1959).

————. *In the Matter of Clear Channel Broadcasting in the Standard Broadcast Band*, 31 FCC 565 (1961).

————. Report and Order, 78 FCC 2d 1345 (1980).

FCC Engineering Department. *Report on Social and Economic Data Pursuant to the Informal Hearing on Broadcasting, Docket 4062, Beginning October 5, 1936*. Washington, D.C., 1938.

Federal Radio Commission. *Annual Report*, Washington, D.C., 1927–34.

Federal Regulation of Radio Broadcasting. 35 Op. Atty. Gen. 126 (1926).

The First 50 Years of Broadcasting. Washington, D.C.: Broadcasting Publications, Inc., 1982.

Flannery, Gerald V., ed. *Commissioners of the FCC, 1927–1994*. Lanham, Md.: University Press of America, 1995.

Fleming, Roger W. Telephone conversation with author, May 31, 1994.

Foust, James C. "A History of the Clear Channel Broadcasting Service, 1934–1980." Ph.D. Diss., Ohio University, 1994.

————. "Technology Versus Monopoly: The Clear Channel Group and the Clear Channel Debate, 1934–1941." *Journal of Radio Studies* 4 (1997): 218–29.

Friedrich, Carl J. and Evelyn Sternberg. "Congress and the Control of

Radio Broadcasting, Part I." *The American Political Science Review* 37 (October 1943): 810–19.

General Electric Company v. Federal Radio Commission, 31 F. 2d. 630 (1929).

Godfried, Nathan. *WCFL: Chicago's Voice of Labor, 1926–78.* Urbana: University of Illinois Press, 1997.

Goodwill Stations v. FCC, 325 F. 2d 637 (1963).

Hansen, John Mark. *Gaining Access: Congress and the Farm Lobby, 1919–1981.* Chicago: University of Chicago Press, 1991.

"Heading for Radio Investigation." *Business Week*, August 21, 1937, 17.

High, Stanley. "Not-So-Free-Air." *Saturday Evening Post*, February 11, 1939, 73–77.

Hofstadter, Richard. *The Age of Reform.* New York: Vintage Books, 1955.

Home Box Office v. FCC, 567 F. 2d. 9 (1977).

Hoover v. Intercity Radio Company, 286 F. 1003 (1923).

Horwitz, Robert Britt. *The Irony of Regulatory Reform: The Deregulation of American Telecommunications.* New York: Oxford University Press, 1989.

Jansky, C.M. Jr. "The Contribution of Herbert Hoover to Broadcasting." *Journal of Broadcasting* 1 (Summer 1957): 241–49.

Jellison, Katherine. *Entitled to Power: Farm Women and Technology, 1913–1963.* Chapel Hill: University of North Carolina Press, 1993.

Kang, Joon-Mann. "Franklin D. Roosevelt and James L. Fly: The Politics of Broadcast Regulation, 1941–1944." *Journal of American Culture* 10 (1987): 23–33.

Krasnow, Erwin G., Lawrence D. Longley and Herbert A. Terry, *The Politics of Broadcast Regulation* (Third Edition). New York: St. Martin's Press, 1982.

"Largest Radio Transmitter on Air." *Literary Digest*, April 28, 1934, 18.

"Lawyer Plays Important Part in Radio Broadcasting." *American Bar Association Journal* 16 (June 1930): 347–48.

Le Duc, Don R. *Beyond Broadcasting: Patterns in Policy and Law.* New York: Longman, 1987.

Lichty, Lawrence W. "The Impact of FRC and FCC Commissioners'

Backgrounds on the Regulation of Broadcasting." *Journal of Broadcasting* 6 (Winter 1961–62): 97–110.

———. "The Nation's Station: A History of Station WLW." Ph.D. Diss., Ohio State University, 1964.

Mackey, David R. "The Development of the National Association of Broadcasters." *Journal of Broadcasting* 1 (Fall 1957): 305–25.

Mander, Mary S. "The Public Debate About Broadcasting in the Twenties: An Interpretive History." *Journal of Broadcasting*, 28 (Spring 1984): 167–85.

McChesney, Robert W. "Free Speech and Democracy! Louis G. Caldwell, the American Bar Association and the Debate over the Free Speech Implications of Broadcast Regulation, 1928–1938." *The American Journal of Legal History* 35 (October 1991): 351–92.

———. *Telecommunications, Mass Media and Democracy.* New York: Oxford University Press, 1994.

McConnell, Grant. *The Decline of Agrarian Democracy.* Berkeley: University of California Press, 1953.

"Name Battles to Head Clear Channel Fight." Chicago *Tribune*, October 24, 1961.

National Farmers Union Archives. University of Colorado at Boulder Library.

National Grange of the Patrons of Husbandry Records. Kroch Library, Cornell University, Ithaca, N.Y.

NBC v. FCC, 132 F. 2d. 545 (D.C. Cir., 1942).

Nord, David Paul. "The FCC, Educational Broadcasting, and Political Interest Group Activity." *Journal of Broadcasting* 22 (Summer 1978): 321–38.

Ornoff, Michael E. "Ex Parte Communication in Informal Rulemaking: Judicial Intervention in Administrative Procedures." *University of Richmond Law Review* 15 (1980): 73–101.

Potts, William. Telephone conversation with author, May 24, 1994.

———. Telephone conversation with author, June 1, 1994.

———. Telephone conversation with author, August 17, 1998.

"QRX." *Time*, May 23, 1938, 25.

Quaal, Ward. Telephone conversation with author, January 5, 1994.

————. Telephone conversation with author, April 27, 1994.

————. Telephone conversation with author, May 5, 1994.

————. Telephone conversation with author, May 12, 1994.

————. Telephone conversation with author, November 12, 1998.

Radio Act of 1912. Public Law No. 264, 62nd Cong., August 13, 1912.

Radio Communications—Issuance of Licenses. 29 Op. Atty. Gen. 579 (1912).

"Radio Waves Played Tricks in WLW Super-Power Days." Cincinnati *Enquirer,* August 22, 1948.

Ray, William B. *FCC: The Ups and Downs of Radio-TV Regulation.* Ames: Iowa State University Press, 1990.

Records of the American Farm Bureau Federation. American Farm Bureau Federation, Park Ridge, Ill.

Records of the Board of War Communications. RG 259, National Archives, College Park, Md.

Records of the Federal Communications Commission. RG 173, National Archives, College Park, Md.

Rinks, Jerry Wayne. "We Shield Millions: A History of WSM, 1925–1950." Ph.D. Diss., University of Tennessee, Knoxville, 1993.

Robbins, William B., Papers. Cincinnati Historical Society, Cincinnati, Ohio.

Rogers, George Harry. "The History of the Clear Channel and Super Power Controversy in the Management of the Standard Broadcast Allocation Plan." Ph.D. Diss., University of Utah, 1972.

Saltzman v. Stromberg-Carlson Telephone Manufacturing Company, 46 F. 2d. 612 (1931).

Sangamon Valley Television Corporation v. FCC, 269 F. 2d 221 (1959).

Sarno, Edward F. Jr. "The National Radio Conferences." *Journal of Broadcasting* 13 (Spring 1969): 189–202.

"Scandal in the Air." *The Nation,* April 27, 1937, 455.

Schuman, Charles. Telephone conversation with author, May 31, 1994.

Seavey, Hollis M. Interview with Layne R. Beaty, October 28, 1986, Broadcast Pioneers Library, Washington, D.C.

————. Telephone conversation with author, May 12, 1994.

Shooshan III, Harry M. and Erwin G. Krasnow. "Congress and the Federal Communications Commission: The Continuing

Contest for Power." *Hastings Communication and Entertainment Law Journal* 9 (1987): 619–33.

Smead, Elmer E. *Freedom of Speech by Radio and Television.* Washington, D.C.: Public Affairs Press, 1959.

Smulyan, Jeffrey. "Power to Some People: The FCC's Clear Channel Allocation Policy." *Southern California Law Review* 44 (1971): 811–47.

"Starts FCC Cleanup." *Business Week*, October 23, 1937, 53.

Sterling, Christopher H. *Electronic Media: A Guide to Trends in Broadcasting and Newer Technologies, 1920–1983.* New York: Praeger, 1984.

Sterling, Christopher H. and John M. Kittross. *Stay Tuned: A Concise History of American Broadcasting.* Belmont, Calif.: Wadsworth Publishing Company, 1990.

Stone, Alan. *Wrong Number: The Breakup of AT&T.* New York: Basic Books, 1989.

"That Radio Channel Plan Is Here." *Business Week*, January 13, 1937, 38.

Tunstall, Jeremy. *Communications Deregulation: The Unleashing of America's Communications Industry.* New York: Basil Blackwell, 1986.

Udelson, Joseph H. *The Great Television Race: A History of the American Television Industry, 1925–1941.* Tuscaloosa: University of Alabama Press, 1982.

United States v. Zenith Radio Corporation, 12 F. 2d 614 (1926).

U.S. Congress. House. Committee on Interstate and Foreign Commerce, *Regulation of Broadcasting: Half a Century of Government Regulation of Broadcasting and the Need for Further Legislative Action.* 85th Cong., 1st Sess., Washington, D.C., 1958.

———. House. Committee on Interstate and Foreign Commerce. *Clear Channel Broadcasting Stations.* 87th Cong., 2d Sess. Washington, D.C., 1962.

———. House. Committee on Interstate Commerce. *Proposed Changes in the Communications Act of 1934 (HR-5497).* 77th Cong., 2d Sess., Washington, D.C., 1942.

———. Senate. Committee on Agriculture, Nutrition and Forestry. *Farm Structure: A Historical Perspective on Changes in the*

Number and Size of Farms. 96th Cong., 2d Sess., Washington, D.C., 1980.

———. Senate. Committee on Interstate and Foreign Commerce. *To Limit the Power of Radio Broadcast Stations*. 80th Cong., 2d Sess., Washington, D.C., 1948.

———. Senate. Committee on Interstate and Foreign Commerce. *Hearings on S. 1973*. 81st Cong., 1st Sess., Washington, D.C., 1949.

———. Senate. Committee on Interstate Commerce. *Radio Control: Hearings on S. 1 and S. 1754*. 69th Cong., 1st Sess., Washington, D.C., 1926.

———. Senate. Committee on Interstate Commerce. *Hearings on S. Res. 113*. 77th Cong., 1st Sess., Washington, D.C., 1941.

———. Senate. Committee on Small Business. *Daytime Radio Broadcasting—1957*. 85th Cong., 1st Sess., Washington, D.C., 1957.

———. Senate. Select Committee on Small Business. *Daytime Radio Stations*. Senate Report No. 1168, 85th Cong., 1st Sess., Washington, D.C., 1957.

Westinghouse Electric and Manufacturing Company v. FRC, 47 F. 2d. 415 (1931).

Wheeler, Burton K. "The Shocking Truth About Radio." *The Progressive*, November 6, 1944, 1, 10.

White, Llewellyn. *The American Radio: A Report on the Broadcasting Industry in the United States from the Commission on Freedom of the Press*. Chicago: University of Chicago Press, 1947; repr., New York: Arno Press, 1977.

Wik, Reynold M. "The Radio in Rural America During the 1920s." *Agricultural History* 55 (October 1981): 339–50.

"WLW Power Cut 90%." *Business Week*, February 18, 1939, 32.

Wolpe, Bruce C. *Lobbying Congress: How the System Works*. Washington, D.C.: Congressional Quarterly, Inc., 1990.

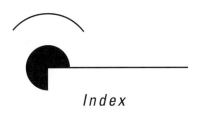

Index

ABC
  and Docket 6741 hearings, 117
  farm programming curtailed by,
    208–209
  and Johnson Bill, 135
  reaction of, to Docket 6741
    reconsideration, 162, 163
  and Twenty-Station Plan, 126, 127,
    138
ABS. *See* Association for Broadcast
  Standards
Administrative Procedure Act, 97
Advertising, 26–27, 59–60, 189
AFBF. *See* American Farm Bureau Fed-
  eration
Agrarian myth, 191
Agriculture U.S.A., 201
Air Force, 168–169
AIRS. *See* Associated Independent
  Radio Stations
Alexanderson transmitter, 15
Allen, Edward A., 57
Allis-Chalmers, 190
Allocation. *See also* Superpower

clear channel formation plan, 29, 31
  and early regulation, 14
  FCC analysis of data on, 60–63
  1936 hearings on, 52–60
American Bar Association
  Standing Committee on Radio Law of,
    48
American Civil Liberties Union, 58, 67
American Farm Bureau Federation, 9,
    132, 187, 191, 192, 195, 198, 199,
    200, 202–203, 206, 212, 213, 214
American Radio, The (White), 8
American Society of Composers,
  Authors and Publishers, 52
American Telephone and Telegraph
  (AT&T), 7, 15, 18, 27, 127
  Class B stations owned by, 19
  and "radiotelephony for hire," 16
AM radio
  and advent of commercial television,
    146–147
  and clear channel debate, 5, 107, 108
  and Docket 6741, 117, 118, 137
  Golden Age of, 3

"Anarchy in the ether," 26
Angell, Jack, 204
APA. *See* Administrative Procedure Act
Armstrong, Edwin Howard, 111, 131
ASCAP. *See* American Society of Composers, Authors and Publishers
Associated Independent Radio Stations, 52
Association for Broadcast Standards, 174, 175
  farm group support sought by, 210
AT&T. *See* American Telephone and Telegraph
Audion vacuum tube, 15
AVCO Corporation, 176–177

Baker, John, 195
Baker, Norman, 63
Barnouw, Erik, 19
Bartley, Robert, 164
Battles, Roy, 167–168, 170, 171, 175, 176, 177, 190
  CCBS work by, 206, 207, 208, 209, 210, 211, 212, 213
Bellows, Henry A., 28
Benjamin, Louise, 17
Bennett, John, 164–165, 171
Berry, Jeffrey, 224
Bestec, Maj. Gen. John B., 170, 171
Biggar, George C., 187
"Big Job, The" campaign, 93–97
Blue Book. *See Public Service Responsibility of Broadcast Licensees*
"Blue" network, 27
BMI. *See* Broadcast Music, Inc.
Bone, Homer, 45
BRECOM (BRoadcast Emergency COMmunications), 169, 170
Brinkley, Joel, 7
Brinkley, John R., 63
British Marconi, 15
Broadcast Bureau, 97
Broadcasting, 13
  birth of, 16–20
  legacy of early regulation of, 14
Broadcasting magazine, 4, 44, 51, 53, 59, 98
Broadcast Music, Inc., 52
Brown, Max, 208, 210, 211, 212
Business Week, 60, 66
Butman, Carl, 31

Caldwell, Louis, 67, 79, 100, 128, 152, 196–197, 200
  and allocation hearings of 1936, 52, 55
  and CCBS lobbying activity, 98
  clear channels and influence of, 48, 50, 51
  and Docket 6741 hearings, 115, 116, 118, 120, 121, 128
  and FCC analysis of allocation data, 61
  and General Order 40, 47
  and international agreement negotiations, 64
  and Johnson Bill hearings, 131, 132, 133, 134, 135, 137
  and NARBA renegotiation, 114
  and superpower hearings, 67
  and Twenty-Station Plan, 122, 126
Caldwell, Orestes H., 26
Canada, international agreements, 63, 64, 65
Capehart, Homer, 134
Case, Norman S., 66, 86, 87, 88
"Case for Clear Channel Broadcasting in Weather Reports to Growers, The," 209
CBS, 28, 47, 84, 87, 88, 127
  and closing arguments of Docket 6741, 129
  and Docket 6741 proceedings, 111, 112
  FM plan and Docket 6741 hearings, 117, 118–120
  and Johnson Bill, 135
  NARBA agreement opposition by, 152
  reaction of, to Docket 6741 reconsideration, 162, 163
  superpower opposed by, 67
  Twenty-Station Plan opposed by, 138
CCBS. *See* Clear Channel Group Broadcasting Service
CCBS Farm Paper Service, 201
CCG. *See* Clear Channel Group
Censorship
  Section 326 of Communications Act on, 116
Central Broadcasting Company, 94
Central Labor Council (Cincinnati), 58
Chain broadcasting investigations, 83–85
Chain programming, 34

Chicago Federation of Labor, 34
Citizens' groups, 7
Class A stations, 19, 20
Class B stations, 18–19, 20–21
   frequencies for, 20–23
   Hoover's authorization of, 18
Class C stations, 20
Class I-A stations, 65
Class I-B stations, 65, 87, 110, 160
Class II stations, 65, 110
   duplication by, according to Docket
      6741, 167 (table)
   prohibition of nighttime broadcasting
      by, 113
Class III stations, 110
Class III-A stations, 65
Class IV stations, 65, 110
Clear channel debate
   and commercial industry, 6–7
   significance of, 221–227
Clear Channel Group, 8, 50, 51, 52, 53,
      62, 71, 79, 80, 81, 85, 87, 192
   disbanding of, 82
   emergence of, 9
   first station to join, 46 (table)
   formation of, 40, 47
   and international agreement
      negotiation, 64
   and superpower hearings, 67
   testimony of, at allocation hearings of
      1936, 54, 55
Clear Channel Group Broadcasting Ser-
      vice, 8, 10, 47, 71, 83, 94, 96, 101,
      108, 178
   and Docket 6741, 109, 112, 115, 119,
      120, 164, 166
   early lobbying activity by, 97–100
   and farm groups, 9, 192–195,
      200–204, 209–215, 224
   and FM broadcasting, 100
   and Johnson Bill hearings, 130–137
   and monopoly charges, 83, 84
   and NARBA negotiations/renego-
      tiations, 114, 185–187
   opposition to, 146
   *Radio for ALL America: The Case for
      the Clears*, 173–174
   reaction of, to Docket 6741 recon-
      sideration, 162, 163, 164
   reaction of, to Docket 6741 decision,
      168–173
   Twenty-Station Plan, 122–127, 138,

      164, 198
   during World War II, 90–93
Clear channels, 20–24
   debate over, during 1930s, 40
   and farm organizations, 185–187
   forerunner to outlets for, 18
   NARBA and frequencies for, 151–152
   and National Farmers Union,
      204–209
   nighttime exclusivity of, 22
   opposition to/opponents of, 86
   piecemeal duplications of, in early
      1940s, 85–90
   in post–Docket 6741 years, 173–177
   and superpower hearings, 66–70
   and Twenty-Station Plan, 122–127
   during World War II, 90–93
Clear channel stations, 3
   early assignment of, 14
   farm programming on, 9
   schism begins between networks and,
      89–90, 101
   supremacy of, 4
Cohn, Marcus, 129
Color television system, 111
Columbia Broadcasting System. *See*
   CBS
Commerce Department, 24, 25
Commercial broadcasting industry
   fracturing of, 7
   triumph of, over noncommercial
      entities, 223
Commercial interest groups, 8, 10. *See
   also* Clear Channel Group Broadcasting Service
Committee for Kentucky, 117
Committee on Administrative Procedure, 98
Committee on Domestic Broadcasting,
   92
Communications Act of 1934, 116, 136,
   223
Computer industry, 226
Congress, 33, 65, 80, 101, 225
   and broadcast policy-making, 7
   chain investigations before, 83–85
   clear channel investigations by, 5
   and Docket 6741 decision, 164, 165
   pressure on FCC about clear channel
      case by, 147–151
   Radio Act of 1927 enacted by, 26
Conrad, Dr. Frank, 16

Cooper, Ed, 131, 132, 133
Corwin, Norman, 58
Courier-Journal Company, 33
Court of Custom Appeals, 25
Cowles Broadcasting Company, 110, 121
Coy, Wayne, 130, 148
Craig, Edwin W., 45, 46, 47, 54, 55, 67,
    81, 91, 114
Craney, Edward B., 98, 99, 110, 121,
    148–149, 202, 203
  and Johnson Bill hearings, 131, 133,
    135, 136
Craven, T. A. M., 58, 60, 61, 99, 110,
    160, 168, 224
  and FCC allocation hearings of 1936,
    54, 55
  mass duplication favored by, 164
  and NARBA renegotiation, 114
  and piecemeal duplication (early
    1940s), 86, 87, 88
  and superpower hearings, 66
Crosley, Powel, Jr., 43, 44, 52, 58, 59,
    68, 93, 128
Crosley Corporation, 41, 43, 118, 152
Cross, John, 164, 167, 168, 174
Cuba, 63, 64, 65, 113, 151, 152, 153
Cuban Missile Crisis, 169–170
Curran, George, 152

Damm, Walter J., 92
Davis, Ewin, 30
Davis, Stephen B., 13
Davis Amendment, 30, 31–32, 49
Day, Doris, 4
Daytime Broadcasters Association, 146,
    155, 156, 157, 162, 170, 174, 175,
    186, 203, 210, 215
Daytime groundwave/skywave signal
    paths, 20 (figure)
Day-time-only stations, 35
Daytime Skywave Case, 153–157
Daytime stations, 157–161
DBA. *See* Daytime Broadcasters Associ-
    ation
DCB. *See* Defense Communications
    Board
DeChant, Tony, 212, 213, 214
Defense Communications Board, 91, 92
Dellinger, J. D., 32
Denny, Charles R., 115, 119, 122, 129
Department of Agriculture, 195
  and *Agriculture U.S.A.*, 201

county agent system of, 191
  National Farm and Home Hour
    produced by, 190
Department of Commerce, 13, 65
  early allocation plans pursued by, 14
  early broadcast licenses issued by, 16
Department of Defense, 170–171
Department of the Treasury, 91–92
Depression (1930s), 50
DeWitt, John H. (Jack), 45, 118, 123,
    124, 131, 157, 168–169, 170, 175,
    176, 195, 221
De Wolf, Francis Colt, 114
Digital television standards, 226
Dill, Clarence C., 29, 45
Dingell, John, 164–165, 171, 172
Diode vacuum tube, 15
Docket 6741, 9, 122, 134, 145, 149–150,
    153, 159, 177, 178, 207, 208, 222
  beginning of hearings, 115–122
  channels duplicated by Class II
    stations, 167 (table)
  clear channels after decision, 173–177
  closing arguments, 127–130
  decision, 164–167
  farm groups in, 195–200
  opening of, 109–113
  reaction to decision, 168–173
  reconsideration of, 160–164
  significance of, 137–138
Docket 8333 (Daytime Skywave Case),
    154–157, 160
Dominican Republican, 64
Donovan, William J., 25
Dorn, William Jennings Bryan, 156
Dr. Laura, 226
Duplication, 45, 46, 48, 54, 55, 80, 99,
    178, 207
  on clear channels, 34, 35
  and Docket 6741 decision, 164, 166,
    167 (table)
  and Docket 6741 reconsideration,
    162–164
  FCC's KOA decision, 193
  piecemeal, during early 1940s, 85–90
  superpower as defense against, 64

Eagan, R. Russell, 152, 153, 169, 200,
    211
Edwards, E. P., 188
8KX (Pittsburgh), 16
Einstein, Albert, 44

Electricity
  delivery of, to farms, 188
Evans, Howard, 53
Everybody's Farm, 189, 190
Everybody's Farm Hour, 189
Ex parte contacts, 97, 98, 165

Fading, 41
Farm Bloc alliance, 191
Farm Bureau. *See* American Farm
    Bureau Federation
Farmers
  and radio, 187–190
Farm groups/organizations
  and Clear Channel Group
      Broadcasting Service, 9,
      192–195, 200–204, 214–215, 224
  and clear channels, 185–187
  and Docket 6741, 115, 116, 195–200
  lobbying by, 190–192
  rival groups/CCBS compete for,
      209–214
Farm Paper Service, 202
FCC. *See* Federal Communications
    Commission
Federal Communications Bar Associa-
    tion, 48
Federal Communications Commission,
    30, 40, 46, 48, 49, 60, 69, 81, 87,
    221
  allocation rules, 79
  analysis by, of allocation data, 60–63
  and broadcast policy-making, 7, 8
  and CCBS personnel, 98
  clear channels examined by, 5, 107
  clear channels in post–Docket 6741
      years, 173–177
  closing arguments of Docket 6741,
      127–130
  criticisms of, 65–66
  Daytime Skywave Case, 153–157
  Docket 6741, 145, 172–173, 177, 178,
      222
  Docket 6741 decision, 164–167, 207,
      208
  Docket 6741 hearings begin, 115–122
  Docket 6741 opened by, 109–113
  Docket 6741 reconsidered, 161–164
  duplication efforts, 86–90
  and ex parte contacts, 97, 98
  "Mayflower Decision" by, 94
  network structure examined by, 71

and reaction to Docket 6741 decision,
    168–173
  significance of Docket 6741, 137–138
  and World War II, 90
Federal Radio Commission, 3, 5, 39, 41,
    53, 66, 192
  allocation efforts by, 14, 28–34
  creation of, 13, 26
  first general counsel for, 47
  1928 allocation plan of, 4, 222
First Amendment, 223
Fly, James Lawrence, 82, 83, 84, 86, 88,
    91, 92, 93, 99, 192
FM broadcasting, 99
  effect of clear channel debate on, 107
FM radio, 5, 147
  and Docket 6741, 111, 117, 118–120,
    137
  emergence of, 9
Ford, Frederick, 164
"4000 Local Community Radio Stations
    or 12 Distant Superpower Giants:
    The Growing Outcry Against
    'Superpower,' " 174–175
FRC. *See* Federal Radio Commission
Frequencies, 14
  Hoover's authorization of, for land-
      based broadcasting, 17
  reassignment of, under NARBA, 82
Further Notice of Proposed Rule Mak-
    ing (FCC), 161

Gary, Hampson, 49
General Electric, 16, 18, 43
  Alexanderson transmitter patented
      by, 15
  Class B stations owned by, 19
General Order 40, 31, 32, 42, 45, 47
General Order 41, 32
General Order 87, 33
Godley, Paul, 121
Golden Age of Radio, 3, 6
Grand Ol' Opry, 4
Groundwaves, 21, 22
Gupton, Gayle, 164
Guy, Raymond F., 136

Haiti, 64
Hansen, John Mark, 191
Harding-Cox presidential race, 16
Harris, Oren, 164–165

Havana agreement, 64
Hawley, Ellis, 17
Haynes, Kit H., 208
HDTV. *See* High-definition television
Heterodyning interference, 29
Hettinger, Herman S., 61
High-definition television, 7
Hitch, Tom, 204
Hitler, Adolph, 93, 94
Hobbyists, 15
  and birth of broadcasting, 16
Hofstadter, Richard, 191
Hoover, Herbert, 16, 17, 18, 20, 22, 23, 24
  and chaos of 1926, 24–26
Hopkins, Harry, 81
Horwitz, Robert Britt, 225
House Committee on Interstate and Foreign Commerce, 70, 83, 84, 85, 164–165, 170, 171. *See also* Congress
House Resolution 714, 172, 173
House Resolution 8210, 172
Hull, Richard, 198, 212
Hunt, Lester C., 121
Hyde, Rosel, 119, 148, 152–153, 160, 164

Independent Broadcasters Protective League, 149
Independent clear channel operators, 107
Industrial Revolution, 190
Intercity Radio Company (New York), 25
Interest groups, 70, 223–225
  in intra-industry regulatory debates, 6, 7
Interference, 17, 41
  and Class B stations, 19
  and skywave signal, 22
"Interim Agreement" (NARBA), 113
International broadcasting agreement negotiations, 5, 63–66
Ionosphere, 21
Iowa Farm Bureau, 197, 200
Iowa Farmers Union, 192

Jansky, C. M., 67
Japan

Pearl Harbor attacked by, 91, 194
Jett, Ewell K., 113, 114, 122, 194
Johnson, Edwin, 130, 131, 133, 134, 135, 137, 171–172
  FCC pressured by, 147–151
Johnson Bill, 138, 145, 149, 164, 199
  Hull's testimony at hearings, 212–213
  and National Farmers Union testimony, 205–206
  Senate hearings on, 130–137
Joint Committee on Radio Research, 188
Joint Communications Agency, 168–169
Journal of Radio Law, The, 48

KDKA (Pittsburgh), 16, 42, 43, 81, 126, 127, 169, 176
Kennelly-Heavyside Layer, 21
KFI (Los Angeles), 22, 88, 117, 173, 176–177, 187, 194, 201
KGO (San Francisco), 33, 45, 124, 127
Kilpatrick, Leroy, 159
King, Charles, 164
KMOX, 208
KOA (Denver), 9, 25, 85–90, 101, 122, 124, 193
KPO (San Francisco), 124
Krasnow, Erwin G., 7, 8, 225
KRVN (Lexington, Nebraska), 208, 211, 212
KSL (Salt Lake City), 47, 88, 124, 173, 187, 212
KWKH, 97
KYW (Philadelphia), 33

Lacey, John, 199, 200
LaFount, Harold, 34, 42, 92
Larrabee, William Henry, 70
League of Women Voters, 28
Lee, Robert E., 164, 166–167, 171, 172
Licenses
  early granting of radio, 14
Limbaugh, Rush, 226
Limited-time stations, 32
Livesay, Ray, 157–159
Lobbying, farm, 190–192
Lone Ranger, The, 112
Longley, Lawrence D., 7, 8
Lynn, John C., 208

Maland, Joseph, 53, 56
Marconi, Guglielmo, 44
Maristany, Carlos, 151
Maritime point-to-point communication,
    14–16
Marsh, Ed, 209
Matheson Radio Company, 86, 89
"Mayflower Decision," 94
McChesney, Robert, 6, 7, 223
McDonald, John, 204
McFarland, Ernest, 134, 137
McFarlane, W. D., 66
McKeller, Kenneth, 45
McNinch, Frank, 66
"Meet Mr. Big" (booklet), 93
Mexico, 63, 64, 65, 203
    and Daytime Skywave Case, 157
    and NARBA negotiations, 82, 151,
        152, 153
Microradio, 226
Miller, Justin, 114
Miller, Ken, 168–169
Minow, Newton H., 164, 165, 171, 172,
    213, 225–226
Missionary Society of St. Paul the
    Apostle, 34
Moore, James, 198
Morse, Wayne, 158
Music copyright, 52
Mutual Broadcasting System, 84, 112,
    126, 135, 152

NAB. *See* National Association of
    Broadcasters
NAEB. *See* National Association of Edu-
    cational Broadcasters
NARBA. *See* North American Regional
    Broadcasting Agreement
NARBA Interim Agreement, 201
NARBS. *See* National Association of
    Regional Broadcast Stations
Nation, The, 66
National Apple Institute, 209
National Association of Broadcasters,
    27, 40, 51, 83, 98, 114, 119, 223,
    226
National Association of Educational
    Broadcasters, 54, 115, 129, 156,
    163, 212
National Association of Regional Broad-
    cast Stations, 40, 51, 53, 56–57,

67, 110
National Association of Television and
    Radio Farm Directors, 167–168
National Broadcasting Company. *See*
    NBC
National Committee for Education by
    Radio, 49, 53
National Council of Farmer Coopera-
    tives, 187, 195, 208
National Farm and Home Hour, 190,
    205
National Farmers Union, 9, 187, 191,
    192, 194, 196, 204–209, 210,214,
    224
National Grange, 167–168, 187, 192,
    194, 195, 206, 208, 212, 213
National Hog Cholera Eradication Com-
    mittee, 209
National Independent Broadcasters, 52,
    57, 67, 92
National Life and Accident Insurance
    Company, 45
National Radio Conferences
    (1922–1925), 17–18, 22, 23, 24
National Wool Growers Association, 209
NBC, 47, 83, 84, 87, 88, 89, 90, 100,
    127
    and closing arguments of Docket
        6741, 129
    creation of, 27, 28
    and Docket 6741 proceedings, 110,
        112, 117
    dominance of, over clear channel
        assignments, 33
    and Johnson Bill, 135
    KOA owned by, 85
    NARBA agreement opposition by, 152
    National Farm and Home Hour
        produced by, 190
    reaction of, to Docket 6741
        reconsideration, 162, 163
    and Twenty-Station Plan, 126, 138
NBC-Blue Network, 90, 112, 190
NBC-Red Network, 90
Networks, 223
    Association for Broadcast Standards
        supported by, 175
    and Docket 6741 hearings, 110–112,
        115
    effect of clear channel debate on, 108
    FCC examination of, 71
    and Johnson Bill, 135–136

Networks (*continued*)
schism begins between clear channel
stations and, 89–90, 101
support for Association for Broadcast
Standards by, 175
Twenty-Station Plan opposed to, 138
New Deal era, 191
Newsom, Hershel D., 208
NFU. *See* National Farmers Union
NIB. *See* National Independent Broad-
casters
Nighttime exclusivity, 70
Nighttime skywave signal path, 21 (fig-
ure)
Nockels, Edward, 33, 54
Noncommercial stations, 14
Normandy invasion (WWII), 93
North American Regional Broadcasting
Agreement, 64, 79, 88, 137, 201
and American Farm Bureau
Federation, 202–203
renegotiating, 108, 113–115, 146,
151–153
shifting of and chain investigations,
82–85

Office of War Information, 93
Offutt Air Force Base, 168–169
Ohio Farm Bureau, 197, 198, 200
O'Mahoney, Joseph C., 121
O'Neal, Edward A., 191, 192, 197
Operating hour assignments, 14
OWI. *See* Office of War Information

Patents, 15
Patton, James, 194, 205–206, 210, 211
Payne, George Henry, 58, 59, 66, 68, 86
Pearl Harbor
Japanese attack on, 91, 194
Peoples Broadcasting Corporation, 197
Point-to-point communication, 14, 15
Populism, 190, 191
Potts, William, 98, 226
Prairie Farmer magazine, 208
Prall, Anning S., 66
Progressive, The, 99
*Public Service Responsibility of Broad-
cast Licensees* (Blue Book), 116

Quaal, 81, 96, 97, 110, 150, 152, 168,
175, 176, 177
CCBS leadership by, 201, 202, 204,
206, 207, 209, 215
Quello, James, 164–165

Radio
and farmers, 187–190
growth in broadcasting of, 13
network dominance of, 5
in World War I era, 14–16
Radio Act of 1912, 14–16, 16, 17, 24, 25
Radio Act of 1927, 18, 26, 29
Radio Corporation of America. *See* RCA
*Radio for ALL America: The Case for
the Clears*, 173–174
Ray, William B., 97
RBC. *See* Regional Broadcasters Committee
RCA, 15, 16, 18, 27, 40, 43, 90, 111
Red Top Brewing Company (Cincinnati), 59–60
Regional Broadcasters Committee, 110,
114, 120, 121, 146, 170, 174. *See
also* Association for Broadcast
Standards
and closing arguments of Docket
6741, 128–129
and Docket 6741 hearings, 115, 117
and Twenty-Station Plan, 126
Regulatory debates
role of commercial interest groups in,
7, 8
Reno, Milo, 192
Report on Chain Broadcasting, 71, 83,
89
Riggs and Greene Broadcasting
Company, 175
Robinson, Ira E., 31, 42
Roosevelt, Franklin D., 44, 65, 66, 82,
91
Rule-making decisions
and Sangamon Valley, 165
Rural Electrification Administration,
188
Rural listeners
allocation survey sent to, 49
clear channel programming to, 9, 95,
96

Rural Living Resolutions Subcommittee, 203
Rural programming, 3, 40, 115, 116, 225. *See also* Duplication; Farm groups/organizations; Superpower
Rural radio coverage maps, 95
Rust, William F., 175, 176

Sangamon Valley Television Corporation v. United States, 97, 165, 166
Sarnoff, David, 44, 111
Satellite companies, 226
Saturday Evening Post, 66
Seavey, Hollis, 98, 152, 159, 164, 202, 203
Second National Radio Conference, 22
Senate Interstate and Foreign Commerce Committee, 13, 18, 83, 99, 147, 170. *See also* Congress
clear channel hearings before, 9, 108
Johnson Bill hearings, 130–137
Senate Resolution 294, 67, 69
Shared-time stations, 32
Shepard, John III, 51, 52, 92, 100, 110, 118
Sholis, Victor A., 83, 84, 85, 92, 114, 123, 133, 150, 151, 193, 195
and "Big Job" campaign, 93, 94, 95, 96
and CCBS formation, 81
and Docket 6741 testimony, 117, 119
Shooshan, Harry M., 225
Shouse, James, 59, 134, 190
Shuman, Charles, 202, 204
Signal Hill Television Company, 165–166
Signal importation debate, 226
Skelton, Red, 4
Skywave interference, 41
Skywave signals, 21, 22, 41, 153–157
Smith, Russell, 196
Spearman, Paul D. P., 56, 115, 127, 197
State Department, 91–92, 114
Station interest groups
formation of, 45–52
Stratovision plan (Westinghouse), 127
Stromberg-Carlson, 33, 118
Subcommittee on Communications (Senate), 147
Subcommittee on Small Business (Senate), 158
Superpower, 64, 79, 107, 122, 166. *See also* White Areas
and allocation hearings of 1936, 53, 57–58
and FCC analysis of allocation data, 63
hearings on, 66–70
National Farmers Union testifies against, 204–205
opposition to, 83
during World War II, 92
Superpower Committee, 66, 68, 69
Supreme Court, 69
KOA decision by, 89, 90
Sutton, George O., 57
Sweeney, Martin L., 70
Sykes, Eugene O., 53, 58
Syndicated radio hosts, 226

Taylor, Archer S., 159, 160
Telecommunications, Mass Media and Democracy (McChesney), 6
Telecommunications Act of 1996, 226
Telegraph, 14
Television, 5
ascendance of, 146
clear channel debate, and effect on, 107
and Docket 6741, 111, 137
emergence of, 9
FCC assignments, 161
high-definition, 7
Tennessee Farm Bureau, 204
Territorial wave frequencies, 20
Terry, Herbert A., 7, 8
Third National Radio Conference, 22
Third Notice of Proposed Rule Making (FCC), 162
Thompson, Frederick I., 86
Tobey, Charles, 130, 131, 132, 133, 135, 137
Tobler, Willis, 199
Transoceanic communication, 15
Trucking organizations
CCBS seeks alliance with, 214
"25 American Radio Stations Hitler Likes Least, The," 93

Twenty-Station Plan, 122–127, 130, 138,
    163–164, 174, 176, 198
    members of, 125 (table)
Tyler, Tracy, 49

United Fruit Company, 15
United States
    Class B frequency zones within, 22
    entry into World War II, 194, 195
    and NARBA renegotiation, 113
    in negotiations of international
        agreements, 63, 64, 65
U.S. Court of Appeals for the District of
    Columbia, 88, 97, 154

Voice of America, 169–170

WABC, 88
Walker, Paul A., 86
WBAP, 124, 176–177
WBZ (Boston), 124, 126, 127, 176
WCAU (Philadelphia), 81
WCBS, 208
WCCO (Minneapolis), 88, 89, 122, 173,
    212, 214
WCFL (Chicago), 34
WEAF, 24, 27, 42, 88, 99
Weather information
    through farm programming, 189
WEEU, 87
W8XO, 41, 44, 69, 93
Weizenecker, Frank, 58
WENR, 127
Westinghouse, 15, 16, 18, 40, 43, 118
    Class B stations owned by, 19
    FRC frequency decision appealed by,
        33
    and Twenty-Station Plan, 127
WFAA, 124, 176–177
WGN (Chicago), 95, 112, 113, 154, 169,
    172–173, 176–177, 187, 205, 208,
    212, 214
WGY (GE), 19, 24, 42, 43
    loss of clear channel assignment,
        32–33
WHAM (Rochester), 33, 175, 176
Wharton School of Finance and Com-
    merce, University of Pennsylvania,
    61

WHAS (Louisville), 33, 117, 133
WHDH (Boston), 86, 87, 88, 90, 193,
    194
Wheeler, Burton K., 67, 68, 80, 99, 108,
    121, 133, 134, 135, 171–172,194
Wheeler, Edward, 131, 133
Wheeler Resolution, 70, 71, 150, 225
White, Llewellyn, 8
White, Wallace H., 130
White Areas, 57, 101, 134, 148, 222. *See
    also* Superpower
    and Docket 6741 hearings, 116, 117,
        120
    and Docket 6741 reconsideration,
        162, 163
    higher power and, 41–44
    and Twenty-Station Plan, 122, 123,
        124, 125
White Bill, 137, 150
White House, 7
WHO (Des Moines), 94–95, 169, 173,
    189, 214
Wik, Reynold, 188
Williams, Andy, 4
Wireless Ship Act of 1910, 14–16
WJAZ (Zenith Radio Corporation), 25
WJR (Detroit), 154, 169, 172–173,
    176–177
WJW (Akron), 90
WJZ (New York), 24, 27, 88, 127
WKAR (Michigan State University),
    196, 206
WLS (Chicago), 187, 208
WLS National Barn Dance, The, 4
WLW (Cincinnati), 9, 42, 50, 53, 65, 66,
    68, 92, 112, 134, 173, 177, 189,
    190
    economic power of, 59–60
    experimental license for, 4, 79, 80
    history behind, 41
    power experiment of, 43–44
    rural population coverage by, 49
    signal power of, 39–40
    during World War II, 93
WMAQ, 113
WNYC, 88, 89, 90
WOI (Ames, Iowa), 129, 194, 196, 198,
    206, 212, 215
World War I era
    radio in, 14–16
World War II, 40, 99, 107
    "Big Job" campaign during, 93–97

CCBS during, 90–93
  farm lobbying during, 191
  United States entry into, 194, 195
WOR (New York), 67
WRC (Washington, D.C.), 22
WRFD, 197, 198, 206, 215
WSAZ (Huntington, Virginia), 159
WSB (Atlanta), 95, 96, 169–170,
  176–177
WSM (Nashville), 45, 49, 119, 154, 168,
  169, 173
WTAM (Cleveland), 90
WWL, 97–98

WXYZ (Detroit), 112

XENT, 63
XER, 63

Yankee Network (New England), 51,
  100, 118, 121
Young, Owen D., 15

Zenith Radio Corporation, 25